Ethics of Environment and Development

Ethics of Environment and Development

Global Challenge, International Response

**Edited by
J. Ronald Engel
and
Joan Gibb Engel**

Illustrations by John D. Petersen

**The University of Arizona Press
Tucson**

© The editor and contributors 1990

First published in Great Britain in 1990 by
Belhaven Press (a division of Pinter Publishers)
25 Floral Street, London WC2E 9DS

Published by arrangement with Belhaven Press:
THE UNIVERSITY OF ARIZONA PRESS
1230 North Park Avenue, Suite 102,
Tucson, Arizona 85719

Library of Congress Cataloging-in-Publication data has been requested.

British Library Cataloguing in Publication data are available.

ISBN: 0-8165-1183-7

*Published in association with The International Union for the Conservation of Nature and
Natural Resources*

Typeset by The Castlefield Press Limited, Wellingborough, Northants.
Printed and bound by Biddles Limited.

Contents

Contributors

Simon Sui-Cheong Chau, Ph.D., senior lecturer at the Baptist College, Hong Kong, is activator for Green Power, Hong Kong, a member of the executive committee of the Hong Kong Conservancy Association, director of the Asian Regional Exchange for New Alternatives, and columnist for the Hong Kong *Economic Journal*. He is the translator of numerous books and the co-author of the *ECCE Translator's Manual*.

Bill Clark, Ph.D., International programme coordinator for Friends of Animals, is a member of the Israeli delegation to the Convention on Trade in Ecological Species (CITES), the IUCN Species Survival Commission's Equid and Antelope specialist groups, and the IUCN Ethics Working Group. Formerly chief curator of Hai-Bar, and wildlife biologist with the Society for the Protection of Nature in Israel, he has published articles in many journals, including *International Wildlife* and *Biblical Archaeology Review*, and is the author of two books on Hai-Bar, *Paper Ark* and *High Hills and Wild Goats*.

David A. Crocker, Ph.D., professor of philosophy, Colorado State University, is co-founder (with Mihailo Marković) and coordinator of the International Development Ethics Association (IDEA) and author of *Praxis and Democratic Socialism: The Critical Social Theory of Marković and Stojanović*. He has published in philosophy journals such as *Inquiry* and *Revista de la Filosofía de la Universidad de Costa Rica*. In 1986–7 Professor Crocker was a senior Fulbright researcher and visiting professor at the University of Costa Rica.

Mawil Y. Izzi Deen (Samarrai), Ph.D., assistant professor, King Abdul Aziz University, Jeddah, is consultant to the Saudi Arabian Center for Science and Technology on building codes and land-use regulations, and author of essays on the relation of environmental protection and Islam, as well as co-author of *Islamic Principles for the Conservation of the Natural Environment*.

O. P. Dwivedi, Ph.D., LL.D., chair and professor, Department of Political Studies, University of Guelph, is chair of the Study Group on Technology and Development, International Political Science Association, and member of the Environmental Assessment Board of Ontario, and the Unesco Man and the Biosphere (MAB) General Scientific Advisory Panel. He has served as WHO consultant to the Department of Environment, India, and Canadian International Development Agency (CIDA) consultant to Papua New Guinea. Professor Dwivedi is co-author of *Hindu Religion and the Environmental Crisis*, editor of *World Religions and the Environment*, and author of numerous books and articles on ethics, environment and public policy.

J. Ronald Engel, Ph.D, professor of social ethics at Meadville/Lombard Theological School and lecturer, Divinity School, University of Chicago, is chair of the IUCN Ethics Working Group, and member of the Eco-Justice Working Group of the National Council of Churches (USA). Professor Engel was a consultant to the biosphere reserve project of Unesco Man and the Biosphere programme (MAB) and is currently doing research for the Lilly Endowment on the ethics of non-governmental organizations. He is the author of *Sacred Sands: The Struggle for Community in the Indiana Dunes* and editor of *Voluntary Associations: Socio-cultural Analyses and Theological Interpretation*.

Denis Goulet, Ph.D., O'Neill Professor in Education for Justice, and fellow of the Kellogg Institute for International Studies, University of Notre Dame, has held visiting professorships in universities throughout the world. He is a member of the programme advisory committee, Overseas Development Council. Professor Goulet has authored numerous books in development ethics, including *The Cruel Choice*, *The Uncertain Promise*, *A New Moral Order*, *Mexico: Development Strategies for the Future*, *Ethics of Development*, and *Incentives for Development: the Key to Equity*.

Eduardo Gudynas, Director, Grupo Ambiente y Desarrollo, Centro de Investigación y Promoción Franciscano y Ecológico, and assistant professor, Department of Ecology and Ethology, Institute of Psychology, University of Uruguay, is regional editor for the Environment Liaison Centre International and member of the IUCN Commission on Education and Training and IUCN Ethics Working Group. The author of numerous articles on biosystematics and ecology of vertebrates, Mr Gudynas is congress coordinator for the 1989 First Latin American Congress of Ecology.

Fung Kam–Kong, B.A., is General Secretary of Green Power, Hong Kong, and a freelance writer on green philosophy and the green movement.

Rajni Kothari, B.Sc., co-chairman, International Foundation for Development Alternatives (IFDA), was founder and editor of the international journal, *Alternatives*, director of the international United Nations University Programme on Peace and Global Transformation, president, People's Union of Civil Liberties, India, chair, Lokayan, and chair, Indian Council of Social Science Research. He is the author of numerous publications on development ethics, including *Rethinking Development: In Search of Humane Alternatives*, *Transformation and Survival: In Search of Humane World Order*, *State Against Democracy: In Search of Humane Governance*, and *Politics and the People: In Search of a Humane India*.

I. Laptev, Ph.D., is chief editor of *Isvestia* and deputy of the Supreme Soviet of the Union of Soviet Socialist Republics. Dr Laptev was previously professor of the Academy of Social Sciences USSR and has published widely in the fields of science, Marxist philosophy, and public policy, including *The World of Man in the World of Nature*.

Mihailo Marković, Ph.D., Ph.D., chair, Committee for Philosophy and Social Theory, Serbian Academy of Arts and Sciences, is vice-president of the World Future Studies Federation, member of the board, International Philosophical Institute, Paris, and member of the Committee for Defence of Freedom of Public Expression, Belgrade. Formerly co-chair of the International Humanist and Ethical Union, and dean of the Faculty of Philosophy, University of Belgrade, Professor Marković is the author of numerous philosophical works, including *Dialectics and Humanism, From Affluence to Praxis, Contemporary Marx, Dialectical Theory of Meaning,* and *Philosophical Foundations of Science.*

Robert J. Moore, Ph.D., D.D., programme officer responsible for cofunding projects of international non-governmental organizations for the Canadian International Development Agency (CIDA), was formerly Guyana's High Commissioner for Canada, executive director of the International Development Information Programme, and head of the Department of History at the University of Guyana. He lectures and writes widely on issues related to Third World development, religion, and global education, and is the author of *Third World Diplomats in Dialogue with the First World.*

Arne Naess, Ph.D., professor emeritus and member of the Council for Environmental Studies, University of Oslo, is chair of Greenpeace, Norway. He has held many distinguished academic positions, including visiting professorships at the University of California at Berkeley and Santa Cruz, and director of the East/West Controversies project for Unesco, 1948–9. Professor Naess is the author of numerous essays and books on philosophy, including *Democracy, Ideology, and Objectivity, The Pluralist and Possibilist Aspects of the Scientific Enterprise, Gandhi and Group Conflict,* and *Ecology, Community, and Life Style.*

C. K. Omari, Ph.D., associate professor of sociology at the University of Dar es Salaam, is chair of the Tanzania National Council of Social Development, chair of the board of governors of the Institute of Social Welfare, and member of the executive council of the International Council of Social Welfare. Professor Omari teaches in the fields of rural sociology and comparative peasant societies. His writings include *Strategy for Rural Development, Sociocultural Factors in Modern Family Planning* and the novel, *Kuanguliwa Kwa Kifaranga.* His edited works include *Towards Rural Development in Tanzania* and *Persistent Principles Amidst Crisis.*

Jimoh Omo-Fadaka, Ph.D., executive chair of African NGOs Environment Network (ANEN), and member of the board of directors of the Environment Liaison Centre in Nairobi, was formerly Regents Professor of Environmental Studies, University of California, Santa Cruz, senior consultant to UNEP on ecodevelopment, and African coordinator for the United Nations University Programme on Peace and Global Transformation. Dr Omo-Fadaka has authored over 100 papers on alternative patterns of development, and the relation of environment and development in developing countries.

Martin Palmer, M.A., director of the International Consultancy on Religion, Education and Culture (ICOREC), Didsbury Polytechnic, Manchester, is religious adviser to WWF International, and religious adviser on conservation to HRH Prince Philip. Mr Palmer coordinated the Assisi Conference on religion and conservation in 1986, and is former director of the Inner City Religion and Environment Centre, Manchester. His publications include *Faith and Nature*, *Worlds of Difference*, and *Genesis or Nemesis — Belief, Meaning, and Ecology*.

John D. Petersen, M.S., is the resident biologist on the Bouverie Audubon Preserve in northern California, and a member of the Ornithologists' Union. His art work is published in *Discovering Sierra Birds*. His posters for the Costa Rican National Park Foundation are displayed in the National Museum of Costa Rica.

Hilkka Pietilä, M.Sc., secretary general of the Finnish United Nations Association, is vice-president, World Federation of United Nations Associations, and member of the council, International Foundation of Development Alternatives. Ms Pietilä has wide international experience, having served in such capacities as advisory member of the Finnish delegation to the United Nations General Assembly, and member of the Finnish delegations to the UN Conference on the Human Environment and the World Population Conference. She is the author of numerous articles on women's issues, ecology and peace. Her books include *In Defence of Human Dignity*.

Holmes Rolston, III, Ph.D., professor of philosophy at Colorado State University, is associate editor, *Environmental Ethics*, research associate, University of Colorado Museum Herbarium, and member of the IUCN Ethics Working Group. He has published widely in the field of environmental ethics in scientific, philosophical and public interest journals and is the author of *Philosophy Gone Wild*, *Science and Religion*, and *Environmental Ethics*.

Ariel Salleh, M.A., senior lecturer in sociology at the University of Wollongong, NSW, Australia, is an editor of the international social theory journal *Thesis Eleven*, and has given lectures, workshops and broadcasts on ecofeminism throughout Europe, the United States and the South Pacific. She has published articles on Green politics, feminism, Marxist theory, and deep ecology in international journals, including *Social Alternatives*, *Environmental Ethics*, and *Philosophy of the Social Sciences*.

S. Sivaraksa, called to the Bar by the Middle Temple, London, and director of the Santi Pracha Dhamma Institute, Bangkok, was founding editor of the Thai journal *Social Science Review*, editor of the journal of the Buddhist Association of Thailand, *Visakha Puja*, and founding member of the Coordinating Group for Religion in Society (CGRS). He is a contributor to the publications of the Asian Forum for Culture and Development, and the author of numerous articles and books on Buddhism, social justice, and alternative development, including *Religion and Development*, *Siamese Resurgence*, *A Socially Engaged Buddhism*, and *Unmasking Thai Society*.

Henryk Skolimowski, D.Phil., professor of philosophy, Program in Humanities, University of Michigan, is associate editor, *The Ecologist*, and a member of the IUCN Commission on Ecology and IUCN Ethics Working Group. Professor Skolimowski has served as a member of the Task Force on Appropriate Technology of the United States Congress and as consultant to Unesco concerning the impact of science and technology on development. He is the author of numerous articles and books on philosophy and ecophilosophy, including *Eco-Theology*, *The Theatre of the Mind*, *Technology and Human Destiny*, and *Ecophilosophy: Designing New Tactics for Living*.

Stephen R. Sterling, M. Env. Sc., consultant in environmental education, is executive editor of the *Annual Review of Environmental Education*, consultant to the Council for Environmental Education, UK, and member of the IUCN Ethics Working Group. Mr Sterling was formerly assistant director of the Council for Environmental Education and was involved in the drafting of *The Conservation and Development Programme for the United Kingdom*. He has published widely in the fields of environmental education and environmental ethics.

Foreword

History teaches us that lasting human happiness can come only from harmony among the inhabitants of the Earth. In terms of public policy, the concept of justice has been used as a device for reducing tensions and promoting harmony among human beings. The addition of the dimension of ecological sustainability has led to the enlargement of the concept of justice to cover the generations yet to be born. Thus, a new Earth ethic has to be based both on intra-generational and inter-generational justice.

Gandhi underlined the importance of making *Antyodaya* (the well-being of the poorest individual) the pathway to *Sarvodaya* (the welfare of the entire human society). In other words, to be sustainable, development must also be equitable. Environmentalists should be as concerned with protecting the livelihood and security of the poor as they are with protecting the livelihood and security of the penguin.

I am glad this book looks at the ethical aspects of sustainable development from the points of view of science, society, and religion. Careless technology, commercial greed, political indifference, and the needs of the poor for the basic necessities of life, together with a rapid growth in human population, have all resulted in a situation where, as stressed by Professor Ronald Engel in his Introduction, no further time should be lost in elevating sustainable development to a global ethic. This is not going to be an easy task, as is clear from the continuing degradation of the environment. Fortunately, however, the realization that nature's patience is not inexhaustible is becoming more widespread at the political, professional, and public levels.

The contributors to this volume have dealt with the many facets of the ethics of our common future in a truly multicultural and authoritative manner. I wish to refer to two issues briefly.

We are aware that biological diversity and cultural diversity are the twin foundations of biological productivity and human versatility. There is, however, inadequate realization of the importance of institutional diversity in technology development and transfer. The growing emphasis on intellectual property rights may stimulate the rapid growth of the age of invention, but will it help or hinder the rapid diffusion of the benefits of ecologically sound technologies in the Third World? Should the pursuit of private profit be the sole motivation for applied research, or should the lasting happiness of all the inhabitants of the Earth be an equally powerful engine of discovery?

What institutions can enable a speedy and effective sharing of the technologies which can strengthen the ecological security of the world, including the protection of the ozone layer and the global climate? How can we achieve a balance between the desire for short-term economic gain and the dedication to a development upon people and the environment became matters of increasing ethical and theological concern.

Since Lutheran theologian Joseph Sittler's historic 'Called to Unity' address at the New Delhi Assembly of the World Council of Churches in 1961, a number of regional and international conferences on the ethics of environment and development have been held by Christian organizations, most pre-eminently the World Council of Churches' Conference on Faith, Science and the Future held at the Massachusetts Institute of Technology in 1979.[9]. This work will continue in 1990 when the World Council of Churches holds a convocation in Seoul on the theme 'Justice, Peace and the Integrity of Creation', and in 1991 when the seventh Assembly of the World Council of Churches takes as its theme 'Come Holy Spirit — Renew the Whole Creation!'

There has also been in recent years a sudden outburst of religiously-inspired movements, institutes, and educational projects seeking to protect the environment and initiate new forms of alternative development. A very partial listing includes the Sarvodaya movement in Sri Lanka, the Buddhist Perception of Nature Project in Thailand, the Seminar 'Terra Mater' and Assisi Nature Council in Italy, the Asian Cultural Forum on Development, Centro de Investigación y Promoción Franciscano y Ecológico in Uruguay, and the Eco-Justice Working Group of the National Council of Churches (USA).

Conferences of Roman Catholic bishops in the Philippines and the Dominican Republic have issued significant pastoral letters on the ethics of environment and development, and in 1988 Pope John Paul II issued the encyclical 'Sollicitudo Rei Socialis' (On Social Concerns) which calls for a morally based concept of 'true development' that respects human rights and demonstrates

awareness of the fact that one cannot use with impunity the different categories of beings, whether living or inanimate — animals, plants and natural elements — simply as one wishes, according to one's economic needs. On the contrary, one must take into account the nature of each being and its mutual connection to an ordered system, which is precisely the 'cosmos'.[10]

Aware of the failures of the major moral traditions of the world to provide adequate environmental ethics for modern civilization, a growing community of philosophers and theologians undertook the task of fundamental ethical reconstruction.[11] In 1979 the English language journal, *Environmental Ethics*, began publication. A comparable body of new thought began to emerge among liberation theologians, development ethicists, and social philosophers around a critique of the dominant paradigm of economic development.[12] In 1987 the International Development Ethics Association (IDEA), founded by David Crocker and Mihailo Marković, held its first international conference in Costa Rica.

Until very recently, however, few connections were made among the groundswells of moral concern taking place in the different sectors of public life. In particular, there was a lack of communication between research scientists and specialists engaged in implementing policy in the natural resource and development fields and the leaders of conscience groups concerned explicitly with the advocacy of moral and religious purposes, including practitioners of the new international discussion. They have also been the motivations driving the rising concern for morality and ethics in world conservation and development.

The year 1980 was a watershed. The launching of the World Conservation Strategy (WCS) that year by the International Union for the Conservation of Nature and Natural Resources (IUCN) in cooperation with UNEP, FAO, Unesco and the World Wildlife Fund (WWF) marked the first official notice that ethics was a matter of explicit concern to the international conservation movement. Modestly tucked into the preface to Chapter 13 of this historic document is the following revolutionary pronouncement:

Ultimately the behavior of entire societies towards the biosphere must be transformed if the achievement of conservation objectives is to be assured. A new ethic, *embracing plants and animals as well as people*, is required for human societies to live in harmony with the natural world on which they depend for survival and well-being. The long term task of environmental education is to foster or reinforce attitudes and behavior compatible with this new ethic.[5]

The same year, 1980, at the 12th General Assembly of IUCN, President Mobutu Sese Seka of Zaire proposed the development of a charter for nature based on the proposition that 'all human conduct affecting nature must be guided and judged'.[6] Two years later the United Nations General Assembly overwhelmingly adopted the World Charter for Nature. This remarkable document, sponsored by Zaire and thirty-two other developing nations, went beyond simply affirming the need for a new ecological morality and took the bold step of defining some of the needed moral content. The Charter put the world body on record as 'convinced that . . . every form of life is unique, warranting respect regardless of its worth to man'.[7]

Also in 1980, the report of the Independent Commission on International Development Issues, *North-South: A Program for Survival*, was published. This forthright attempt to restructure the international economic and political arrangements which continue to perpetuate hunger and poverty in the Third World included an appeal similar to that of the World Conservation Strategy for a change in global moral values. The primary difference is that while the WCS concentrated upon environmental issues, the Independent Commission concentrated upon social concerns. Writing in his introduction, 'A Plea for Change', the chair of the commission, Willy Brandt, pointed out that world development ought not to be confused with economic growth and is more than an economic process. It is fundamentally a matter of moral commitment to human solidarity:

the new generations of the world need not only economic solutions, they need ideas to inspire them, hopes to encourage them . . . They need a belief in man, in human dignity, in basic human rights; a belief in the values of justice, freedom, peace, mutual respect, in love and generosity, in reason rather than force.[8]

While these developments were taking place in the United Nations, a similar transformation was occurring in the attitudes of many of the religious communities of the world. The impact of science, technology, and economic the last three decades in response to a felt need for a new way of life that is both socially and environmentally *good*. It seeks to provide a synoptic overview of the contemporary moral challenge of sustainable development and the similarities and differences in its interpretation by ethicists throughout the world. The picture that emerges is stimulating, for it indicates that persons in diverse cultures are seeking critically and constructively to answer Brundtland's call for a new holistic global ethic.

There is an ambiguity in the call for an ethic of sustainable development that needs to be noted at the outset. In ordinary language, 'ethics' and 'morality' are often used interchangeably. However, 'morality' most properly refers to judgments and actions regarding what is right or good, and 'ethics' to the reasoning such judgments and actions require.[2] For this reason the term 'ethics' is frequently used as an equivalent for moral philosophy. In this book it will be used more broadly to refer to disciplined reflection about morality, moral problems and moral judgments. One need not be a philosopher to be concerned for ethics; however, one must be concerned to submit one's moral values and judgments to rigorous intellectual scrutiny.

It is not clear whether Bruntland's call is for a new holistic ethic in this latter sense, or whether it is assumed that the meaning of sustainable development is clear and the task is to make it a matter of moral obligation. The authors of this book are not convinced that we yet know what sustainable development ought to be. They assume that if we are to make adequate moral judgments about our treatment of the environment and the direction of contemporary development, and if we are to move toward better forms of behaviour, there must be disciplined and widespread ethical reflection. If sustainable development is to succeed as a new way of life on Earth, its moral content must be thoroughly debated and understood.

The growing concern for ethics in world conservation and development

The prevailing opinion at the time of the founding of the United Nations in 1945 was that the nations of the world would cooperate to found a new international economic and social order on principles of justice and human rights. This hope never completely died. Over the years, respected world figures, among them Indira Gandhi, His Holiness the Dalai Lama, Pope John XXIII, and HRH Prince Philip, have made appeals similar to those of Brundtland for the necessity of public moral transformation, while internationalists such as Dag Hammarskjöld, Julian Huxley, Nicholas Polunin, and Sir Peter Scott have sought to make the moral dimensions of conservation and development part of the deliberations of international organizations.

The notion that sustainable development should be 'elevated' to a global ethic may be traced to the United Nations Conference on the Human Environment at Stockholm in 1972.[3] At this conference and its associated meetings, developing nations placed economic justice on par with the concern of many industrialized nations for environmental protection.[4] While the positions of the various parties to the debate have changed since 1972, the twin moral principles of social justice and environmental responsibility have remained permanent features of

Introduction
The ethics of sustainable development
J. Ronald Engel

The Norwegian Prime Minister, Gro Harlem Brundtland, opened the 1988 World Conference on the Changing Atmosphere with the call for 'a new holistic ethic in which economic growth and environmental protection go hand-in-hand around the world'. With these words she placed the ethic of sustainable development squarely at the centre of hope for global change. Brundtland was speaking not only for herself but for the United Nations Commission on Environment and Development which she chaired. Its 1987 report, *Our Common Future*, concluded that 'human survival and well-being could depend on success in *elevating sustainable development to a global ethic*'.[1]

What would it mean to elevate sustainable development to a global ethic? What kind of 'ethic' is this? In what way is it 'new'? What kind of 'environmental protection' is meant? What kind of 'economic growth' is intended? Are steady-state economies precluded? Before we accept 'sustainable development' as a new morality as well as a new economic strategy, we need to know what ecological, social, political, and personal values it serves, and how it reconciles the moral claims of human freedom, equality, and community with our obligations to individual animals and plants, species, and ecosystems. Most important, if we are morally serious, we must know on what grounds it may be said that sustainable development is a *true* ethic for human beings on planet Earth.

Whatever its ethical novelty, the moral questions that provoked the proposal to elevate sustainable development to a global ethic are not new. Under various guises they have been debated in international forums since the 1960s when 'development' was first widely perceived as a problematic concept and the 'environment' emerged as a major international concern. These questions have been urgent but neglected considerations since the advent of the modern industrial era. Indeed, what is the 'new holistic ethic' of sustainable development but the latest attempt to answer the perennial question of the purpose of human activity on the face of the Earth — the elemental moral question of what way of life human beings ought to pursue?

This book is an expression of a growing interest in these fundamental ethical concerns — an interest publicly expressed in virtually all parts of the world in

Introduction
The Ethics of
Sustainable Development

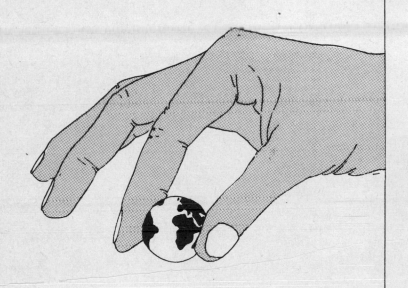
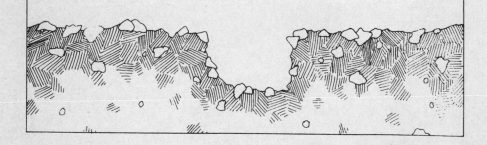

Pitt, Holmes Rolston, III, Henryk Skolimowski, Kathy Sreedhar, and Stephen Sterling. The manuscript could not have been prepared for publication without the steadfast research and technical assistance of Barbara Jo Sorensen and Richard Speck, the help of Kathryn Cogan and Leah Haworth, or the support of Joanne Esters-Brown and Paula Swain-Harmon at Meadville/Lombard Theological School. Laurie Abbott and Spencer Lavan provided valuable assistance with problems of translation. We have had a most supportive and knowledgable editorial director in Iain Stevenson of Belhaven Press. Finally, it has been a distinct pleasure to work with our illustrator, John D. Petersen, who generously donated his time and creative ability to the project.

We take full responsiblity for editing the volume, including the degenderizing of all textual material with the exception of quotations from primary sources.

Although separated by many hundreds of miles, and in many cases still unacquainted except through letter or telephone, we feel a deep sense of companionship with all those who have contributed to this volume.

J. Ronald Engel
Joan Gibb Engel
Chicago
May, 1989

Preface

This volume had its inception in the workshop sponsored by the Ethics Working Group of the International Union for the Conservation of Nature and Natural Resources (IUCN) at the 1986 Conference on Conservation and Development in Ottawa. A need was expressed for a book that would begin to clarify, from a multicultural perspective, the ethical principles at stake in the concept at the centre of the World Conservation Strategy — 'sustainable development'. The publication of *Our Common Future* in 1987 by the World Commission on Environment and Development gave new impetus to the idea of sustainable development and further pointed to the need for a book on the 'ethics of our common future'.

The present work meets this need in a number of respects. It brings together in one volume the thinking of persons well equipped to provide an ethical interpretation of sustainable development — authorities in the fields of environmental ethics and development ethics. It also brings together the work of those who are addressing the questions of environment and development from the differing perspectives of religion and humanistic philosophy.

Though they speak from necessarily individual biases, the ethicists assembled here are concerned to span the gaps between theory and practice, fact and value, science and public policy. They constitute a rare intellectual leadership in our world today, persons with capacities for both critical and constructive moral thought.

Equally important, their essays represent diverse cultural, philosophical, and religious traditions of East, West, South and North, as well as the growing consciousness of the special contributions of the cultures and experience of women.

Future works cannot help but amend the weaknesses of this volume. They will represent neglected viewpoints, address neglected issues, sharpen self-criticism and challenge the positions expressed here. Yet we see this book as a pioneering effort in what it is hoped will be a creative period in human social thought — a period when leading thinkers from all cultures will join to address the ethics of environment and development as one unified subject matter and in global perspective.

When, after the long drought-ridden North American summer of 1988, the rains returned, and we decided, after several set-backs, to proceed with editing this volume, it was our joy to receive renewed aid and encouragement from persons throughout the world. We want to acknowledge the long-standing support and guidance of Jeffrey McNeely and Walter Lusigi, the generous and timely help of Robin Pellew, and the valuable suggestions of Wolfgang Burhenne, David Crocker, Rick Davis, Denis Goulet, Nancy Nash, Howard Parsons, David new Earth ethic? This is an area which merits debate and discussion and the reaching of a consensus which will make our common future bright.

A second major area of concern is the growing violence in the human heart. We talk about a 'non-aggression pact with nature' but incidents of aggression among members of the human race are growing in number. Over $1 trillion are being spent each year on so-called defence arrangements by both rich and poor nations. But finding a few million dollars for the conservation of biological diversity or land and water productivity requires considerable effort.

Gandhi asked: 'How can we be non-violent to nature unless the principle of non-violence becomes central to the ethos of human culture?' This question is even more valid today than when he posed it over fifty years ago. It is the central dilemma which the authors of this book seek to address.

M.S. Swaminathan
President, International Union for the
Conservation of Nature and Natural Resources

disciplines of environmental ethics and development ethics.

These connections began to made in 1986 when the International Conference on Conservation and Development met in Ottawa to review the progress of the World Conservation Strategy and to map its revision. Moral concerns were prominent in the deliberations of the conference, evidenced by the title chosen for the conference proceedings, *Conservation and Equity*, the inclusion of a workshop on Ethics, Culture and Sustainable Development sponsored by the Ethics Working Group of IUCN, and the vote of the conference to include a new section on ethics in the revised World Conservation Strategy.[13]

Also in 1986, and for the first time in world history, representatives of five world religions met with one another and with leaders of the international conservation movement to share their beliefs regarding the moral imperative to care for the environment and to join in an ecumenical worship service to celebrate the glory of creation. The meeting took place in Assisi, Italy, as part of the 25th anniversary of the World Wildlife Fund; afterwards, WWF International initiated a permanent programme in religion and conservation.[14] The United Nations Environment Programme has also taken initiatives to link religious ethics and conservation, and in 1988 the first Global Conference of Spiritual and Parliamentary Leaders on Human Survival was held at Oxford.

This is only a sketch of what appears to be a very widespread and profound change in human attitudes throughout the world.

However, Bruntland's assertion that ethics, as much as technics, is essential to progress in the protection of the environment and the elimination of poverty is not necessarily shared by other world leaders. Indeed, to all appearances, the prevailing opinion among professional specialists, business, and political leaders alike is that the economic, managerial, technical, and scientific dimensions of conservation and development, mixed with a good dose of *realpolitik*, are sufficient to cope with the problems of providing adequate resources for human consumption and material progress. It is assumed that once people understand the harmful consequences of environmental mismanagement, their behaviour will change.

There is also good reason to be sceptical of the new interest in morality and ethics. Evocations in public arenas of moral principles are often little more than pious hopes that hide brutal realities, flourishes designed to legitimate policies that have been decided on other than moral grounds. It is difficult to make even the most accepted moral principles operational in a world of sovereign and antagonistic states.

But the fact remains that our present political and economic arrangements are only retained because they are perceived to be legitimate, and their legitimacy rests ultimately on the perception that they are ethically justified.[15] History teaches that once this ethical justification is challenged by new moral sensibilities, and legitimacy withdrawn, the arrangements are likely to change. The alternative is for those who wield power to accept the power of morality and genuinely seek the larger good. For all their 'realism', those who dismiss the role of morality in human action are not doing justice to human nature. Leaders of movements for social transformation have always understood that in order to change a situation one must appeal, sooner or later, explicitly or implicitly, to moral as well as material considerations.

The contributions of ethics

There are at least five practical reasons for the new interest in morality and ethics. Each builds on the others and introduces one of the tasks that 'ethics', defined as *disciplined reflection by persons in all walks of life on moral ideas and ideals*, is being asked to perform. The fifth, defining a new social paradigm for sustainable development, incorporates the preceding four, and is the principal concern of the authors in this book.

First, there is a new awareness of the *role of values* in human activity. Social scientists have long stressed the political, social, and economic determinants of human behaviour, but recent attention also has focused upon the 'missing concept' of culture.[16] This shift is associated with the rejection of the assumption that value neutrality and impartial objectivity are possible in the practice of science, policy formation, and professional activity. One philosopher of science Stephen Toulmin, writes:

Instead of viewing the world of nature as onlookers from outside, we now have to understand how our own human life and activities operate as elements within the world of nature. So we must develop a more coordinated view of the world, embracing both the world of nature and the world of humanity — a view capable of integrating, not merely aggregating, our scientific understanding, and capable of doing so *with practice in view* . . . Nowadays, scientists have always to consider themselves as agents, not merely observers, and ask about the moral significance of the actions that comprise even the very doing of science.[17]

The moral values and cognitive beliefs of a culture play a crucial role in how well human societies adapt to the natural environment and what kind of political and economic relationships they maintain.[18] This basic truth has been rediscovered in international environment and development circles for several reasons: a growing awareness that approaches to sustainable development must differ depending on the cultural heritage and religious traditions of a society; a recognition that ecologically sound knowledge is a part of the cultural traditions of native and other traditional societies; and an awareness of how modern cultural values have destroyed sustainable patterns of land and resource use.[19]

The first task that ethics is being asked to perform, therefore, is to *understand and evaluate* the moral codes woven into cultures — what they are and how they function to enhance or distort the relationships of human beings to one another and to the Earth.

Second, there is a new appreciation of the way in which moral ideals *motivate* persons to care for the world around them, often to the point of considerable self-sacrifice. This appreciation has come simultaneously with the recognition that appeals to self-interest or fear of human extinction have been overdone by the environmental movement and may be counter-productive. Many recent events testify to the power of moral outrage to kindle social movements for environmental preservation and alternative development. These include the much-publicized Chipko ('hug the tree') movement in India; the protest of the T'boli people in the Philippines against dams in South Cotabato; AGAPAN in Brazil ('attack today and ever . . . defending life!'); the Daintree River rainforest blockade in Australia; the actions of Greenpeace and other green groups in Europe, and the Kenya Women's Greenbelt movement. Additional evidence of the power of moral motivation to effect substantial changes in our relationships to people and the rest of life comes from movements such as green consumerism, ethical investment, and voluntary simplicity. No less important is the increasing self-awareness of many scientists, resource managers, and development experts regarding their personal moral motivation for professional and public service.

Thus ethics gives voice to the moral conscience of persons, provides a language that expresses their moral intuitions, and empowers them to share their feelings with others. It enables leaders of movements for progressive social change to draw creatively on the root symbols of their religious and cultural traditions, and encourages recontact with the originating moral motivations of the modern conservation and alternative development movements. With the help of ethics, these moral motivations, eloquently expressed in the life and work of such prophetic figures as Henry David Thoreau, Albert Schweitzer, Mahatma Gandhi, Louis Lebret, E.F. Schumacher, and Wangari Maathai, will continue to inspire non-violent movements for the betterment of human life.

A third reason for the new interest in ethics is its role in *clarifying the values* at stake in policy decisions and *giving moral reasons* for alternative courses of action. Contemporary environment and development issues are loaded with moral implications that need to be understood and carefully weighed before intelligent choices can be made. For example, many persons working with grassroots constituencies on such issues as planned parenthood or wildlife preservation find that an ability to think well and speak persuasively about the various rights and duties involved is essential to the success of their efforts. Without these, the possibility of significant change is foreclosed and action is taken on the basis of habit or custom, personal preference, or political or technical feasibility.

At a more abstract level, many feel a keen need to clarify the values that inform public policy statements on environment and development issues. Documents such as the World Conservation Strategy and the World Charter for Nature are peppered with moral concepts such as 'democracy', 'equity', and 'respect for nature' which, though crucial to their message, are often used in a vague and even contradictory fashion.[20] Terms such as 'ecological integrity', while useful, often blur the many kinds of values found in the natural world. Yet the internal coherence of public policy statements, and consequently their practical effectiveness, depends upon reasoned justification for the values and choices espoused. Ethical clarity cannot be generated casually, but requires the same kind of rigorous intellectual attention as that given scientific, technical, and legal considerations.

Fourth, ethics is helping to *resolve* some of the outstanding value conflicts that thwart conservation and development projects. One of the most prominent of these is the presumed conflict between 'resource conservation', which stresses efficient, long-term utilization of natural resources, and 'ecocentrism', which stresses preservation of values inherent in natural landscapes.[21] To those of an ecocentric persuasion, resource conservation reflects an anthropocentric and technocentric world view. The ecocentric position, in turn, is considered romantic and misanthropic.

This conflict is reflected in the international policy statements of the environmental movement. The World Charter for Nature, for example, affirms both that every form of life warrants respect *regardless of its worth to man* and that 'ecosystems and organisms . . . shall be managed to achieve and maintain *optimum sustainable productivity*'.[22] Similarly, the World Conservation Strategy has been criticized for its resource conservation orientation, yet it contains in Sections 3.1 and 13.12, two direct references to obligations to other species. *Our Common Future* also fails to integrate 'our moral obligation to other living beings' with its overriding concern for better resource management and economic betterment.[23]

Ethics can help in such conflicts, not by proving one side right and the other wrong, nor by providing a merely theoretical resolution removed from the real world, but by redefining the issue so that the values in each position that are worthwhile, yet which are perceived to be in opposition, may be seen as potentially reinforcing and achievable in concert. In the case of resource conservation versus ecological preservation, ethically-informed leaders in both the environment and development communities have indicated that the underlying moral concern of advocates of resource conservation is stewardship of natural resources on behalf of distributive justice within and between generations. If this is the case, the basic issue is not between instrumental and intrinsic values but between two kinds of intrinsic value — social justice and ecological integrity — both of which, in any defensible moral approach to life, are worthwhile ends, both of which require efficient, long-term instruments of support (technical and otherwise), and each of which can potentially contribute to the enhancement of the other.[24]

The fifth reason for the new interest in ethics has to do with the task most central to this book: the role of ethics in helping to define a *new social paradigm* which will promote sustainable development in each culture and region of the world. Thomas Kuhn's use of 'paradigm' in *The Structure of Scientific Revolutions* to refer to standard examples of scientific work which embody a set of conceptual, methodological and metaphysical assumptions has been expanded by ethicists and social scientists in such a way that 'dominant social paradigm' is now taken to mean the collection of norms, beliefs, values, and habits that form the world view most commonly held within a culture and transmitted from generation to generation by social institutions.[25] The culminating function of ethics in this century, its contribution to human and ecological liberation, will be its critique and reform of the dominant social paradigm of modern global development.

The Ottawa Conference on Conservation and Development concluded that 'we need an alternative society, another type of development that is linked with structural transformation'. While 'new solutions will incorporate mixtures of the old, . . . concrete solutions to environmental problems will largely depend on a new organizational capacity of society as a whole, *based on the cultural values of different communities, their creativity and their potential for innovation*'. Five broad criteria for the 'emerging paradigm of sustainable development' were identified by the conference:[26]

- integration of conservation and development;
- satisfaction of basic human needs;
- achievement of equity and social justice;

- provision for social self-determination and cultural diversity;
- maintenance of ecological integrity.

The Ottawa conference was one more expression of the growing consensus — broadly shared within the international conservation community, and increasingly recognized in the international development community — that not simply this or that part of the present global development pattern needs to be corrected, but that the entire model of modern industrial development is seriously awry. Not only the economic values of competition and consumption but the expectation of unlimited material growth; not only the prevalence of technology but the view of the world as a machine; not only the hierarchies of power, wealth, status, or sex but the idea of hierarchy itself; not only the dichotomy of resource conservation versus ecocentrism, conservation versus development, humanity versus nature, theory versus practice, intrinsic versus extrinsic values but the need to think in dichotomies at all. In other words, the basic world view or image of social and cosmic reality in terms of which scientific, moral, political, and most other questions have been asked and answered since the beginning of the modern industrial era is being questioned.

Many factors contribute to this questioning. There have been changes in the environment and social and economic relations, changes in technology, changes in scientific models, changes in metaphysics, changes in economic data and theory, changes in global politics. But no factor has been more influential than ethics for the simple reason that the failure of modern society is primarily experienced as a failure to provide a fulfilling and sustainable way of life, a *good* life, for *all*.

In the shift of paradigms from 'modern' to what some are calling 'post-modern', ethics is asked to be both critic and builder. For how else do we achieve distance from the paradigm that envelopes us than by taking a self-critical ethical posture towards the most basic assumed values of our culture? Is what I take for granted good? Is it humanly fulfilling? Does it achieve what it purports to achieve? Is the world better for it? And how else do we envisage a 'new holistic ethic' of sustainable development except on the basis of moral creativity?

The moral challenge of sustainable development

A number of issues confront any serious effort within the cultures and religions of the world to define a new moral paradigm. The four essays in Part One introduce the most important of these, and suggest some basic directions that must be taken to respond to them.

The primary issue, as Rajni Kothari suggests, which sets the terms for any and all talk of 'the ethics of sustainable development', is the lack of a shared moral language in which to think and deliberate about the meaning of world order. All previous ways of defining the nature of the global problems of our time are secondary to this fundamental need.

The faith that the future is open and contingent in important respects upon human choice, that individual persons can identify with people in other cultures, with the dispossessed, with the community of life on Earth, and that humans have the capacity to make universal moral judgments, is essential to any possibility of

creating a new world order. Without it such statements as the Universal
Declaration of Human Rights and the World Charter for Nature are meaningless.
Yet this faith is being severely challenged by both the resurgent absolutisms and
the widespread relativism of our time. The authors of this volume each see this
issue in different ways but are united in the conviction that universal moral
principles are possible and can inspire effective personal and institutional
commitments. Furthermore, they believe that cultural diversity is best preserved
and strengthened by inclusive moral principles that promote relationships of
mutual respect between all persons.

As Kothari suggests, each culture and religion of the world can contribute to
the needed sense of global solidarity and to the creation of the moral vocabulary
required to hammer out a new concept of world order. The truth of his claim is
brought home by the chapters that follow. Each author seeks, out of the resources
of a particular culture or religion, to make precisely such a contribution.

A second issue that Kothari introduces is the considerable ambiguity in the
term 'sustainable development'. Two irreconcilable meanings are current: one is
genuinely rooted in ethics and points to a true alternative mode of development;
the other, ethically vacuous, is essentially camouflage for maintaining the
economic growth that created the crisis to begin with. It is essential, Kothari
argues, that the two be carefully distinguished.

The authors of this book are quite sensitive to this issue. Given the common
association of 'sustainable development' with the limited goal of resource
conservation — growth with equity — many are sceptical that a broader, more
demanding ecological definition will be successfully communicated by the term.
In the viewpoint of several of the authors, neither the World Conservation
Strategy nor the report of the World Commission on Environment and
Development go far enough in dissociating the term from the dominant Western
paradigm. A critique of these documents is therefore a part of their analysis.

In order to break its association with a limited, instrumental view of
conservation and development, and in order to suggest some of the positive moral
dimensions of the new social paradigm, most of our authors grope for a richer
symbolic language with which to speak about the concept of sustainable
development — 'authentic integral development' (Goulet), 'ecological/holistic
world view' (Sterling), 'reverential development' (Skolimowski), 'ecosophical
development' (Naess), 'noosphere' (Laptev), 'just, participatory
ecodevelopment' (Crocker), 'communalism' (Omo-Fadaka), 'desirable society'
(Sivaraksa).

However, along with the shared suspicion, there is also agreement that, at least
in principle, there is nothing inherent in the term 'sustainable development' to
keep it from becoming the name for an alternative post-modern social paradigm
and a new moral conception of world order. 'Sustainable', by definition, means
not only indefinitely prolonged, but nourishing, as the Earth is nourishing to life,
and as a healthy natural environment is nourishing for the self-actualizing of
persons and communities. The word 'development' need not be restricted to
economic activity, much less to the kind of economic activity that now dominates
the world, but can mean the evolution, unfolding, growth, and fulfilment of any
and all aspects of life. Thus 'sustainable development', in the broadest sense, may
be defined as *the kind of human activity that nourishes and perpetuates the historical*

fulfilment of the whole community of life on Earth. Several authors attempt some such broad interpretation.

This issue is not really dealt with, however, as both Kothari and Denis Goulet point out, unless the origin, thrust, and destructive impact of the dominant social paradigm of world development are clearly identified. Only then is it possible to achieve adequate critical distance from the forces that structure our lives so as to appreciate the degree to which the new paradigm more truly expresses the human potential. Indeed, the necessity for, and nature of, the alternative only become evident as the oppressive character of the regnant paradigm is understood.

A number of chapters include an analysis of the dominant development paradigm and reasons for its moral inadequacy. Although there are overlaps, these analyses vary significantly. Taken together, they throw light from many different angles on the world most of us take for granted, yet which is not inevitable and can be changed. The labels the authors use to designate the dominant paradigm of world development reflect differing emphases — 'anti-development' (Goulet), 'Western world view' (Sterling), 'unsustainable development' (Gudynas), 'money economy' (Omari), 'top-down development' (Omo-Fadaka), 'patriarchy' (Pietilä).

Denis Goulet introduces a third issue. Throughout most of recent history, advocates of alternative development have been at political odds with advocates of ecological integrity, appealing to different constellations of value and different constituencies. The promise of the present situation is that these two wings of protest against the dominant social paradigm will form a new and powerful alliance. This book is itself a step toward the new alliance since it brings together leading writers in the fields of environmental ethics and development ethics. The primary challenge posed by this combination of moral concerns is to define the paradigm of sustainable development so that neither the value of economic justice nor the value of ecological integrity is treated instrumentally. The need, Goulet writes, is to locate 'environmental concerns at the heart of normative discourse on development'.

A shift in social paradigms requires a shift in types of moral reasoning. Sustainable development, conceived as a moral ideal, challenges the traditional separation in ethics of theory from practice. The kind of ethics that Goulet recommends is one with which many authors in this volume have sympathy — most explicitly Mihailo Marković, David Crocker, and Jimoh Omo-Fadaka. These authors share a commitment to ethics as *praxis*, a productive, free, and creative activity that integrates theory and practice, albeit in different ways and with different rhythms. Such activity, far from being the prerogative of specialists, is the birthright of all persons. Indeed, it is the mark of a truly 'developed' society that its citizens are not only permitted, but provided with the means, in the words of Marković, 'to bring freely to life their potential creative powers'. None of these powers is more important than the capacity for moral reflection and choice.

This understanding of ethics requires the theorist to be a person of action, engaged in the processes of change as well as reflection. A distinguishing fact about the authors of this volume is that they are so engaged. Each is socially active on behalf of the values he or she prescribes, and each writes out of first-hand acquaintance with the political, economic, and environmental conditions that support as well as thwart the achievement of these values. As persons of practical experience and wisdom, their words speak directly to all persons who are similarly engaged in exercising moral leadership in difficult circumstances.

Religion, science and sustainable development

Some of the most vigorous responses in recent years to the global environment and development crisis have come from leaders of the world's religious traditions. Their responses are unexpected and perplexing to those accustomed to equate concern for conservation and social justice with humanist, science-based value systems. While religious traditions have without question influenced the way in which modern societies impact the environment and shape economic institutions, at the beginning of the modern era a dualism developed in many societies between religious and secular life. As a consequence, with certain notable exceptions, modern religious communities have devoted little explicit ethical attention to environment and development issues.

However, given the role that traditional religions have played in the course of human history to sustain complex human communities over many generations, it is not surprising that in response to the overwhelming needs of our age — needs in large part created by the failures of secular society — perceptive religious leaders should discover that they have wisdom to contribute to the quest for a sustainable way of life and a responsibility to engage with others in the search for a new public environmental ethic.

The kind of wisdom that religious philosophers and ethicists have to offer to the common quest for a new development paradigm stems from a different analysis of the moral plight of human beings than that offered by other thinkers. For the religions of the world, the moral failure of human beings to live in peace and justice with one another and the rest of creation is rooted in a deep, *spiritual failure*. The human will is in bondage to forces of evil or structures of reality that alienate it from the true ground of its being. This bondage is evident in the greed, lust, selfishness, and craving for pleasure and power that are the real motivating powers behind the dominant materialistic world view. Thus no amount of attention to new moral ideas of sustainable development and no amount of new moral resolve can by themselves put the world on a sustainable development path. For the religions of the world, a change in the human will itself is necessary, a deliverance from the bondage of the human spirit. This can only be done with the help of spiritual disciplines that restore the proper relationship of human beings to the ground of being, disciplines that depend upon religious insight and ultimately, upon faith.

As noted in the previous historical overview, the new interest in the religious bases for conservation and development ethics has taken practical form in projects by religious communities throughout the world, and in new efforts at collaboration between religious leaders and conservationists. Martin Palmer, who directed the conference at Assisi in 1986, describes the dialogue now under way between religious leaders and conservationists and provides an overview of some of the key theological, ethical and practical insights which five of the world faiths (Hinduism, Buddhism, Judaism, Christianity, and Islam) have to offer the search for viable ethics of sustainable development. This introductory review is essential background for the more detailed chapters on the world faiths that follow, including the analysis by Holmes Rolston, III on the sometimes conflicting, sometimes reinforcing, moral claims of traditional belief and modern science.

In addition to discussions of the religious ethics of Hinduism by O.P. Dwivedi, Buddhism by Sulak Sivaraksa, Judaism by Bill Clark, Christianity by Robert J. Moore, and Islam by Mawil Y. Izzi Deen (Samarrai), C. K. Omari discusses the resources of the religious traditions of indigenous African peoples, Simon Sui-Cheong Chau and Fung Kam-Kong discuss the ancient wisdom of Taoism and Chinese Buddhism, and Hilkka Pietilä frames her essay with an appeal to the ancient religions of the Goddess.

Many of these essays reflect the changing course of the academic discussion that began with Lynn White's 1967 thesis that the cultural roots of the modern aggressive pursuit of science and technology lay in late medieval Christianity. White argued in general that 'every culture, whether it is overtly religious or not, is shaped primarily by its religion', and specifically that 'not only modern technology but also the unhesitatingly exploitative approach to nature that has characterized our culture are largely reflections of value structures emerging from the matrix of Latin Christianity'.[27] The discussion that White initiated led to a series of attempts to fix the blame for the environmental crisis on one or more body of religious belief, and to find new, more adequate religious grounds for contemporary, principally Western, culture. Many thinkers sought to find in Asian religions, for example, the respect for nature that they saw missing in the West. Other historians doubted if any cultural tradition had provided truly adequate environmental ethics for either ancient or modern human societies, and warned that, even if they had, religions cannot be easily exported from one society to another.[28]

As the essays in this book indicate, this discussion has now reached a much more productive stage. The emphasis now is upon a retrieval of those basic symbols and doctrines within each tradition which undergird positive environment and development ethics, and the translation of those symbols and doctrines into clear prescriptions for public policy and personal behaviour. There is also a readiness among members of the world faiths to learn from one another. In their essays, Robert J. Moore and S. Sivaraksa show that the capacity to engage in cultural self-criticism can exist side by side with profound faith and religious self-affirmation. This new dialogical and comparative perspective has emerged in the context of a deepening appreciation of the fact that the roots of our ecologic crisis are wider than any particular cultural inheritance and reach deep into human nature itself.

Along with an increasing appreciation in recent years of the potential contributions of religion to a new global ethic of sustainable development, there has been a commensurate loss of trust in the capacities of modern science and technology to provide the knowledge and means required to bring human societies into harmony with their environment and one another. Many of the essays are sharply critical of the mechanistic science that has dominated Western society in the modern epoch; some hold it directly responsible for our current crisis.

Rolston provides a clarifying analysis of the respective contributions of science and religious (and cultural) tradition in the new social paradigm of sustainable development. Using a rich illustrative set of specific moral dilemmas involving conservation and development, he demonstrates how science and tradition sometimes conflict, sometimes complement, and sometimes criticize one another. By showing the dialectical and plural character of these two primary forms of culture, Rolston refuses to adopt a pro or anti stance towards either. The question is rather what kind of science and what kind of tradition are most adequate as bases of moral valuation. This statement of the issue sets the terms neatly for the subsequent essays. While the approaches of the authors differ, sometimes radically, most appear to agree that a new social paradigm of sustainable development will require the selective transformation of both modern science and the historic religious and cultural traditions, as well as necessitate the development of a greater mutuality between them.

Some of the authors, such as Stephen R. Sterling, are hopeful that the new scientific epistemology that has emerged in recent decades will provide the basis for a world view more in keeping with the best insights of traditional religion. Others, such as Eduardo Gudynas, see the reconciliation of tradition and science occurring through the transformation of science into a more participatory, needs-orientated social enterprise.

In reading the following essays, it is important to understand that the 'religious' dimension of human experience is not limited to particular religious traditions but encompasses a great variety of ways in which humans experience and interpret transcendence, or the ultimate in existence.[29]

Many of the authors would agree with the notion of transcendence suggested by Goulet when he speaks of the need for a 'higher telos', an end-value to which both nature and human freedom are subordinate, if the norms of ecological integrity and social justice are to be unified and if scientific inquiry is to find its proper place in the total process of human knowing, valuing, and acting. Yet many of the same authors would hesitate to equate that higher telos with any special heritage of religious belief, or limit it to a belief in God — to a 'one' or 'whole' that embraces as well as transcends the 'many', including the Earth and all its creatures. For Kothari, transcendence is to be found in the 'sanctity of the Earth'; for Skolimowski, it is in the experience of 'the sanctity of life'; and for I. Laptev, it is a creative evolutionary principle, immanent in the dialectical interaction of history and nature, in and through which human beings and the rest of nature are brought to their highest fulfilment. Other authors, such as Crocker and Marković, would be uneasy with Goulet's formulation if it implied any non-contingent restraint beyond human conversation itself and the salvific novelty that conversation inserts in the processes of history.

Unity and diversity in international response

One of the principal discoveries made in the preparation of this book is the degree to which ethicists in diverse centres of world culture are seeking to respond to the moral challenge of sustainable development in terms of an emergent ecological world view. Equally striking are the differences in the ways in which they are interpreting the ecological vision in light of their respective cultural traditions.

Broad agreement exists that the key to a normative understanding of sustainable development is to be found in the idea of 'individuals-in-community' as the basic feature of life on Earth. Biologically and socially, in nature and culture, this is the way things essentially *are* and — healed, enriched and fulfilled — this is the way things *ought* to be. The science of ecology, originally defined as 'the science of communities', teaches us that the Earth is best described as a mosaic of coevolving, self-governing communities consisting of diverse forms of life, with intricately balanced, interdependent parts and processes.[30] The ecological vision accepts this description of fact as also a description of value. Thus to speak of the world as composed of so many autonomous individuals, so many species, or so many impersonal corporations or nation-states, is to abstract from the way things are and to risk diverting attention from the primary object of practical moral concern: the harmonious realization of individuals-in-community.

According to the ecological world view, human communities involve unique kinds of cooperative and conflicting relationships that bind their highly integrated individual members; these relationships are embedded in, and dependent upon, more 'loose' kinds of relationships that bind diverse forms of existence into 'mixed' communities of plants, animals and people. Each element, organism, and individual within the mixed community exists for itself, for others, and for the whole; which is to say, each community displays intrinsic, extrinsic, and systemic values. The terms 'land' and 'bioregion', which have enjoyed increased usage in recent years, refer to such inclusive and holistic contexts of interdependent community.[31]

All human cultures acknowledge moral duties to individual human beings. The ecological vision expands our ideas of moral obligation to include not only all organisms, but the interactions between individual organisms in ecosystems — most properly, the ecosystemic order itself. Rolston argues that to deny moral value to ecosystems because they are not integrated in the same way as centralized individual organisms is to make a *category* mistake. In thinking about the value of social and biotic communities we should be concerned for a 'matrix of interconnections between centres, not for a single centre'. He goes on to say:

Ecosystems are in some respects more to be admired than any of their component organisms because they have generated, continue to support, and integrate tens of thousands of member organisms . . . We want to love 'the land', as Leopold terms it, 'the natural processes by which the land and the living things upon it have achieved their characteristic forms (evolution) and by which they maintain their existence (ecology)'. *The appropriate unit for moral concern is the fundamental unit of development and survival.* Loving lions and hating jungles is misplaced affection. An ecologically informed society must love lions-in-jungles, organisms-in-ecosystems, or else fail in vision and courage.[32]

It follows that the meaningful choices of our age are not between the individual and the community, or between the environment and people, but between different kinds of 'mixed communities' of people, animals, plants, and minerals — between those individuals-in-community whose development path is ecologically sustainable and socially just and those whose path is not.

As a number of the following essays show, the ecological vision of reality is in some respects a very old image of reality. It is found in the traditions of native peoples and in the world's great historic religions and cultures. It has erupted into our consciousness today in part as a consequence of the new science of ecology and in part due to the recovery of the ancient truths of these traditions, truths which once created sustainable societies. We are beginning to learn again the lessons of moral restraint and self-limitation; that the true meaning of human freedom is individual and collective self-government. But an ecologically-informed vision of sustainable development is also a new creation, something uniquely within *our* power to choose. Never before have human societies had the power and duty to *plan* sustainable development and never before have we lived on the threshold of a truly planetary culture.

The multiple dimensions of the emerging ecological world view are reflected in the essays that follow. The ecological vision variously informs a systems cosmology, a theory of democracy, a new scientific epistemology, a strategy for global justice. In this respect, the essays mirror the actual multidimensional character of the social transformation struggling to take place throughout the world. Many changes are occurring that appear to be unrelated but yet are connected by their common grappling with the new world view. One place where these various dimensions converge is in the idea and practice of community-based ecodevelopment.[33] The moral value of participatory public institutions that function within the constraints of particular ecosystems is a recurring theme of these essays.

There are also important differences that distinguish these essays. In addition to those that define the various approaches to human salvation taken by the great religions of the world, there are significant broad cultural differences as well. Ethicists are appropriating the ecological world view and formulating a new paradigm of sustainable development in ways most appropriate to their own society's culture and historical situation. In addition, and this point cannot be minimized, there are significant conflicts that divide these essays from one another and from other ethical approaches. The reader is therefore required to weigh these essays with care. Each of us must come to our own understanding of how best to interpret the ecological vision and give ethical content to the idea of sustainable development.

A brief overview of some of the major cultural differences that will be encountered in the following chapters may be of help.

Western Europe and North America were the originating centres of the modern development paradigm and they are still among its most powerful progenitors. It is revealing that the shared concern of the essays in this section of the book is to go to the historical and epistemological foundations of the Western project — in the words of Stephen Sterling, whose comprehensive summary of the Western world view and its alternative, the ecological world view, introduces this section, 'to examine and challenge the Western world view "from the inside"'. Each essay seeks to provide a philosophical and historical critique of the dualistic Western world view and to envisage a more holistic alternative. The epistemological issue is paramount: each seeks to find grounds in a kind of knowing and valuing that is outside, or underneath, the ordinary accepted norms of Western culture on the basis of which they may be criticized and transformed.

No unanimity exists as to the nature of these grounds. Sterling finds them in recent developments in the philosophy of science, especially systems theory. Skolimowski locates them in the *sui generis* character of human moral valuation itself. Arne Naess, whose writings on deep ecology constitute perhaps the best known challenge in the Western environmental movement to the dominant Western development paradigm, finds them in the affirmation of 'intrinsic value' as articulated in the first principle of the deep ecology platform: 'The welfare and flourishing of human and non-human living beings has value in itself'.

Eastern Europe faces a problem similar to that of the West. It too is a major progenitor of the modern paradigm of world mastery and control. In spite of differences in political and economic philosophy, basically the same underlying technological world view informs both. However, the Eastern European and Soviet thinkers represented here believe that humanist philosophy in the tradition of Karl Marx and Friedrich Engels has the capacity to evolve toward a more inclusive ecological perspective that will correct the vast social and environmental imbalances of industrial society; that indeed, because it is a scientific philosophy, it will, given time, necessarily so evolve. They also suggest that because it prescribes a scientifically planned collective economy, it has capacities, unavailable in the philosophies of free market societies, for implementing sustainable development.

Building on the work of the early Marx and the Russian scientist Vladimir Vernadski, a principal architect of our contemporary ecological vision of the biosphere, Laptev argues the need to situate human evolution in the larger evolutionary adventure of the planet. In his view, the emerging paradigm of sustainable development marks a new stage in planetary history, the stage at which, through human reason and productive activity, the biosphere becomes the 'noosphere' and the relations among persons and between society and nature are mutual and universal. Marković, a humanist or revisionist Marxist, roots the failure of the Western paradigm of development in its pessimistic view of human nature and argues for what he sees as a more positive vision of human nature in democratic socialist humanism as the moral basis for a new paradigm.

Latin America is a vast region of diverse peoples and cultures. It is also a continent in ferment. What Crocker says in his case study of Costa Rican development can be said about many parts of the region: 'Costa Ricans are no longer making or failing to make development decisions within a generally accepted paradigm. Rather, they are groping for a "new development path" and debating various proposals for social change'. This means, he believes, a development path beyond free market liberalism, statist socialism, or even the 'growth with equity' model of progressive social democracy.

Contemporary Latin American ethical reflection on sustainable development is conditioned by the weaving together of three main cultural threads: Roman Catholic Christianity; secular humanism; and native traditions. Out of this unstable amalgam have come some of the most original theology, literature, and social experimentation of the late twentieth century. Because of its general openness to new ideas, drive for liberation from Northern dominance, and intense cultural creativity, Gudynas and Crocker believe that the region can now benefit in a practical way from ethical reflection on the fundamental ends and means of development. Gudynas provides an introduction to the various schools of thought about the ethics of sustainable development that have vied with one another in Latin America since 1972, and concludes with his own proposal for a new form of socially responsible, participatory science and a kind of ethics that considers all human actions in social ecological terms. Based on contemporary Costa Rican social experimentation and *praxis* philosophy, Crocker proposes four normative principles of 'just, participatory ecodevelopment': the satisfaction of basic human needs; democratic self-determination; environmental respect; and equal opportunity for personal self-realization.

In the views of Omari and Omo-Fadaka, Africa is also seeking a moral vision of development beyond capitalism or socialism but, unlike Latin America, it is a vision that has already in large part been found. Omari and Omo-Fadaka argue that only by reclaiming and updating the traditional moral patterns of community-based social and economic life can Africa move beyond its present impasse and enter a development path that is culturally authentic, equitable, and ecologically sound. As Omari explains, in many African societies land was a community property, owned by past, present, and future generations as one entity. The moral and religious values associated with this practice still have the potential to promote equitable distribution and environmental stewardship. While most of these communal practices have been destroyed by the impact of Western economic development, Omo-Fadaka believes that with the help of poets, priests, philosophers, and artists, they could live again and the political will be found to address Africa's overwhelming environmental and social problems.

Some of the most important sources of inspiration and insight available in the world today for revisioning environment and development issues are to be found in the international feminist, 'women in development', and ecofeminist ethics movements. In the past decade there has been a remarkable convergence of thinking by feminist writers in many parts of the globe regarding the fundamental systematic relationships between poverty, environmental destruction, and sexism (and other sorts of domination) and the roots of these oppressive relationships in the patriarchal social structures and cultural ideologies of most human societies. This convergence is seen in the chapters by Hilkka Pietilä (Finland) and Ariel Salleh (Australia) in this volume, as well as in the work of Rosemary Ruether (USA), Irene Dankelman (Holland), Maria Mies (West Germany), and Vandana Shiva (India).[34] The perspective of women in developing countries is especially crucial to the ecofeminist analysis: women and their associated environments bear enormous burdens at the hands of the dominant forces of global development; at the same time, feminine experience and women's knowledge of how to produce and conserve life have much to teach the rest of humankind about how to create a sustainable and non-violent world.

An agenda for ethics

When one task is accomplished, it opens the way for work to begin on the next. The profound moral purpose that began to be articulated in international discussions only two or three decades ago — to find a new way of life on Earth that is ecologically sound and socially just — has been accomplished in at least one important respect. As the chapters in this book indicate, ethicists in many parts of the world are now thinking in converging directions about a new social paradigm of sustainable development. However different their methods of approach, their grounds for moral truth, their cultural and social context, this fact stands out: they share the agenda of elevating sustainable development to a global ethic, an ethic that recognizes and promotes the mutuality of ecological and social values in concrete living communities.

Exactly what the moral dynamics of this mutuality are is not yet clear. How freedom, equality, and public participation may be reinforcing principles in human social life is difficult enough to define — so difficult, that it has taxed the best human minds for centuries. To ask how these enduring social values can reinforce one another and also promote the complex and diverse values of the natural world, and how, moreover, the values that human beings discover in their relationships to nature can reinforce these social values, is to issue an unparalleled challenge to human capacities for moral understanding. In what specific ways, for example, does human freedom depend upon the freedom of nature, and the freedom of nature depend upon human freedom? Yet this kind of understanding is required if the new paradigm of sustainable development is to serve as the basis for significant social change — if it is to help define specific, practical development goals, and provide guidance in the inevitable conflicts that arise when social and ecological obligations are considered within the same framework of action.

One task on the agenda of the ethics of sustainable development is to reconceptualize our inherited moral ideas so that they can do justice to the full complexity of interactions within and between biological and social communities.

This task is much too large for any single ethicist or combination of ethicists working in isolation in different parts of the world, or for any one school of thought or particular cultural, scientific, philosophical, or religious perspective. It requires that ethicists and scientists from different religious, philosophical, and cultural backgrounds have the opportunity to work in close and sustained collaboration with one another. As Goulet, Palmer, Gudynas, Omo-Fadaka, Pietilä, and Dwivedi argue in separate sections of this work, and as I have maintained in writings elsewhere, ecofeminist ethics must be integrated with ecophilosophy; the leaders of the various religions of the world must continue their dialogue with one another and with more secular points of view; environmental ethicists and development ethicists must expand the dialogue that is just now beginning between them; professional ethicists must find new ways to collaborate with their peers in the fields of environment, development and resource management; and serious collaboration must begin between ethicists and educators, artists, writers and other creators and bearers of human culture.[35]

Most urgent of all, ways must be found for ethicists to work directly with grassroots constituencies on particular projects, so that the moral principles necessary to the success of sustainable development will be built, as Omo-Fadaka so rightly insists, from the ground up rather than from the top down.

Equally important is a second issue on the agenda: how to implement moral principles more effectively in practice. Here ethicists and others are asked not so much for 'strategies' of action — such terminology smacks of the mechanistic and patriarchal paradigm which has created our problems in the first place — as for help in perceiving new political possibilities for achieving moral ideals.

Independent public-regarding voluntary associations committed to various aspects of environmental protection and economic and social justice now exist in most societies of the world and their significance for social transformation is referred to frequently in the pages that follow. They are often effective despite difficult political and social circumstances. The formation of cross-cultural, cross-disciplinary, and cross-sectorial coalitions can strengthen them.

Ethically-informed persons have the opportunity to expand customary notions of what is politically possible by helping associations of concerned citizens understand the moral dimensions of the public issues they face, the full complement of values entailed by a responsible development path, and how the various constituencies they represent may be morally motivated to support those values. Citizens working together are the agents that alone can advocate, educate, experiment, in a word, *morally create* the new sustainable communities of the future.[36]

Neither the task of ethical definition nor the task of ethical effectiveness can be successfully pursued apart from one another. This is especially evident in the creation of the single most important kind of coalition required for sustainable development to become a reality: the coalition between advocates of ecological integrity and advocates of social and economic justice. In recent months, coalitions of non-governmental organizations concerned with poverty, human rights, population, and environmental issues have begun to appear in different parts of the world and this has been made possible in part by the recognition that their goals are ethically coherent and mutually reinforcing.

Making Common Cause Internationally, a Policy Statement and Action Plan for International Development, Environment and Population NGOs, endorsed by the International Council of Voluntary Agencies, and further supported by the Rome Development Forum, March 1988, reads in part:

We affirm both the integrity, stability, and beauty of the ecosystem and the imperative of social justice. We recognize that poverty, environmental degradation, and population growth are inextricably related and that none of these fundamental problems can be successfully addressed in isolation . . . We will succeed or fail together.[37]

If sustainable development is to be elevated to an effective global ethic, it will depend upon the emergence of this kind of holistic moral understanding and action in every society of the world.

Notes

1 World Commission on Environment and Development, *Our Common Future* (Oxford: Oxford University Press, 1987), 308. Emphasis added.
2 William K. Frankena, *Ethics* (Englewood Cliffs, New Jersey: Prentice Hall, 1973), 4.
3 Lynton Keith Caldwell, *International Environmental Policy: Emergence and Dimensions* (Durham, North Carolina: Duke University Press, 1984).
4. See the Stockholm Declaration of the United Nations Conference on the Human Environment, An Independent Declaration on the Environment (the Dai Dong

Declaration), Declaration of the Third World and the Human Environment (the Oi Committee Declaration) in Burns H. Weston, Richard A. Falk and Anthony A. D'Amato, eds, *Basic Documents in International Law and World Order* (St Paul, Minn.: West Publishing Co, 1980).

5 International Union for the Conservation of Nature and Natural Resources, *The World Conservation Strategy: Living Resource Conservation for Sustainable Development* (Gland, Switzerland: IUCN, 1980). Emphasis added. In addition to the passage in Section 13.1, the WCS calls for a new environmental ethic in Sections 1.2 and 8.10 and explicitly states a moral obligation both to future generations of people and to other species in Sections 1.5 and 3.1–2.

6. UN General Assembly, 'Draft World Charter for Nature. Report of the Secretary General', Thirty-sixth sess., Agenda Item 23, A/36/539, 13 October 1981, Annex I, Appendix II, 14–15.

7 'The World Charter for Nature' in Wolfgang E. Burhenne and Will A. Irwin, *The World Charter for Nature: A Background Paper* (Berlin: Erich Schmidt Verlag GmbH, 1983), 9.

8 Independent Commission on International Development Issues, *North-South A Programme for Survival* (London: Pan, 1980), 12.

9 Paul Abrecht and Roger L. Shinn, eds, *Faith and Science in an Unjust World*, 2 vols (Geneva: World Council of Churches, 1980).

10 *Origins: NC Documentary Service* 17 (3 March, 1988): 645.

11 For an introduction to this literature, see J. Ronald Engel, 'Ethics' in David C. Pitt, ed., *The Future of the Environment: The Social Dimensions of Conservation and Ecological Alternatives* (London: Routledge, 1988), 23–45.

12 See Denis Goulet, *The Cruel Choice: A New Concept in the Theory of Development* (New York: Athenaeum, 1971); David Crocker, 'Hacia una Etica del Desarrollo', *Revista de Filosofía de la Universidad de Costa Rica* 25, 62 (1987): 129–41; Godfrey Gunateilleke, Neelan Teruchelvam, and Radhika Coomaraswamy, *Ethical Dilemmas of Development in Asia* (Lexington, Mass.: Lexington Books, 1983).

13 Peter Jacobs and David A. Munro, eds, *Conservation with Equity: Strategies for Sustainable Development* (Gland, Switzerland: IUCN, 1987). A draft chapter on ethics for the revised edition of the World Conservation Strategy, 'Building a World Conservation Ethic', was presented by the Ethics Working Group to the 17th General Assembly of IUCN in 1988.

14 *The Assisi Declarations: Messages on Man and Nature from Buddhism, Christianity, Hinduism, Islam and Judaism* (Gland, Switzerland: WWF International, 1986). A sixth religious declaration on conservation was published by the Baha'i International Community. WWF International also publishes *The New Road, A Bulletin on the WWF Network on Conservation and Religion*.

15 Denis Goulet, 'The Ethics of Power and the Power of Ethics' in *The Cruel Choice: A New Concept in the Theory of Development* (New York: University Press of America, 1985).

16 Peter Worsley, *The Three Worlds: Culture and World Development* (Chicago: University of Chicago Press, 1984), 41. See also Caldwell, *International Environmental Policy*, 262.

17 Stephen Toulmin, *The Return to Cosmology: Postmodern Science and the Theology of Nature* (Berkeley: University of California Press, 1982), 255–6.

18 Stephen Boyden, *Western Civilization in Biological Perspective: Patterns in Biohistory* (Oxford: Clarendon Press, 1987); Roy Rappaport, *Ecology, Meaning and Religion* (Richmond, California: North Atlantic Books, 1979).

19 Osvaldo Sunkel, 'Beyond the World Conservation Strategy: Integrating Development and the Environment in Latin America and the Caribbean' in Jacobs and Munro, *Conservation with Equity*, 37.

20 Although studies have been made of the concepts in these documents, none have been undertaken from an ethical perspective. See R. Cosijn, *An Analysis of Key Terms of the World Conservation Strategy* (Amsterdam: Netherlands Commission for International

Nature Protection, 1986); and International Council of Environmental Law, *World Charter for Nature: Commentary* (Bonn: IUCN Commission on Environmental Policy, Law and Administration, 1986).

21 T. O'Riordan, *Environmentalism* (London: Pion, 1981).

22 Burhenne and Irwin, *World Charter for Nature*, 9–10. Emphasis added.

23 World Commission, *Our Common Future*, 57.

24 J. Ronald Engel, 'Ecology and Social Justice: The Search for a Public Environmental Ethic' in Warren R. Copeland and Roger D. Hatch, eds, *Issues of Justice — Social Resources and Religious Meanings* (Macon, Ga.: Mercer University Press, 1988), 243–67. Another value conflict that thwarts contemporary conservation efforts involves animal rights advocates, on the one hand, and advocates of both resource conservation and ecological ethics, on the other. Again, ethicists are seeking ways to resolve this issue in ways which do justice to the full variety of values at stake. See Mary Anne Warren, 'The Rights of the Nonhuman World' in Robert Elliot and Arran Gare, eds, *Environmental Philosophy: A Collection of Readings* (University Park: The Pennsylvania State University Press, 1983), 109–31; J. Baird Callicott, 'Animal Liberation and Environmental Ethics: Back Together Again' in *In Defense of the Land Ethic: Essays in Environmental Philosophy* (Albany: State University of New York Press, 1989), 49–61.

25 Thomas Kuhn, *The Structure of Scientific Revolutions*, 2nd edn (Chicago: University of Chicago Press, 1970); Dennis Pirages and Paul Ehrlich, *Ark II: Social Responses to Environmental Imperatives* (San Francisco: W. H. Freeman, 1974).

26 Peter Jacobs, Julia Gardner and David Munro, 'Sustainable and Equitable Development: An Emerging Paradigm' in Jacobs and Munro, *Conservation with Equity*, 19–20. Emphasis added.

27 Lynn White, Jr, 'Continuing the Conversation' in Ian Barbour, ed., *Western Man and Environmental Ethics*, (Reading, Mass.: Addison-Wesley, 1973), 60.

28 For a review of this discussion see J. Baird Callicott and Roger T. Ames, 'Epilogue', *Nature in Asian Traditions of Thought: Essays in Environmental Philosophy* (Albany: State University of New York Press, 1989).

29 Herbert W. Richardson and Donald R. Cutler, eds, *Transcedence* (Boston: Beacon Press, 1969).

30 Donald Worster, *Nature's Economy: the Roots of Ecology* (Garden City, New York: Doubleday, 1979).

31 The popularity of the writings of Aldo Leopold on the 'land ethic' have contributed to this. See Baird Callicott, ed., *Companion to A Sand County Almanac* (Madison: University of Wisconsin Press, 1987).

32 Holmes Rolston, III, *Environmental Ethics: Duties to and Values in the Natural World* (Philadelphia: Temple University Press, 1988), 174, 176. Emphasis added.

33 See F. Berkes, ed., *Common Property Resources: Ecology and Community-based Sustainable Development* (London: Belhaven, 1989); J. Ronald Engel, 'The Ethics and Symbolism of the Biosphere Reserve Concept' in W.P. Gregg, Jr, S.L. Krugman and J.D. Wood, Jr, eds, *Proceedings of the Symposium on Biosphere Reserves*, Fourth World Wilderness Congress, 14–17 September, 1987, YMCA of the Rockies, Estes Park, Colorado (Atlanta: US Department of the Interior, National Park Service, 1989), 21–32.

34 Hilkka Pietilä, 'Women as an Alternative Culture Here and Now', *Development* 4 (1984); Ariel Salleh, 'Deeper than Deep Ecology', *Environmental Ethics* 6 (1984): 335–41; Rosemary Ruether, *New Woman New Earth* (New York: Dove Press, 1975); Irene Dankelman and Joan Davidson, eds, *Women and Environment in the Third World* (London: Earthscan, 1988); Maria Mies, *Patriarchy and Accumulation on a World Scale* (London: Zed Books, 1986); Vandana Shiva, *Staying Alive: Women, Ecology and Development in India* (London: Zed Press, 1989).

35 J. Ronald Engel, 'Promoting the Development and Adoption of Environmental Ethics' in Philip Hughes and Charmian Thirlwall, eds, *The Ethics of Development: Choices in Development Planning* (Port Moresby: University of Papua New Guinea Press, 1988), 55–65.
36 J. Ronald Engel, ed., *Voluntary Associations: Socio-cultural Analyses and Theological Interpretation* (Chicago: Exploration Press at Chicago Theological Seminary, 1986).
37 *Making Common Cause Internationally, a Policy Statement and Action Plan for International Development, Environment and Population NGOs* (Geneva: International Council of Voluntary Agencies, 1988).

Part One
Global Challenge

1 Environment, technology, and ethics

Rajni Kothari

Twenty, even ten, years ago one had still to establish the 'case' for the environment. To this end, beginning with the Stockholm conference, a major intellectual and political effort was mounted, an effort that has proved successful. Unfortunately, this very success has been co-opted by the status quo, with the result that while everyone talks of the environment, the destruction of nature goes on apace, indeed at an increasing pace. The environment is proving to be a classic case of 'doublespeak', a lot of sophistry, and not a little deliberate duplicity and cunning.

A decade ago, there was reluctance on the part of national governments and international agencies to include the environmental dimension in their strategies of development. This reluctance has given way to acceptance, and 'sustainable development' has become a universal slogan. Yet nothing much seems to have changed in mainstream development policy. There is no genuine striving towards an alternative perspective on development, no ethical shift that makes sustainable development a reality. 'Sustainability' has been adopted as rhetoric, not as an ethical principle which restructures our relationship with the Earth and its creatures in the realm of knowledge and in arenas of action.

In the absence of an ethical imperative, environmentalism has been reduced to a technological fix, and as with all technological fixes, solutions are seen to lie once more in the hands of manager technocrats. Economic growth, propelled by intensive technology and fuelled by an excessive exploitation of nature, was once viewed as a major factor in environmental degradation; it has suddenly been given the central role in solving the environmental crisis. The market economy is given an even more significant role in organizing nature and society. The environmentalist label and the sustainability slogan have become deceptive jargons that are used as convenient covers for conducting business as usual. This is particularly the case with the world's privileged groups, whose privileges are tied to the status quo, and who will therefore hold on to those privileges as long as they can.

But there are other voices which give a different meaning to sustainability, one which is rooted in ethics, not in monetary policy, and which goes hand in hand with the striving towards an alternative mode of development. Without such striving, sustainability is an empty term, because the current model of development destroys nature's wealth and hence is non-sustainable. And it is ecologically destructive *because* it is ethically vacuous — not impelled by basic values, and not anchored in concepts of rights and responsibilities. Thinking and acting ecologically is basically a matter of ethics, of respecting the rights of other beings, both human and non-human.

This chapter will address these two opposing meanings of 'sustainability' and their respective development paradigms. It will differentiate between sustainability as a narrow economic ideal and sustainability as an ethical ideal, between sustainability of privileges and sustainability of life on Earth. Once the conflict was between 'environment' and 'development'. I now see a conflict between the two meanings of 'sustainable development', because sustainability has become everyone's catchword, even though it means entirely different things to different people.

Later I shall lay out the profile of an alternative design for development, one which is environmentally and ethically sound, and at the same time economically, socially, and politically just. But before I do, it is necessary to provide an analysis of the reasons why the present mode of development which once held out such promise and gave rise to the vision of 'continuous progress for all' has come to grief. In what follows, I shall provide such an analysis in the context of the fast-changing processes of history, their philosophical underpinning, and their consequences for the politics of development. We shall see that it is more from the striving of ordinary folk as they face the modern trauma that new possibilities might emerge than from the doings of counter-elites spawned by social movements, though the catalytic role of the latter should not be underestimated. The issue is less whose efforts should succeed than which interventions are likely to endure because they are ethically grounded.

The crisis in world order

We may begin with some fundamentals. The most fundamental point to grasp is that we live in a period of profound transformation which is engulfing and interlocking diverse regions, cultures, and ecosystems into a common enterprise, and in the process giving rise to new conflicts waged on a scale unheard of in earlier times. Whereas thinkers from time immemorial have defined the human predicament as the need to overcome conflict through some kind of a social order, most of them thought in terms of a single society, or of conflicts between two or more societies. *For the first time we are realizing that the human predicament is on a world scale.* And all actors in it, and perhaps most of all the weakest and the most deprived among them, need to think in terms that cover all persons and societies. The end of colonialism, the unprecedented increase in population, the urgency of the economic problem, the sudden sense of the bounties of nature drying up, and a feeling of scarcity of basic resources in place of a feeling of continuous progress — all point, on the one hand, to a scenario of growing conflict that will become worldwide in scope, and on the other hand, to the need to work out new solutions based on a new structure of human cooperation.

It is only by thinking in terms of a new concept of ordering the world as a whole that there can be any salvation for a humanity that has lost its moorings. This will require new ways of attending to human problems; but it is not impossible to do this once the problems become clear, and we are able to move out of the old grooves in which we habitually think.

It is necessary to grasp this point. For it is only at times of deep crisis that major changes become possible, for better or for worse, and human beings are capable of both. It is a time when we can either seize the opportunity by deciding to control our future and usher in a new era, or we may miss the opportunity and be pushed into a downward course by forces beyond our control, after which it may be difficult to retrieve lost ground. That we are caught in such a historic moment should be clear to anyone who reflects on the concrete realities of the world we live in and the developments taking place in different parts of this world — in economics, in politics, in the availability and distribution of resources, in the relationship between food and population, in patterns of trade and control of technology, and in the strategic and power relations in which the different nations and regions find themselves confronting each other.

The causes of world crisis

Now while it is recognized that the contemporary human condition is one of a deepening crisis, perception as to the nature of the crisis and its causes has changed over the last two decades. For a long time — and this view still persists — the crisis was perceived in terms of an ideological struggle between different ways of life and systems of belief, not infrequently associated with a struggle for power between rival blocs of countries. A very large part of human energy and world resources was devoted to this conflict, which is by no means over and which in no small way accounts for the terrible arms race that enveloped the world and still persists. Later, attention focused on something more immediate and very pressing, but which had somehow escaped human sensitivity for so long: the great economic schism that is dividing the world into extremes of affluence and deprivation, with concentrations of poverty, scarcity, and unemployment in one vast section, and over-abundance, over-production, and over-consumption in another and much smaller section. Furthermore, both these are in a relationship in which resources from the poorer regions have for long been drained, and continue to be drained, through new instruments of appropriation. The last few years have witnessed an increasing concern with this single problem of poverty and inequity on a global scale, though it must be admitted that very little has been done systematically to solve it; indeed, it has been getting worse.

All these perceptions of the nature of the human crisis are still relevant. But perhaps one needs to think beyond single dimensions and look to more fundamental causes. After all, the fact that a century of unprecedented material progress has also been one of sprawling misery and increasing domination of the world by just a few powers suggests that there is something basically wrong with our world and the global structures that have permeated it. Indeed, there *is* something basically wrong with the way modern humanity has gone about constructing its world.

Industrialization was supposed to be an end to the condition of scarcity for humankind as a whole; in fact, it has made even ordinary decent existence more scarce and inaccessible for an increasing number of human beings. Modern education was supposed to lead to continuous progress and enlightenment for all, and with that a greater equality among men and women; in fact, it has produced a world dominated by experts, bureaucrats, and technocrats, one in which the ordinary human being feels increasingly powerless. Similarly, modern communication and transportation were supposed to produce a 'small world' in which the fruits of knowledge and development in one part of the globe could become available to all the others; in fact, modern communication and transporation have produced a world in which a few metropolitan centres are sucking in a large part of world resources and depriving the other regions of whatever comforts, skills, and local resources they once used to enjoy. Surely then there is something more deeply wrong with the structure of this world than the mere production of nuclear weapons or the economic handicap of the poorer countries. The world in which we live is indeed very badly divided, but the divisions are more fundamental than those of ideology, or of military or economic power. Perhaps there is something wrong with the *basic model of life* humankind has created in the modern age.

Colonizing the future

That this might indeed be the case is indicated by the rupture that has occurred for the first time in world history between the present and the future, the future including both the very young among us and the yet-unborn generations. While rational anticipation and prudence in preparing oneself against the future were inherent in all earlier thought, the future consequences of present action were never as morally relevant and urgent as they are today.

This is a result of the basic way of life we have created in the modern age, especially our creation of modern technology. Technology has a powerful impact on beings that have no voice in decisions regarding how technology is to be used. As the growing economic, energy, and environmental crises are now showing us, decisions taken at one point in time have the power to affect future generations in ways that are by and large irreversible. The consequences of what our parents and the older generation among us did — the ravaging of nature, the depletion of resources, the pattern of investment, the stockpiling of armaments, the building of highly centralized economic and political structures that are difficult to change (except by long struggle and violence) — are being felt by the younger generation of today. How is one to assure that the interest of the younger generation and the yet-to-be-born generations of the future are somehow represented in the present? They have no voice in the decision-making processes of modern society, least of all in representative systems of government of which only the old (whom we prefer to call 'adults') have a monopoly. It was once an assumption of planning and of prudence generally that one must sacrifice or postpone gratification in the present so that the future generations can live a better life. In fact, modern civilization does just the opposite. We are so involved in our own gratification in the present, stimulated by the mass media and advertisement agencies, that we are sacrificing the life chances of future generations.

Thus, just as decisions made in the metropolitan centres of the world and their ever-rising consumption of finite resources are adversely affecting millions of people in far-off places, decisions made by the present generation are affecting and will continue to affect the future of the young and the yet-unborn generations. These are serious questions to which the present models of politics and economics provide no answer. They call for a different kind of consciousness, one which takes a total view of existence; empathizes with the weak, the distant, the unborn, and the inarticulate; and intervenes in legislative and administrative processes at various levels of the world without, however, degenerating into some kind of brahminical class that arrogates to itself all knowlege and wisdom. As yet such consciousness (which no doubt exists here and there) is still very dim and, at any rate, not very influential in the decision-making processes of business and government. But the need for someone to represent the future — the 'last child', the 'seventh generation' — in the decisions made in the present cannot be overemphasized.[1]

Sustainability cannot be real if the future itself is colonized. Sustainability therefore cannot be realized by those who have only learned how to act in the short term. For real lessons in sustainability we need to turn to peoples and cultures that have acted on behalf of future generations. Women, particularly Third World women, who produce sustenance for their children are intimately in touch with the future through their nurturance. It is little wonder that ecology movements, like Chipko in India, spring from these cultural pockets which have conserved the qualities of caring — caring for the 'last man' as Gandhi asked his countrymen to do, or the 'last child' as I would like to put it.[2] The native Americans, who also have a special commitment to the future as part of their understanding of nature's ways, have conceptualized it in an even more telling way: to use and protect nature's creation 'so that seven generations from this day our children will enjoy the same things that we have now'. Oren Lyons, spokesman for the traditional circles of elders, has been carrying this message into the contemporary world, pleading:

Take care how you place your moccasins upon the earth, step with care, for the faces of the future generations are looking up from earth waiting their turn for life.

Today belongs to us, tomorrow we'll give it to the children, but today is ours. You have the mandate, you have the responsibility. Take care of your people — not yourselves, your people.[3]

Colonizing nature

That our basic model of life is wrong is also indicated by what we have done to other species and forms of life as well as to inanimate nature. We increasingly destroy other animal species, vegetation, the chemical sources of life, and the seabeds and rocky lands whose bounty has been the source of so much imagination, wonder, joy, and creativity. Springing from the unending acquisitiveness of our technological way of life and a concomitant decline in our sensitivity to other humans, we have been on a rampage that threatens our common organic bond with the whole of creation — and thus both our own survival and that of other species.

Modern humanity, and in particular Western technological humanity, has accummulated wealth by denying the rights of others to share in nature's bounty. These 'others' include marginal communities (tribes and small villages), future generations, and other species. Inequality, non-sustainability, and ecological instability all arise from the selfish and arrogant notion that nature's gifts are for private exploitation, not for sharing. In contrast to this rapaciousness, many cultures of the world have based their relationship with nature on the assumption that human beings are members of the Earth family, and must respect the rights of other members of the family. In traditional India, human beings were believed to be part of the cosmic family — *Vasudhevkutamkam*. The belief that trees and plants, rivers and mountains have intrinsic value created ethical constraints on human use of the environment. Hunters and gatherers have always apologized to nature before killing plants and animals. Rural women in India offer leaves to the tree goddess, *Patnadevi*, before collecting fodder from the forest.

The living Earth has a right to life, and that right is the primary moral argument for sustainable life. As Aldo Leopold has pointed out, ethics is the recognition of constraints put on an individual as a member of a community, and the ecological ethic simply enlarges the boundaries of the community to include soils, waters, plants, and animals, or collectively, the land.[4] The modern West is slowly rediscovering the ethics of nature's rights as the basis for conservation and ecological recovery. The Earth is no longer just a bundle of resources. As James Lovelock has suggested, she is *Gaia*, a living being.[5] Animals are not just resources and game for human consumption. Peter Singer has argued for animal liberation as a component of human liberation.[6] And Christopher Stone has raised the issue of whether trees have rights.[7] The women of Gharwal, the backbone of the Chipko movement, who risked their lives to save their trees, clearly believe that trees have rights, and that the rights of trees are of a higher order than those of human beings because trees provide the *conditions* for life on Earth.

Sustainability ultimately rests on the democracy of all life, on the recognition that human beings are not masters but members of the Earth family.

Human capacities for a new world order

None of these issues — the rampage of technology, the divisions of global society, the sacrifice of the life chances of future generations, or the destruction of other species and other sources of life and sustenance — were adequately raised in earlier philosophical discussions about the human predicament. The predicament that faces humankind today includes all these issues; and the salvation that we must work out for ourselves and for the whole of nature must address itself to all these issues. In this sense, the crisis that we face is far more total than ever before.

And yet, human beings throughout history have shown an almost infinite capacity for identifying their own immediate purposes with larger purposes. We have come a long way from the primeval stage when we identified with just a few of our kind and cared little for others. Today we are able to identify not only with our own national or regional collectivity but with the whole of the human species, and even with non-human species. Our capacity to symbolize and identify with abstract entities enables us to think in cosmic terms and embrace entities and identities that range from the ephemeral to the eternal.

Nor is this entirely new. At many times in history humanity has shown a striking empathy for the whole of creation. The intellectual and religious movements that led to a deep sense of regard for life in all forms and an abhorrence of violence in all forms, including violence to other forms of life, had their mainsprings in this innate human power to symbolize and identify with creation and to revolt against human excesses. This is what powerful movements like Buddhism and Jainism represented in my own land. Similar movements took place in other regions. It is true that often, as in India, this kind of feeling for life produced a rather quiescent attitude toward life's purposes and even a metaphysic that undermined humanity's self-confidence. It will be necessary to guard against this kind of defeatist religiosity. But such an attitude is by no means inherent in developing a larger identity with creation.

The conclusion I draw is that if there is to be a moral imperative for sustainable development, there needs to be a sense of sanctity about the Earth. Concern for the environment has to emanate from the basic human capacity to experience the sacred, the capacity to wonder at the blessings that are still with us, to seek after the mysteries of the cosmic order, and a corresponding modesty of the self and its claims on that order. Respect for life has to be a fundamentally spiritual notion, based on faith in the inalienable rights of all living beings. The basic sanctions behind them are not contractual but transcendental. They are not primarily claims bestowed by law but are inherent in the very nature of life.

Humanity, then, does have the capacity to create a new world order. Indeed, of all the species only humanity has the capacity to transform its history on a global scale. Human beings are the abstracting animals, the historical animals, the aesthetic animals, the animal that through language, memory, empathy, and will — including the will to transcend the temptations of the moment — can integrate sense perceptions with intricate systems of knowledge, awareness, and morality, as well as with the as yet unknown and unravelled realms of mystery and wonder. Indeed, it is out of these unique capacities that our ultimate salvation must emerge. The predicaments that we face, however, are immediate; we need to move quickly beyond all the structures we have created — political, socioeconomic, and technological — and evolve new criteria for human effort and cooperation.

It is not that humanity must sacrifice all its activities, knowledge, and institutional structures, or surrender all its achievements and start all over again in a clean, new state. Evolution does not take such form. It is rather that our view of which values and purposes should inform our actions and institutions must be consciously *re*-viewed; and, wherever choices are called for, these should be exercised. We have the capacity to exercise such choices. Maybe some small technological 'breakthrough' in one field or another will again lull us to sleep. But we now know that all such breakthroughs are temporary and cannot take the place of a fundamental restructuring of society. Gadgets may temporarily overpower the mind, but ultimately the mind must come into its own and address itself to the moral questions of life.

The point is that every few hundred years a new challenge presents itself. And each time, it calls for new understanding and a new paradigm of action. Ours is one such moment in the history of humankind and the universe.

The ethics of sustainable development

Contemporary concern for sustainable development is an authentic moral concern to the degree that it poses an alternative to the dominant model of modern development. Its moral significance lies not in the specialized concerns of experts and counter-experts (whether they be professional ethicists, scientists, or technicians), but in a vision of a new way of life that is at once comprehensible and accessible to all human beings.

One can identify four primary criteria for sustainable development when it is conceived as an ethical ideal: a holistic view of development; equity based on the autonomy and self-reliance of diverse entities instead of on a structure of dependence founded on aid and transfer of technology with a view to 'catching up'; an emphasis on participation; and an accent on the importance of local conditions and the value of diversity. To these we must add two still more basic concerns, or rather two broad considerations that should inform all our concerns. One is a fundamentally normative perspective on the future, particularly from the viewpoint of the coming generations for whom we are responsible. The other is a cosmic view of life as sacred.

The report of the World Commission on Environment and Development, *Our Common Future*,[8] is misleading if it suggests that the so-called 'underdeveloped' countries can experience the life they see on Western television programmes without further degradation of the global environment. 'Our common future' cannot lie in an affluence that is ecologically suicidal, and socially and economically exclusive. It can, and must, lie in a curtailment of wants, as Gandhi constantly reminded his countrymen and others.[9] We have more than enough empirical evidence that the destruction of the biosphere lies first and foremost in the wasteful lifestyles of the world's privileged groups, and that the problem of poverty emanates from this same source. Consumption, as an end in itself, excludes the rights of others, both because it makes heavy demands on resources, but also because, in self-gratification, it is blind to others' needs.

The moral approach to development suggested here also involves a certain understanding of how we can most authentically know and relate to the rest of nature. The presumption that the role of science and technology was to develop nature in the service of humankind has turned out to be an illusion. It was based on a view of science itself as an instrument of human power over nature, other men and women, other forms of life, and all the qualities of being that constitute the cosmic order. This must give place to the original purpose of science, namely, seeking to understand the mysteries of nature with a deep sense of humility and wonder. True science is practised by persons with a fundamental philosophical scepticism about the scope and limits of human knowledge, who never for a moment assume that all is knowable and that secular knowledge provides the key to 'mastering' the universe. Such a moral vision will make for a partnership between science and nature, and — equally vital — between scientists and all peoples whose lives are rooted in the wisdom of their ancestors. There is a vast area of research and development that lies ahead in this field. The scientist will have to take on a more modest role as a participant in a total system of relationships. As was stressed earlier in this chapter, one of the basic postulates of an alternative philosophy of development is to treat life as a whole and not in fragments. This calls for a perspective on science that is oriental rather than occidental, feminist rather than *macho*, rural rather than urban, one that draws on the accumulated wisdom of centuries (each succeeding century and generation refining the inherited pool) rather than one that rejects all that is past and traditional.

The shift to sustainable development is primarily an ethical shift. It is not a technological fix, nor a matter of new financial investment. It is a shift in values such that nature is valued in itself and for its life support functions, not merely for how it can be converted into resources and commodities to feed the engine of economic growth. Respect for nature's diversity, and the responsibility to conserve that diversity, define sustainable development as an ethical ideal. Out of an ethics of respect for nature's diversity flows a respect for the diversity of cultures and livelihoods, the basis not only of sustainability, but also of justice and equity. The ecological crisis is in large part a matter of treating nature's diversity as dispensable, a process that has gone hand in hand with the view that a large portion of the human species is dispensable as well. To reverse the ecological decline we require an ethical shift that treats all life as indispensable.

Notes

1 Rajni Kothari, *Transformation and Survival: In Search of a Humane World Order* (New Delhi: Ajanta, 1988).
2 Sundarlal Bahuguna, ed., *Chipko Message* (Chipko Information Centre, Parvatiya Navjivan Mandal, P.O. Silyara, Tehri Gharwal, 1984); Core Group of the United Nations University's Major Project on Peace and Global Transformation, *The Last Child* (Delhi: Lokvani, 1990).
3 Oren Lyons, 'An Iroquois Perspective' in Christopher Vecsey and Robert W. Venables, eds, *American Indian Environments: Ecological Issues in Native American History* (New York: Syracuse University Press, 1980).
4 Aldo Leopold, *A Sand County Almanac and Sketches Here and There* (London: Oxford University Press, 1949).
5 James Lovelock, *Gaia: A New Look at Life on Earth* (London: Oxford University Press, 1979).
6 Peter Singer, *Animal Liberation* (New York: Random House, 1975).
7 Christopher Stone, *Should Trees Have Standing? Toward Legal Rights for Natural Objects* (Los Altos, California: William Kaufmann, 1974).
8 World Commission on Environment and Development, *Our Common Future* (Oxford: Oxford University Press, 1987).
9 J. D. Sethi, *Gandhi Today* (New Delhi: Vikas Publishing House, 1978).

2 Development ethics and ecological wisdom
Denis Goulet

The ecological imperative is clear and cruel: nature must be saved or we humans will die. The single greatest threat to nature — menacing, irreversible destruction of its regenerative powers — comes from 'development'. This same 'development' is also the major culprit in perpetuating the 'underdevelopment' of hundreds of millions. The task of eliminating degrading underdevelopment imposes itself with the same urgency as does the task of safeguarding nature. These twin concerns have spawned two ethical streams of protest among policy theorists and development practitioners. One stream is concerned wth protecting nature, the other with promoting economic justice. Almost always, the two streams have flowed in opposite directions. This is tragic because it is the identical pseudodevelopment which lies at the root of both problems. The only antidote to pseudodevelopment is a working ethic of what many are calling 'sustainable development', but which I prefer to call 'integral authentic development'. Such an ethic joins the two normative streams — a regard for environmental wisdom and a concern for universal economic justice.

The task of development ethics today is to formulate this ethic of integral development, locating environmental concerns at the heart of normative discourse on development.

The simple thesis defended here states that there can be no sound development ethic without environmental wisdom, and vice versa, no environmental wisdom is possible without a solid ethics of development. The urgent task at hand consists in assuring that development ethics enter into the formulation of environmental policy and conversely that environmental ethics be a prime consideration in the formulation of developmental policy. Great difficulty and confusion, however, attend the task of bringing the two ethical streams together. Fundamental problems of language and meaning, disagreements of diagnosis, policy preference, and value assessment cloud the concepts. Conflicting development paradigms compete for legitimacy; there exist antagonistic ways of defining the essential tasks of ethical reflection; and the terms 'ecology' and 'environment' evoke irreconcilable associations.

Analysis of these divergencies leads to the conclusion that environmental wisdom is compatible only with *certain* images of development and only with *certain* approaches to the conduct of ethical reflection. A normatively sound concept of development is consonant only with *some* conceptions of the environmental or ecological task. What is needed is an overarching framework of dynamic synthesis, a philosophical vision which reconciles the alleged opposition between human freedom and the integrity of nature. One must, in other words, articulate a conceptual scheme in which the demands of three distinct ethical values — justice, freedom, and respect for nature — all become *relativized*. No single one of these values can be taken to have absolute worth; more importantly, each can only be defined and delimited in its proper boundaries with relation to the other two.

Development paradigms: Critiques and alternatives

Nowadays, development is increasingly denounced as a very bad thing. The noted French agronomist, René Dumont, calls the performances of the last forty years a dangerous epidemic of misdevelopment. He argues that in Africa, development has simply not occurred and that Latin America's new wealth, won at the price of massive pollution, urban congestion, and a monumental waste of resources, has not benefited the majority of the continent's population. For Dumont, misdevelopment, or the mismanagement of resources in both the socialist and capitalist worlds, is the main cause of world hunger, afflicting 'developed' countries as severely as it does Third World nations.[1]

In an earlier work, the present author termed much alleged progress to be antidevelopment because it is the antithesis of authentic development, the qualitative improvement in a society's provision of life-sustaining goods, esteem, and freedom to all its citizens.[2] Other writers strike the same theme. The late Swiss anthropologist, Roy Preiswerk, and his colleagues judge that change processes have produced maldevelopment, a faulty orientation in rich and poor countries alike.[3] Authors like the African, Albert Tévéidjrè, and the Haitian, Georges Anglade, reject dehumanizing economic development and recall that the greatest wealth any nation possesses is its poor people themselves.[4]

The most categorical attack comes from those who totally repudiate development, both as a concept and as a project. The French economist, Serge Latouche, condemns development as a tool used by advanced Western countries to destroy the cultures and the autonomy of nations throughout Africa, Asia, and Latin America.[5] The Montreal-based Monchanin Intercultural Centre, through its quarterly review, *Interculture*, tirelessly promotes the thesis that development must be rejected since it is the instrument which destroys native cultures and their political, juridical, economic, and symbolic meaning systems.[6] The Cultural Survival movement headquartered at Harvard University has likewise struggled since its creation in 1972 to prevent 'development' from destroying indigenous peoples and their cultures.[7]

Most national governments and international financing agencies, however, still define development as maximum economic growth and a concerted drive towards industrialization and mass consumption. The success stories praised world-wide are Korea and Taiwan, twin paragons of capital-intensive and high-technology economic growth allied to success in competitive international trading arenas.[8] Development reports remain discretely silent, however, as to the costs in political repression attendant upon these economic successes.[9] The World Bank, the Organization for Economic Cooperation and Development, the International Monetary Fund, and most national planning agencies still promote strategies which treat maximum aggregate growth as synonymous with genuine development.

Notwithstanding the residual hegemony still enjoyed by growth models in policy arenas, a new development paradigm is now in gestation. One sign of its ascending legitimacy is that rhetorical homage must now be paid to its values even by those who pursue traditional growth strategies. In place of mere economic growth, this alternative development model grants primacy to basic needs satisfaction, the elimination of absolute poverty, the creation of jobs, the reduction of dependency, respect for cultural values, and ecological responsibility.

Two recent formulations of this alternative paradigm reveal how value-laden and ethical in nature is any serious talk of development. In September 1986 the Marga Institute held a week-long seminar in Colombo, Sri Lanka, on ethical issues in development. Theorists and practitioners concurred that any adequate definition of development must include five dimensions:

- an economic component dealing with the creation of wealth and improved material conditions of life;
- a social ingredient measured as well-being in health, education, housing, and employment;
- a political dimension embodying values such as human rights, political freedom, enfranchisement, and some form of democracy;
- a cultural dimension in recognition of the fact that cultures confer identity and self-worth to people;
- a fifth dimension called the 'full-life paradigm', which refers to the ultimate meanings of life and history as expressed in symbols and beliefs.

A seminar held some years earlier on the essential components of Latin American development reached nearly identical conclusions. Its comprehensive definition of development revolves around economic growth, distributional equity, participation/vulnerability, and transcendental values.[10] David Pollock explains the inclusion of 'transcendental values' by asking if heightened economic equity is the ultimate goal. He asks:

Does man live by GNP alone? Should we not take advantage of our longer-term vision and ask what kind of person Latin America may wish to evolve by the end of this century? What are the transcendental values — cultural, ethical, artistic, religious, moral — that extend beyond the current workings of the purely economic and social system? How to appeal to youth, who so often seek nourishment in dreams, as well as in bread?[11]

Indeed, development choices *are* value-laden. They pose anew, and in a new mode, the ancient philosophical questions: what is the relation between the fullness of good and the abundance of goods; what are the foundations of justice in and among societies; what criteria govern the posture of societies towards the forces of nature and technology? If providing satisfactory answers to these questions is what makes a country truly developed, it follows that not every nation with a high per capita income is truly developed.[12]

What renders these ancient moral questions specifically developmental and the old answers given to them obsolete is the unique cluster of modern questions. First, there is the vast scale of most human activities — the size of our cities, bureaucracies, and factories, the sheer volume of images and fantasies which assault the senses. There is also the technical complexity and the specialized division of labour ensuing therefrom, so that no single set of skills — manual, intellectual, or artistic — is adequate to cope with the needs of unity, integration, and openness to change. In a technically complex world it becomes nearly impossible to answer such simple questions as, 'what is the good life', and the relation between goods and the good. A third feature of modern life, the web of interdependence, transforms local happenings into global events and causes international conflicts to impinge on local destinies. Finally, and most dramatic, there is the ever-shortening time lag between changes proposed to human communities and the deadline they face for reacting to them in ways which protect their integrity. Mass media, modern medicine, and technology constantly affect the consciousness, values, and destinies of people, leaving them scant time to take counsel with their traditions or their images of the future so as to shape a wise response.

Thanks to these distinctive modern conditions, the moral questions all societies faced in the past have become contemporary developmental questions. By and large, however, these normative questions have been ignored or poorly answered by either development experts or ethicists. Galbraith chides fellow economists for not having 'the final requirement of modern development planning: a theory of consumption . . . a view of what the production is ultimately for.[13] Most development experts flee such value-laden questions, branding them unscientific or impressionistic. For their part, ethicists rarely take development processes and conflicts as the raw materials of their moral reflection. By thus remaining outside the dynamics and constraints of social change, ethicists risk imprisoning themselves within sterile forms of moralism which are useless or positively harmful. The answers to normative questions posed by development do not pre-exist in any ethical doctrine. Neither ancient wisdoms interpreted in static fashion nor uncritical modern scientific approaches suffice to produce such answers. These can issue only from new dialogues between ancient wisdoms and modern visions in modes which avoid ethnocentrism, dogmatism, and ideological manipulation.[14]

The ethical task is especially difficult because the very language of development conceals two ambiguities. An identical term designates both the goal of change processes — namely, some vision of a better life — and those very processes themselves seen as means to reach the goal. Moreover, the term 'development' can be used either descriptively or normatively. One speaks descriptively when listing a country's GNP growth rates, trade balance, or rate of savings and investment. But one may shift to normative language and condemn these very accomplishments by branding them modernization without development or by decrying the failure of quantitative growth to produce human development. These twin ambiguities are unavoidable, for development is both a goal and a means thereto, a label for what *is* as well as a pointer to what *ought to be*.

Serious discourse on development is impossible except in ethical terms. As the North American political scientist, David Apter, notes: 'Perhaps the most important consequences of the study of modernization is that it brings us back to the search for first principles. By this I mean that it requires the unity of moral and analytical modes of thought'.[15] Development ethics must take its place alongside economics, politics, anthropology, and planning as a tool for analysing and solving development problems which, by definition, are inseparably economic, social, political, cultural, technical, and ethical in nature. Success in this enterprise presupposes, however, a certain way of 'doing ethics'.

Ethics: The means of the means

Is any ethical approach commensurate to the task of integrating the diagnostic, policy, and value domains of development? To state what must not be done is easy; to specify what is needed is less so. Evidently, no abstract deductive ethics can serve. The discipline of development is an art, not a science: it deals not with orderly or perfect patterns of logic or design but with decisions and actions taken in domains of high uncertainty. Great practical wisdom is required in development affairs. Wisdom brings unity out of multiplicity after facing contradiction and complexity. In this it is distinguished from naiveté, whose unity of meaning is gained by fleeing from contradiction and complexity. No development ethics can be adequate if it is either ethnocentric or reductionist. No valid ethics can cease adhering to general ends as values, but it must bring the value charge (or density) of those ends to bear on the world of political and economic power by entering into their dynamics.

The French philosopher, Gustave Thibon, seeks some way of converting power to a higher ethic. In a critical study of Nietzche, published in 1975, he restates 'the Nietzschean ideal of sanctification of power':

Heretofore power and purity could coexist, one separate from the other. It was possible, without causing too much damage, for the first to remain spiritually impure and the second materially ineffectual simply because power had limited means at its disposal: the worst whims of caesars did not totally threaten the equilibrium and survival of humanity. But nowadays power disposes of almost infinite means of destruction; therefore, can we seek salvation elsewhere than in the union of force with wisdom?[16]

Ethics cannot exorcize evil from realms of political power simply by preaching noble ideals. Somehow ethics must get inside the value dynamisms of the instruments utilized by development agents and become, as it were, a 'means of the means'.

Nor can ethicists rest content with portraying ideal ends and passing adverse judgment on the means used by politicians, planners, or others to achieve social justice. This approach likewise fails because it remains outside the real criteria and the constraints of decision-making. One may legitimately claim for ethics the role assigned to sociology by Ralf Dahrendorf:

'It is the sociologist's business to consider what a modern, open, civilized society might look like and what roads might lead to it. That is the domain of theory. It is also the sociologist's business once he is equipped with his theories to take part in the process of changing reality in making what is reasonable real. This is the domain of practice.[17]

Genuine ethics is a kind of *praxis*, by which I mean that it generates critical reflection on the value content and meaning of one's social action.[18] Unlike the mere extrinsic treatment of means, ethical praxis conditions choices and priorities by assigning relative value allegiances to essential needs, basic power relationships, and criteria for determining tolerable levels of human suffering in promoting social change.[19] Alternative development strategies have varying impacts on populations victimized by poverty, class privilege, economic exploitation, or political domination. This is why an ethic of social justice and equity needs to harness concrete instruments in support of the struggle conducted by social classes at the bottom of the stratification ladder. It is a hollow, if not a hypocritical, exercise to speak rhetorically about human dignity unless one builds social structures which foster human dignity and eliminate what impedes it: endemic disease, chronic poverty, an unjust system of land tenure, or political powerlessness. A vital nexus links any society's basic value choices to its preferred development strategy and to the criteria it applies in making specific policy decisions, be they over employment, investment, taxes, or education.

In sum, development ethics as 'means of the means' requires not that moralists pose ideal goals and pass judgment on the means used by others to pursue these or other goals, but rather that decision-makers versed in the constraints surrounding vital choices promote the values for which oppressed and underdeveloped groups struggle: greater justice, a decent sufficiency of goods for all, and equitable access to collective human gains realized in domains of technology, organization, and research. This stance, while practical, differs qualitatively from an ethic of pure efficiency in social problem-solving or the mere rationalization and defence of elite interests.[20] The difference lies between a view of politics as the art of the possible (manipulating possibilities within given parameters) and that of politics as the art of creating new possibilities (altering the parameters themselves). Development practitioners ought to adopt as their 'moral imperative in development' those strategies which, utilizing existing social forces, implement the values to which they give their allegiance. In practice this means preferring strategies, programmes, and projects (and even modes of reaching decisions) which assign more importance to ethical considerations than to mere technical criteria of efficiency.

Under ideal circumstances ethicists would share responsibility for the practical consequences of joint decisions taken by teams of development planners, economists, and technicians. Unless economists, planners, and technicians assess the ethical import of their decisional criteria from inside the dynamics of their respective specialties, however, they will fall prey to the determinism of what Jacques Ellul calls 'pure technique'.[21] Conversely, ethicists need the critical input made by problem-solvers if they are to avoid purely extrinsic moralism.

Development ethics has a clear mandate to adopt an intrinsicist methodology or procedure. Its need for a clear view of its tasks and functions is no less acute. The first task of development ethics is to raise aloft certain banners proclaiming:

- the primacy of needs wants (what economists call 'effective demand'); the obligations incumbent on favoured nations and populations to practise effective solidarity with those less favoured (these obligations are based on justice and not merely on optional charity);
- that the demands of justice are structural and institutional, not merely behavioural or reducible to policy changes;
- that the role of development politics is one of creating new frontiers of possibility and not that of merely manipulating resources (wealth, power, information, and influence) within given parameters of possibility previously defined in some static form.

But it is futile to raise banners without justifying and defending them. Development ethics has to make its intellectual case for the values just enunciated. It will have to argue persuasively the reasons why solidarity should be the norm and not some exclusionary 'triage' or lifeboat ethic. If it is true, as Garrett Hardin claims, that there are limits to altruism, development ethics must discover how these limits are to be transcended.[22]

Its second essential task is to formulate ethical strategies for a multiplicity of sectoral problem-solving domains, ranging from population policy to investment codes, and from aid strategy to norms for technology transfers and criteria for evaluating human rights compliance.

Ethicists can strategize only by entering into the technical and political constraints of any problem domain and rendering explicit the value costs and benefits of competing diagnoses and proposed solutions to problems. They must also establish criteria and procedures by which technical, political, and managerial decision-makers may choose wisely and implement at the lowest possible cost what the sociologist, Peter Berger, calls 'a calculus of pain and a calculus of meaning'.[23]

Three distinct rationalities converge in decision-making: technological, political, and ethical rationality.[24]Each has a distinct goal and a peculiar animating spirit or basic procedure. Problems arise because each rationality approaches the other two in reductionist fashion, seeking to impose its view of goals and procedures on the decision-making process. The result is technically sound decisons which are politically infeasible or morally unacceptable, or, in other cases, ethically sound choices which are technically inefficient or politically impossible. From observing experimental innovations in negotiation (in arenas as disparate as resettlement schemes in dam construction sites or the political empowerment of peasant associations seeking to redefine criteria of credit eligibility in large World Bank projects), I have concluded that to avoid reductionism, the three rationalities must operate in a circular, not a vertical, pattern of interaction.

Only from within the constraint systems enveloping any development decision can ethicists draw out the value costs and implications of those decisions and actions. The largest and most important constraint system is the environment — natural and artificial — encompassing all human efforts. Development ethics may well undergo the most severe test of its ability to orientate and guide — while operating as a 'means of the means' — in the domain of environmental policy.

The ecology of integral development

Ecology has now become a household word. Here lies some illuminating symbolism for, in its Greek etymology, 'ecology' designates the science of the larger household, the total environment in which living organisms exist. Indeed, whenever it is faithful to its origins and inner spirit, ecology is holistic: it looks to the whole picture and the totality of relations. As a recently certified pluridisciplinary field of study, ecology embraces four distinct, interrelated subjects: environment; demography; resource systems; and technology. Its special contribution to human knowledge is to draw a coherent portrait of how these four realms interact in patterns of vital interdependence.

Ecological wisdom is the search for optimal modes and scales in which human populations may apply technology to resource use within their environments. Ecology, both as an intellectual discipline and as a practical concern, ineluctably presupposes some philosophy of nature. Traditional human wisdoms long ago parted ways, however, in their fundamental conceptions of nature and their views as to how human beings should relate to it. All wisdoms acknowledge humans to be part of nature and subject to its laws and constraints. The common destiny of all natural beings, humans included, is generation and corruption; they are born, grow, get old, and die. But certain world views more than others have elevated humans above their encompassing nature and assigned them a cosmic role of domination over that very nature of which they are a part. Thus the interrogatory words which serve as the title of one publication, *Man in Nature, Guest or Engineer?*[25]

Nature and human liberty have come to be perceived as opposing poles in a dichotomy. The paradox lies in this: that human beings are not physically compelled to respect nature but they need to do so *if* they are to survive and preserve the existential ground on which to assert their freedom. Since this is so, there can be no ultimate or radical incompatibility between the demands of nature and the exigencies of human freedom, those of environmental sanity, wise resource stewardship, and technology. Theoretical and practical problems arise when one is not looking at the whole picture. Looking at the whole picture enables one to transcend numerous apparent antinomies, chief among which is the putative contradiction between anthropocentric and cosmocentric views of the universe.

Robert Vachon, a Canadian philosopher of interculturalism, believes that Orientals perceive humanity, nature, and the divine not as autonomous realities but as non-dualistic dimensions of life which share interconnection and harmony with all dimensions of being. Vachon defines the oriental vision of reality as holistic because it grants priority to totality over opposition or polarity.[26]

Similarly, the opposition between human freedom and nature can be subsumed under a larger whole. That larger whole is integral development, a normative concept embracing three elements: the good life; the best foundations of life in society; and the proper stance toward natural and man-made environments. As the French ecologist, Bernard Charbonneau, insists, freedom itself is nature and both form part of a larger whole.[27]

It is a difficult task to reconcile nature and freedom because the emphasis on one or the other has given birth to distinct ethical orientations. Those who stress the integrity of nature have formulated an ethic whose highest values are conservation of resources, the preservation of species, and the need to protect nature from human depredations. Those who stress human freedom have framed an ethic whose primary values are justice (which takes the form of an active assault upon human poverty, branded as the worst form of pollution) and the need to 'develop' latent or potential resources into their actualized state. Both ethical orientations adhere to all five values. What sets the two apart is the rank order they assign to these separate values. A 'nature' emphasis locates development and the elimination of human misery below biological conservation and resource replenishment in the hierarchy of values, while a 'freedom' orientation places development and the active conquest of justice in resource allocations above environmental protection or the preservation of endangered species. In truth, however, all these values should enjoy parity of moral status and stand on an equal footing. The reason is simply that any long-term, sustainable, equity-enhancing combat against poverty requires wisdom in the exploitation of resources, just as the preservation of species cannot be persuasively held out as a priority goal if the human species is threatened with degrading poverty or extinction. Nature itself is diminished or wounded when its human members are kept 'underdeveloped'; those human members cannot become truly 'developed' if their supportive nature is violated.

It may well be that no world view can successfully integrate the concepts and requirements of nature and freedom except around some higher *telos*, or end-value, to which both nature and human freedom are subordinate. Because neither nature nor freedom can be taken as absolute values, diverse philosophies and religions assign different value weights to each. Even within a specific world view competing interpretations arise as to the 'proper' weight to be assigned. To illustrate: throughout its history, Christianity has harboured tendencies towards either exaggerated supernaturalism, in which the realms of nature and human activity are treated merely as arenas in which human beings test their virtue or save their souls, or towards excessive naturalism, in which God's transcendent and mysterious salvation is reduced to a better way of organizing human society. There have flourished within Christianity schools of interpretation favouring an exaggerated theocentric humanism which assumes that anything given to man is stolen from God, and an imbalanced anthropocentric theism in which God becomes a glorified projection of popular human values.

The Christian theologian, Teilhard de Chardin, overcomes either imbalance in his view of religion which is both fully transcendent and fully human. He searches for 'the reconciliation of progress and detachment' — of passionate and legitimate love of the greater Earth and the unique quest for the Kingdom of Heaven:

So long as the world appears to me merely as an opportunity for gaining merit, and not an enduring monument to build up and bring to perfection, I shall be but one of the lukewarm, and judging me by my religion men will regard me as below standard, and a turncoat. And who would dare to say they were utterly wrong?[28]

Thus, Teilhard refuses to relegate the world and its secular tasks to a level of secondary importance, or to treat time and history as mere epiphenomenal springboards from which to 'save one's soul'. Instead, he adopts a cosmic vision of reality which is both valued intrinsically and rendered 'open' to suprahistorical transcendence. Within this perspective, it becomes a grave dereliction of duty — in theological parlance, a mortal sin — for a Christian to abuse nature or to abuse his or her freedom.[29]

The French Christian philosopher, Jacques Maritain, taking up a theme defended seven centuries earlier by Thomas Aquinas, explains that neither nature nor human freedom can be properly prized or valued unless the entire realm of historical time and space is seen as a world of *infra-valent ends*.[30] Thus, human efforts deployed to conquer frontiers of knowledge, to institute justice and fraternity in political institutions, to create and distribute wealth in economic endeavours, or to craft beauty in artistic enterprises are not merely *means* for gaining the ultimate end, which is blessed union and happiness with God. These activities are themselves ends, and as such they are intrinsically precious. Nevertheless, the entire order represented by these temporal activities is subordinate to a higher, more absolute transtemporal end.

Bearing in mind this transtemporal end, it does appear that some kind of anthropocentric vision of the universe is unavoidable. Nature cannot defend itself; humans must now assume the task. The exploitation of planet Earth has gone beyond the threshold where nature can defend and replenish itself. The urgently needed symbiosis between nature and the human species can only result from placing human responsibility at the centre of the task of conserving nature. Things have gone wrong not because humans held an anthropocentric view of the universe (they could not do otherwise!) but because they erred in defining the value content of their own development and freedom. Freedom *from* constraining nature is indeed a positive value, but it is not an absolute one. Freedom *from* constraints is a value because it allows freedom *for* human fulfilment or realization. But that very realization substantively consists in establishing full harmony with nature, with the cosmos, with the whole universe, and with its ultimate principle.

Genuine development emerges from the living aspirations of communities of need to affirm themselves as truly human. Similarly, a veritable active respect for nature is to be found more solidly entrenched in non-elite populations who are the repositories of traditional culture than in the coterie of new experts who call themselves systems analysts, resource planners, futures modellers, or ecologists.[31]

Consequently, a new respect for tradition is just as essential for sound developmental planning as it is for ecological strategizing. Most traditional wisdoms have normatively stipulated that human freedom and intervention must respect nature. And they have understood, in turn, that nature is an indispensable ally to sustain, support, and provide for the expansion of that same human freedom. An ethic of authentic development is, therefore, *ipso facto* an ethic of ecological wisdom. It is part of sound development to enjoin and practice ecological wisdom, just as it is part of ecological wisdom (integrally and comprehensively understood) to achieve sound and harmonious human development. Clearly, what is called for is not some passive stance in which no human interventions will be made upon nature to promote economic growth of some sort. Rather, the scope and content of that growth will be redefined, or rather renegotiated, to assure just and adequate access to essential goods by all as well as to protect biosystemic sustainability.

Conflicts over priorities will continue to arise. Cruel choices, such as whether the risk of irreversibly damaging some ecosystem should be incurred in order to attend to the immediate needs for food or fuel of an impoverished populace, will not be eliminated or rendered any easier to make; and no pre-existing answer, normative and operational, is to be found or discovered anywhere. Correct answers must be negotiated in an arena of decision-making, and via a process engaging the representatives of the three rationalities — technical, political, and ethical. But it will be understood by all parties, and they will be committed to safeguarding, that neither the developmental nor the ecological value may be treated instrumentally, as a mere means to realizing the other. For both are end values, although neither is absolute.

The essential task of development ethics is to render development decisions and actions humane. Otherwise stated, it is to assure that the painful changes launched under the banners of development and progress do not result in antidevelopment, which destroys nature, human cultures, and individuals and exacts undue sacrifices — all in the name of profit, some absolutized ideology, or a supposed efficiency imperative. A comprehensive development ethics which incorporates environmental wisdom is the conceptual cement which binds together multiple diagnoses of problems to their policy implications through an explicit phenomenological study of values.

Most fundamentally, the primary mission of development ethics is to keep hope alive. By any purely rational calculus of future probabilities, the development enterprise of most countries is doomed to fail. The poor can never catch up with the rich as long as the latter continue to consume wastefully and to devise ideological justifications for not practising solidarity with the less-developed. In all probability, technological and resource gaps will continue to widen and vast resources will continue to be devoted to destructive armaments. Catastrophes generated by environmental folly or demographic tunnel vision, to say nothing of radiation poisoning, are likely scenarios of despair. Exacerbated feelings of national sovereignty will, in all likelihood, continue to coexist alongside an ever more urgent need to institute new forms of global governance and problem-solving. By any probable rational scenario projectible over the next fifty years, development will continue to wreak ecological destruction, and it will remain the privilege of a relative few, while underdevelopment will continue to be the lot of the vast majority. Only some transrational calculus of hope, situated beyond apparent realms of possibility, can elicit the creative energies and vision which authentic development requires. The French social critic, Jacques Ellul, writes eloquently of the need for hope in a time of abandonment. Ellul speaks in a theological vein, arguing that human beings cannot count on a *Deus ex machina* salvation from whatever gods they believe in. Only the human race can extricate itself from the human impasses — nuclear, ecological, economic, and political — it has itself created. Yet, human beings will despair of even attempting to create a wisdom to match their science, says Ellul, unless they have hope, and grounds for hope, in some God who has entrusted the making of history to them.[32]

In analogous fashion, I believe that development ethics must summon persons and societies to become their best selves, to create structures of responsibility, of justice, and of what Ivan Illich calls conviviality to replace exploitation and aggressive competition.[33] If René Dubos and other sociobiologists are correct in thinking that but a tiny fragment of human brain power has been utilized up to the present, and if neither Africans, nor Asians, nor Latin Americans need become consumers of a single pattern of modern civilization in order to become 'developed', it follows that the present dismal scenario is not ineluctable.[34] Robert Vacca, in *The Coming Dark Age*, gloomily forecasts a world with no future.[35] Development ethics offers a corrective view by reminding us that futures are not predestined. Yes, the most important banner development ethics must raise aloft is that of hope — hope in the possibility of creating new possibilities. Modern men and women have grown properly sceptical of facile utopias, but they also understand that far more changes than were ever anticipated are possible.

Development ethics pleads normatively for a certain reading of history, one in which human agents are simultaneously the stewards and the makers of history even as they bear witness to values of transcendence.[36] There is profound truth, even as there is literal exaggeration, in Marx's notion that till the present we have only witnessed prehistory. The beginning of authentic developmental human history arrives with the abolition of alienation. Development's true task is precisely this: to abolish all alienation — economic, social, political, and technological.

This long view of history and of development as a historical adventure is the only guarantee that development processes will assure a future. Solidarity with the planet of which we human agents are the responsible stewards, and with future generations of our descendants, is the ethical key to achieving a development which is at once human and sustainable. The late L.J. Lebret, a French pioneer in development ethics, defined development as a revolution leading to universal solidarity.[37] Here, in capsule form, we find a complete agenda for the tasks and methods facing development ethics — to institute a universal revolution of solidarity.

Notes

1 René Dumont and M. F. Mottin, *Le Mal-développement en Amérique latine* (Paris: Les Editions du Seuil, 1981), 19.
2 Denis Goulet, *The Cruel Choice: A New Concept in the Theory of Development* (Washington, D.C.: University Press of America 1985), 215–235.
3 Centre Europe-Tiers Monde (CETIM), *Mal-développement Suisse-Monde* (Genève: CETIM, 1975), 11.
4 Albet Tévoédjrè, *La Pauvreté, richesse des peuples* (Paris: Economie et Humanisme, 1978); and Georges Anglade, *Eloge de la pauvreté* (Montreal: ERCE, 1983).
5 Serge Latouche, *Faut-il refuser le développement?* (Paris: Presses Universitaires de France, 1986).
6 'No to Development?' *InterCulture* (Spring–Fall 1987): 95.
7 David Maybury-Lewis, 'Dear Reader', *Cultural Survival Quarterly*, 11 (January 1987): 1.
8 Lawrence J. Lau, ed., *Models of Development: A Comparative Study of Economic Growth in South Korea and Taiwan* (San Francisco: Institute for Comparative Studies, 1986); and Arnold C. Harberger, ed., *World Economic Growth, Case Studies of Developed and Developing Nations* (San Francisco: Institute for Contemporary Studies, 1984).
9 Selig S. Harrison, 'Dateline South Korea: A Divided Seoul', *Foreign Policy* 67 (Summer 1987): 154–175.

10. David H. Pollock, 'A Latin American Strategy to theYear 2000: Can the Past Serve as a Guide to the Future?' in David H. Pollock and A.R.M. Ritter, eds., *Latin American Prospects for the 80's: What Kinds of Development: Deformation, Reformation, or Transformation?* 1 (Ottawa: Norman Patterson School of International Affairs, Carleton University Conference Proceedings, November 1980): 1–37.

11 Ibid.

12 Denis Goulet, 'The United States: A Case of Anti-Development?', *Motive* (January 1970): 6–13.

13 John Kenneth Galbraith, *Economic Development in Perspective* (Cambridge, MA: Harvard University Press, 1962), 43.

14 Robert Vachon, 'Développement et libération dans une perspective interculturelle et cosmique', *Bulletin Monchanin* 8 (1975): 3–30.

15 David Apter, *The Politics of Modernization* (Chicago:University of Chicago Press, 1965), 5–6.

16 Gustave Thibon, *Nietsche ou le declin de l'Esprit* (Paris:Fayard, 1975), 75. Translation mine.

17 David Walker, 'Ralf Dahrendorf's Vision for the London School of Economics', *Change* 8 (June 1976): 24.

18 Richard J. Bernstein, *Praxis and Action* (Philadelphia: University of Pennsylvania Press, 1971).

19 Peter L. Berger, *Pyramids of Sacrifice* (New York: Basic Books, 1974); and Denis Goulet, 'Pyramids of Sacrifice: The High Price of Social Change', *Christianity and Crisis* 34 (1975): 231–7.

20 Tibor Mende, *From Aid to Recolonization*(New York: Pantheon, 1973), 86–129.

21 Jacques Ellul, *The Technological Society* (New York: Alfred A. Knopf, 1965) J. Ellul, *The Technological System* (New York: Continuum, 1980); and Charles Frankel, 'Morality and U.S. Foreign Policy', *Worldview* 18 (June 1975): 13–23.

22 Garrett Hardin, *The Limits of Altruism*, (Bloomington:Indiana University Press, 1977); also Garrett Hardin, *Exploring New Ethics for Survival: The Voyage of the Spaceship Beagle* (New York: Penguin Books, 1971).

23 Berger, *Pyramids of Sacrifice.*

24 Denis Goulet, 'Three Rationalities in Development Decision-Making', *World Development* 14 (1986): 301–17.

25 S.J. Samartha and Lynn de Silva, eds, *Man in Nature, Guest or Engineer?* (Columbo: The Ecumenical Institute for Study and Dialogue, 1979).

26 Robert Vachon, 'Relations de l'homme à la nature dans les sagesses orientales traditionnelles', *Ecologie et Environnement* (Cahiers de Recherche Ethique) 9 (1983): 157, 160.

27 Bernard Charbonneau, *Je fus, essai sur la liberté* (Pau: Imprimerie Marrimpouey Jeune, 1980), 149–56; also B. Charbonneau, *Le Feu Vert: Auto-critique du Mouvement Ecologique* (Paris: Editions Karthala, 1980).

28 Henri de Lubac, *La Pensee religieuse du Pere Teilhard de Chardin* (Paris: Aubier, 1962), 349.

29 Madeleine Bartelemy Madaule, 'La Personne dans la perspective Teilhardienne', *Essais sur Teilhard de Chardin* (Paris: Fayard, 1962), 76.

30 Jacques Maritain, *Integral Humanism* (Notre Dame, Ind.: University of Notre Dame Press, 1973), 134.

31 Denis Goulet, 'Culture and Traditional Values in Development', in Susan Stratigos and Philip J. Hughes eds, *The Ethics of Development, The Pacific in the 21st Century* (Port Moresby: University of Papua New Guinea Press, 1987), 165–78.

32 Jacques Ellul, *Hope in a Time of Abandonment* (New York: Seabury Press, 1973).

33 Ivan Illich, *Tools for Conviviality* (New York: Harper and Row, 1973).

34 René Dubos, *Man Adapting* (New Haven: Yale Univesity Press, 1978).

35 Robert Vacca, *The Coming Dark Age* (Garden City, NY: Doubleday, n.d.).
36 Denis Goulet, 'Makers of History and Witnesses to Transcendence', in *A New Moral Order: Studies in Development Ethics and Liberation Theology* (Maryknoll, NY: Orbis Books, 1974), 109–42.
37 L.J. Lebret, *Développement =Révolution Solidaire* (Paris: Les Editions Ouvrieres, 1967).

3 The encounter of religion and conservation
Martin Palmer

The elderly and saintly Tibetan abbot leaned across the table and with rather sad and inquiring eyes said gently: 'It does seem to me that the sort of ideal political society certain conservationists want is a benevolent dictatorship where the people are told what is good for them and the laws thus promulgated are vigorously applied.'

In Africa, expatriate conservationists erect a massive electrical fence around a nature preserve to keep the local people out. The only way they can legally visit the preserve is by car, but how many Africans can afford a car?

At a meeting of senior conservation officers from around the world, a Christian theologian tells the story of Dr Faust, who sold his soul to the Devil in order to enjoy certain short-term financial and other benefits, but who ultimately had to pay the price for his pact. Why does a theologian feel the need to tell this story to such a group? Because he feels that the relationship between conservation and the multinationals is a Faustian one and a warning bell needs to be rung.

A Hindu priest, a brahman, attending a discussion of the impact of cattle grazing on former rainforest lands, speaks of the wheel of karma wherein every action has its return, and challenges those present to tackle the root of the problem — their own diets.

A senior rabbi, a leader of an Islamic international organization, and the head of a major Catholic order combine to express surprise that, in most discussions of ecology and conservation, issues of justice and peace do not appear on the agenda.

The dialogue begins

These are but a few vignettes of the emerging encounter between the world's major faiths and the conservation movement. Their significance lies in the critical light they cast upon the need for serious attention to conservation ethics and the positive role religious communities might play in meeting that need.

One bar to dialogue between religion and conservation in the past has been the inability of many conservationists to see that their viewpoint is a creation of certain cultural and philosophical forces. Their views, as much as those of

Hindus, Christians, and Marxists, are value-laden. 'Man, like the spider, spins out of himself the world which he inhabits.[1] This simple insight has been ignored by many exponents of conservation. Hiding behind the presumed objectivity of science, they have failed to understand that in their missionary urge to save the world they carry with them a host of cultural presuppositions. Some of these are the conceptual seeds of the very forces of destruction they seek to halt. Thus, it is not surprising that when conservationists start to talk about ethics, they run into difficulties.

One of the more extraordinary statements of the World Conservation Strategy was its call for the creation of a 'new ethic':

Ultimately the behavior of entire societies towards the biosphere must be transformed if the achievement of conservation objectives is to be assured. A new ethic, embracing plants and animals as well as people, is required for human societies to live in harmony with the natural world on which they depend for survival and well-being. The long term task of environmental education is to foster or reinforce attitudes and behavior compatible with this new ethic.[2]

This statement appears in a document prepared by organizations which had heretofore paid scant attention to any value system, let alone belief system, other than their own science-based conservation ethic.

Yet the dialogue would not have begun if the conservation movement had not made important critiques of the role of belief and formal religion in modern civilization. There is little doubt that until Lynn White asserted that a link existed between the exploitative orientation of Western culture as manifest in the factors leading to the ecological crisis and the biblical injunction to 'dominate' nature, Christians had done little to explore their own teachings on the environment.[3] Stung into action by White's historical analysis, Christian theologians and activists have since tried to rehabilitate the reputation of Christianity within the conservation movement. Without the sting of White, it is unlikely that they would have acted with such vigour.

Another example comes from Buddhism. In recent years Buddhists, stung by the criticism of conservationists, have looked hard at the way in which some monks have been used by the whaling industry. Because of the vegetarian creed of Buddhism, Japanese monks for centuries performed funeral rites when people killed whales. The rite apologizes to the spirit of the whale. This fine intention has become corrupted in recent decades by providing a religious justification for the horrendous whaling exploits of the Japanese. The work by Buddhists to put their own house in order on this issue has led to a deeper awareness of the profound teachings on nature within the faith.

Overall, at least until recently, the encounter of religion and conservation has been confused and at times counterproductive. At exactly the moment when conservation needed responsible, ethical critique, the major faiths did little but belatedly endorse general conservation policies which at times actually countered their own ethics and beliefs. Meanwhile, the conservation movement often makes powerful use of language and symbolism derived from the very core of religious faith. For example, it can be argued that one of the main sources of impetus for the conservation movement and the peace movement alike is the apocalyptic vision of the Judeo-Christian tradition.

The intriguing and unsettling interaction between the major world faiths and the growing international conservation movement was given a new shape and direction in 1986. For its 25th anniversary, World Wildlife Fund International issued an invitation to the five major faiths of the world to come on pilgrimage to Assisi, birthplace of the Roman Catholic patron saint of ecology, Francis. The intention was simple, the consequences enormous. The faiths were invited to come and share with the conservation movement their understanding and vision of nature and of our responsibility, place, and purpose within the natural world. But it was seen from the outset as a two way encounter — the great faiths sharing their beliefs and challenging certain cherished shibboleths of the conservation movement, and the conservation movement sharing the scientific data and insight which reveals the daunting scale of our abuse of nature and challenging the faiths to turn their fine phrases into positive action.

Each faith was invited to come 'proud of what it had to offer but humble enough to learn from others'. But what exactly did these five faiths, Buddhism, Christianity, Hinduism, Islam, and Judaism have to offer?

The intention of the remainder of this chapter is to look at what these five faiths contribute to our emerging understanding of the diverse ways in which nature is perceived and the diverse kinds of conservation ethics possible in the world today. In this brief space, I will only be able to touch upon the theological, ethical, and practical insights which these major faiths have to offer to our efforts to achieve sustainable development.

The key point to be made is that, at last, the debate between religionists and conservationists has begun in earnest. There are many painful things to be said on both sides. Conservationists need to recognize their cultural roots and learn that many of their analyses and prescriptions uncritically accept Western, utilitarian, anthropocentric norms. Likewise, the great faiths and their cultures need to realize how urgent the environmental crisis is, and learn how to express to this generation the eternal truths they bear regarding our relationship with nature. Both sides also need to be aware of the challenges presented by other cultures — ancient indigenous cultures, as well as religio-political cultures such as Marxism. For too long, Westerners have sought to mould all other viewpoints to accord with their desire for one truth or one way — scientific, religious, or ideological. The encounter of ecology with faith has shown that we can truly celebrate and learn from diversity while avoiding unnecessary division. That in itself would seem to be a fundamental ethical norm which needs to be explored in the years immediately ahead.

Hinduism

There is no doubt that the most challenging perspective to be offered at Assisi in 1986 came from Hinduism and Buddhism. The reason for this is quite simple. The view of time with which these two faiths operate is totally different from that of the West, be that the Christian West or the scientific West. The West uses a linear model of time. Time moves from A to Z. It runs essentially forward. This is captured in the hymn, 'God is working His purpose out as year succeeds to year', or in the scientific myth of gradual, upward evolution. The Western model inevitably leads to anthropocentrism, since human beings are seen as the summation, even if only for the present, of the processes of history and evolution. In the Hindu and Buddhist world views, time is not linear but cyclical, and this deeply affects the way the world is viewed, humanity is viewed, and ethics are viewed.

In Hinduism, the cyclical nature of existence is captured in the stories of lords Brahma, Vishnu, and Shiva. Their essential natures are expressed in their titles: Brahma is the creator of each new world and universe; Vishnu is the sustainer of the worlds and universes; while Shiva is both the destroyer and the recreator. Shiva brings each world and universe to an end when it has run its course and has degenerated into the state of ignorance and violence. Yet it is from this destruction that the new worlds and universes arise. The passing of one world or universe is essential for the arising of the next. Thus, Shiva is seen as the destroyer who creates. It is this cyclical rise– decline–rise model which underpins the Hindu understanding of life. And just as the worlds and the universes are brought to be, degenerate, die, and are then brought to new incarnations for the process to run again, so it is with our lives, and the lives of all sentient beings. This is captured in the following verses from the *Brihad Aranyaka Upanishad*:

Even as a caterpillar . . . reaches out for another blade of grass and draws it over to it, in the same way the soul, leaving the body and unwisdom behind, reaches out to another body and draws itself over to it.

And even as a worker in gold, taking an old ornament, moulds it into a form newer and fairer, even so the Soul leaving the body and unwisdom behind, goes into a form newer and fairer: a form like that of the ancestors in heaven, or of the celestial beings, or the gods of light . . . or a form of other beings.[4]

This reincarnational, cyclical perspective has immediate consequences for conservation because all life is composed of souls (*atman*) which are passing from lower to higher forms, and occasionally moving in the opposite direction. Thus, the human soul has not always been a human soul. This simply happens to be the form in which the soul is currently reborn. Given that popular Hindu thought ascribes up to 83,000 rebirths to each soul, the range of incarnational possibilities is immense! All particular forms of being are thus linked and ultimately transcended by the *atman* as it seeks reunion with the Ultimate. Karan Singh, in the *Hindu Declaration* made at Assisi, put it most succinctly:

The Hindu viewpoint on nature . . . is permeated by a reverence for life, and an awareness that the great forces of nature — the earth, the sky, the air, the water and fire — as well as various orders of life, including plants and trees, forests and animals, are all bound to each other within the great rhythms of nature.[5]

The corollary is also stated by Singh, namely, that 'the divine is not exterior to creation, but expresses itself through natural phenomena'. Thus does all creation become sacred and of equal value.

The ethical consequences of this perspective for conservation are clear to see even if somewhat hard for many in the West to stomach — literally! If the divine is present in all life, then the taking of life will disturb the chain of being, the wheel of *samsara*, and will affect the life of the person who has taken the life. This is the law of *karma*. Every action begets a reaction.

The strong vegetarian ethic of Hinduism is derived from the belief in karma, as is the general attitude of using but not killing life, an attitude well exemplified in the status of the sacred cow. Here, in what Gandhi described as India's greatest gift to humanity, we can see a model for sustainable development which pre-dates most of the world's extant faiths and cultures. The cow is venerated as Mother, for from her comes food, drink, fuel (dung) and, at her natural death, leather. What use would it be to eat flesh when she can provide so much more, for so much longer, while alive? This makes economic sense, and in Hinduism, the economic is subsumed within the religious — the basis for the respect and veneration which the cow is accorded. 'Cow protection' is the key to the Hindu attitude to the rest of creation and unlocks its distinctive ethical bias. As Gandhi said: 'In its finer or spiritual sense, the term "cow protection" means the protection of every living creature'.

Let us illustrate how this works morally and experientially by considering the recent claim by a fast food chain that it has made x billion hamburgers. To devout Hindus, this claim is a proclamation of suffering — the death and destruction of millions of cattle. And there before our eyes is the cycle of karma. Suffering on such a vast scale inevitably entails a similarly vast effect. To graze the cattle needed to provide this quantity of hamburgers, it has been necessary to destroy millions of acres of rainforest. The climatic and general environmental affect of this is only now becoming apparent, but it is 'obvious', to those who view life from the vantage point of a belief in karma, that ultimately the suffering we caused to the cattle, not to mention to the forest and the creatures of the forest, will rebound on us. We will suffer.

The Hindu concept of karmic law; of the total spiritual interrelatedness of all life; of the divine within all life; leads to a relativizing of the position of humanity. Humans are important, and it is better to be a human being than to be, let us say, a buffalo. However, better than being a human being is to be a demigod. Because the divine is present in all life, there is no basis for human beings to claim that we alone are either 'made in the image of God' or specially chosen by God. This provides a radically different starting point for any consideration of our role, our rights, and our responsibilities towards nature.

Buddhism

A similar concept of the cyclical pattern of birth, growth, maturation, decline, death, and rebirth is to be found within Buddhist teachings. Buddhism gave the world the moving Jataka stories — tales of the previous lives of the Buddha. Many tales tell how the Buddha was once an animal such as a mighty elephant or a monkey king. These tales are enormously popular among Buddhist layfolk. Their message — that all life is interlinked and caring — lays the foundation for the Buddhist ethics of nature. The Dalai Lama expressed this clearly in the following way:

Have you ever wondered what a beautiful place this world would be if everyone would treat all animals and life in the same manner? And realize the fact that, whether it is more complex groups like human beings, or simpler groups such as animals, the feeling of pain and appreciation of happiness is common. All want to live and do not wish to die. As a Buddhist, I believe in the interdependence of all things, the interrelationship among the whole spectrum of plant and animal life, including the elements of nature which express themselves as mountains, valleys, rivers, sky, and sunshine.[6]

Buddhism is conservation minded at its core, yet it is hard to find 'proof texts' in the way that the West, with its biblical traditions, expects. One has to search long and hard in the Pali Canon, Lotus Sutra, or other major works to find explicit environmental teachings. Rather, it is the set of basic assumptions upon which Buddhism rests which provides conservation norms and values. It has been the particular gift of Buddhism to develop the community of monks and nuns which constitutes the *sangha*. The role of the *sangha* is to pass on the teachings of the Buddha, called the *dharma*, from generation to generation, and to help individual monks seek enlightenment. The central role of the *sangha* in Buddhist life is indicated by the basic 'creed' of Buddhism, known as the Triple Gem: 'I take refuge in the Buddha; I take refuge in the *dharma*; I take refuge in the *sangha*.'

The following text from the *Buddhist Declaration* at Assisi gives the Buddhist interpretation of karma and rebirth:

A philosophical system (Buddhism) which propagates the theory of rebirth and life after death, maintains that in the continuous birth and rebirth of sentient beings (not only on this planet but in the universe as a whole) each being is related to us ourselves, just as our own parents are related to us in this life. And just as our own parents have been indispensable to our upbringing in our present lifespan, in another particular span of our life another sentient being has given us the spark of life.[7]

The author of this section of the Declaration then tells what this means in practice:

In my faraway country, I still remember what my parents said: they told us that various spirits and forces are dormant in the rivers, mountains, lakes, and trees. Any harm done to them, they said, would result in drought, epidemics, and sickness in human beings, and the loss of the fertility of the earth.

This sense of the interrelatedness of nature, combined with the emphasis on non-violence, has led to the development of Buddhist monasteries as sanctuaries for wildlife. Ecologists now turn to the ancient Buddhist monasteries to find ecologically balanced reserves.[8] The Thai Buddhist temple of Wat Phai Lom is famous as the breeding place of the open-billed stork.[9]The existence of sacred mountains in places such as Sri Lanka and Japan has also ensured that these areas are under the protection of the Buddha and the *sangha*.

One of the key ethical concepts found in Buddhism, especially in Mahayana Buddhism, is compassion. Buddhism teaches that we all live in illusion. Insects and human beings are on the same level because all beings are caught up in believing that what they are or have now is real or has the potential to be real. In the Theravada tradition, this means that even the concept of myself, of 'I', is illusion. We are trapped in the cycle of rebirth because of our ignorance and our false understanding of reality. It was therefore with compassion that the Buddha taught, wishing to show people the path to follow to escape rebirth and illusion. As Buddhism moved out from its north Indian homeland, and especially as it travelled in China and Japan, there arose salvational figures, known as *bodhisattvas*. These beings are fully enlightened beings who, if they so wished, could cease to be and enter nirvana. However, they have held back from taking the final step in order to help suffering life either move up the ladder of awareness and reincarnation, or escape from the cycle of rebirth altogether.

Because Buddhism sees all forms of life caught up in illusion, its teaching of the compassion of the Buddha and the bodhisattvas applies to all life. This is seen clearly in the following quote from the Sikshasamuccaya of the Vajradhvaja Sutra:

A Bodhisattva resolves: I take upon myself the burden of all sufferings, I am resolved to do so. I will endure it. . . . And why? At all costs I must bear the burdens of all beings, in that I do not follow my own inclinations. I have made the vow to save all beings. All beings I must set free. The whole world of living beings I must rescue, from the terrors of birth, of old age, of sickness, of death and rebirth, of all kinds of moral offense, of all states of woe, of the whole cycle of birth and rebirth, of the jungle of false views . . . from all these terrors I must rescue all beings.[10]

Sad to say, this gentle and compassionate perspective on nature and on ourselves has been badly mauled over the last hundred years as Western or Marxist ideas and values have marched — sometimes literally — into Buddhist countries. It is a well-attested fact that virtually all Japanese were vegetarian (except for eating fish) prior to the 'opening' of Japan in the mid-nineteenth century.[11] The accounts of the destruction of what was apparently an exceptionally harmonious relationship with nature in Tibet by the Chinese over the last thirty years make a particularly tragic tale. Finally, the tables are turning, albeit slowly, and possibly too late. Finally the voices of the compassionate ones are being heard in the West.

Judaism

The twin sources of Jewish ethics are the Torah (the five books of Moses, Genesis, Exodus, Leviticus, Numbers and Deuteronomy) and the Talmud (a collection of commentaries, stories and legal decisions bearing upon core concerns in Judaism and in the Torah). Between them they present a dramatic picture of humanity's role in creation. Many people are familiar with the biblical texts of Genesis which spell out the superior role and status of humanity in the created order. However, one has no real understanding of Judaism if one does not also understand what the Talmud has to say about all this. An example will help to put the biblical texts into the ethical framework of Judaism as a way of life. In Genesis Adam is given mastery and dominion. He names (thereby having power over) the animals and birds. Then he is given the Garden of Eden as his dwelling place. Adam is in control. But then the Talmud tells this story:

Adam walked in the Garden on the first day. He smelled wonderful scents and enjoyed the beautiful sights. The aroma of the ripened fruit drew him to the trees. He reached for an apricot that hung from a branch. The fruit lifted itself so that he could not touch it. He reached for a pomegranate. The fruit evaded his hand. Then a voice spoke, 'Till the soil and care for the trees and then you may eat.'[12]

Judaism, unlike Hinduism and Buddhism, does not hesitate to state that humanity is the top of the tree, the final and greatest creation of God. But neither is it deluded into thinking that this gives humanity *carte blanche* to act as it wishes towards the rest of creation. Again, the Talmud tells us of the great debate which took place between God and the angels when God declared that he would create humanity. The angels, with some justification, pointed out that having created a pretty reasonable world, God is now about to cause disruption and misuse by creating humanity. The debate continued for some time, until the Earth itself joined in and said that she would feed and sustain humanity. But the tension continues. The abuse and misuse of the world by humanity is a fact and one which has drawn forth much commentary from the rabbis down the centuries. It was summarized in the *Jewish Declaration on Nature* made at Assisi in 1986:

The essential thrust of these teachings is that animals, even the most powerful among them, are ultimately helpless before people. We rule their kingdom as God rules ours. The way that we exercise our power over the rest of God's creatures, over those who ultimately cannot defend themselves against us, must be the way of love and compassion. If it is not, then we ourselves have made the choice that the strong can do what they like to other living beings and to each other. If such policies prevail, the world will soon be destroyed by us.[13]

Contained within this statement are two key factors which shape Jewish ethical considerations regarding nature. The first is responsibility; the second is finality. Unlike those faiths with a cyclical view of time, Judaism posits a creator God who commences creation, time, and life at a certain specific point. Time moves from its beginning to its end. Once it reaches its end, that's it. There is no concept in mainstream Judaism of reincarnation of cycles in time or creation. Each life is lived once only. Whereas in a reincarnational faith each lifetime adds a tiny bit to a greater sum total of endeavour, in linear faiths such as Judaism, what a person does with this one life is what he or she will be judged upon for the rest of eternity. This is why responsibility becomes such a crucial concept in Jewish ethics. If this is the one life and there is also only one world for just one time, then the moral imperative to 'get it right' is very high. This means Judaism is underpinned by a strong and clear ethical responsibility to care for nature. In the interfaith liturgy at Assisi immediately prior to the issuing of the Declarations, Rabbi Arthur Hertzberg, vice-president of the World Jewish Congress, said this:

The rebirth of nature, day after day, is God's gift, but humanity is the custodian of this capacity of the Earth to renew itself. As we consume any one of the products of divine bounty, we must first say the appropriate grace. The world is his, and we are but sojourners. At the very least, we must leave the palace of our Host no worse than we found it.

Accordingly, Judaism finds in the Torah, the Talmud, and other authoritative sources, ethical norms to guide humanity. For example, the Talmud pictures

God, before he created humanity, looking at the world and describing it as a larder, but with no one to make use of it. A larder is only of use if it is kept stocked. Any larder which is simply emptied by its users will cease to be of use within a very short period of time. Sustainable development pre-Bruntland Commission! There is within Judaism a strong moral obligation to prepare for the future — often for a future which we will never see. The continuity of linear history depends upon the willingness of those alive now to plant and plan for the future. Otherwise, there will be no future. Another Talmudic tale captures this perception:

A wise rabbi was walking along a road when he saw an old man planting a tree. The rabbi asked him, 'How many years will it take for this tree to bear fruit?' The man answered that it would take seventy years. The rabbi asked, 'Are you so fit and strong that you expect to live that long and eat its fruit?' The man answered, 'I found a fruitful world because my forefathers planted for me. So will I do the same for my children.'[14]

Judaism gives us an uncompromising picture of our superiority and of our responsibility as a result of that superiority. It teaches that when God created the world out of chaos, he left some parts of it unfinished. Not all the *tohu vavohu*, the primal chaos, was ordered. The job was given to us, his partners, on trust. We are not merely the work of God's hands; we are not merely the top of creation; we are not merely the creatures who are responsible; we are God's co-creators.

Crucial to Jewish ethics are the concepts of justice and peace — factors often missing in conservation discussion. The central message of Judaism is that our responsibility under God is to act justly and seek for peace!

What is good has been explained to you; this is what the Lord asks of you: only this, to act justly, to love tenderly, and to walk humbly with your God (Micah 6:8).

The welfare of the natural world is caught up with the welfare of the people:

Sons of Israel, listen to the word of God, for God indicts the inhabitants of the country: there is no fidelity, no tenderness, no knowledge of God in the country, only perjury and lies, slaughter, theft, adultery and violence, murder after murder. This is why the country is in mourning, and all who live in it pine away, even the wild animals and the birds of heaven; the fish of the sea themselves are perishing (Hosea 4:1–3).

The moral welfare and political and economic state of the nation have to be taken into account if nature is to be part of a wholesome society. *Sustainable* development is not enough. Development for whom, run by whom, for the benefit of whom?

In the end, Judaism's ethical code returns to its source — the living, creator God who has shared his creation with humanity in a special way; whose image is in each person; who is not in his creation, but his creation is of him. Ultimately, any conservation ethic in Judaism has to be viewed as part of our responsibility for all aspects of life — personal, societal, environmental — to that which is above and beyond all our efforts, the living God.

Christianity

Christianity shares with Judaism not just its sacred books, but also its basic assumptions about the nature of God, creation, and humanity's special role within creation. It also shares the linear perspective on time and life but with an added dimension. Judaism believes that there will be an end of time, when God will send his Messiah, his anointed one, to restore all life to the way of God. In Christianity, the concept of a flow from alpha to omega has to be interpreted in the light of the life, death, and resurrection of Jesus Christ. The effect of this on Christian ethics is twofold. First, it leads to a deep sense of the sinfulness of humanity; second, it leads to the belief that, here and now, the future is possible, that in Christ there is an end of the old ways of life. Through new life in Christ, the Christian believes that he or she can share in the future kingdom of God when, as the book of Isaiah puts it:

The wolf lies with the lamb, the panther lies with the kid, calf and lion cub feed together. The infant plays over the hole of the cobra; into the viper's lair the young child puts his hand. They do no hurt, no harm, on all my holy mountain, for the country is filled with the knowledge of God as the waters cover the sea (Isaiah 11:6–9).

Father Lanfranco Serrini, Minister General of the Franciscan order, Frati Minori Conventuali, expressed all this very simply at Assisi:

Through his almighty word, God created all things visible and invisible. He created them freely and wisely to manifest his glory and infinite love. And the Lord God continues to provide for all his creatures in a most generous manner: he unfailingly gives them life and sustains them.

Even when men and women disobeyed their Creator and were enslaved by the disharmony they thus introduced into their relationships with God and creatures, the infinitely faithful Lord continued to love them. Indeed God saved humanity by sending his Son, Jesus Christ, who is the Divine Word and the eternal Wisdom made human.

In his faithfulness to what he has made and declared to be very good, God the Father sends his life-giving Spirit to renew humanity and the whole Earth, arousing in human beings a firm hope in the life of the world to come, a world of justice, peace, and harmony.

People carefully comb the New Testament looking for clear injunctions on how to behave environmentally, or how to care for animals. Such attempts are always disappointed, for Christianity offers few rules. Instead it sets out certain basic assumptions and parameters within which each individual is expected to try and live faithfully. Just as for Jews, the Torah needs the Talmud, so, for the majority of Christians, the Bible needs the Church Fathers, the Church liturgy, tradition, and so on. It is in its ability to present a grand vision of the past and future that Christianity works best, not when it is asked to provide moral rules and regulations.

Christianity's view of history presents certain ethical challenges. First, Christianity sees the created order, as Father Serrini said above, as basically good. Into this created order comes humanity which, through rebellion, disturbs the whole harmony of life. Not just human life, but all life. And the disruptive element of humanity is still all too plainly at work. Christians are quite hard-

headed about that. For it was the depravity and 'lostness' of humanity that led it
to kill the Son of God, hanging him upon a tree to die. Thus, on one level there is
quite a pessimistic view of humanity and its relationships with God and creation.
However, as the *Christian Declaration on Nature* at Assisi puts it:

the heart of the Christian faith resides in its proclamation of God's merciful fidelity to
himself and to the works of his hands. Christians believe that God the Father has not
abandoned men and women to their sinful ways but has sent the Savior to bring
redemption and healing to everyone and to all things. . . . They [Christians] maintain
that, risen from the dead and ascended into heaven in his glorified humanity, he reconciles
all things visible and invisible, and that all creation is therefore purposefully oriented in
and through him, towards the future revelation of the glorious liberty of God's children,
when, in the new heaven and the new earth, there will no longer be death, mourning,
sadness or pain. . . . Christians therefore cannot be pessimistic about the future of the
world.[15]

In Christian thought, all humanity is endowed with great power to master the
world. Through sin, this mastery has all too often been abused, leading to death
and destruction of human beings and of nature. Yet, through the power of Jesus
Christ, Christians believe they can become instruments of the will of God for all
his creation. Christianity holds humanity to be 'made in the image of God'. The
ethical consequences of such a belief are spelled out very succinctly in the
following prayer:

Christ has no body now on earth but ours,
No hands but ours,
No feet but ours.
Ours are the eyes through which his compassion looks out on the world;
Ours are the hands with which he blesses all people now;
Ours are the feet by which he goes about doing good.

Islam

The key term in Islamic environmental ethics is 'viceregent' — one who exercises
delegated power on behalf of a great authority of power. It is instructive to look
at what the Qur'ān has to say about how and why humanity was created:

Behold, your Lord said to the Angels: 'I will create a viceregent on Earth'. They said: 'Will
You place there one who will make mischief there and shed blood, while we celebrate Your
praises and glorify Your Holy Name?' He said, 'I know what you do not know.' And he
taught Adam the nature of all things: then He placed them before the Angels and said:
'Tell Me the nature of these if you are right.' They said: 'Glory to You of Knowledge. We
have none, except what You have taught us.' (Sūrah 2:30–32)

The Qur'ān teaches that humanity is not only the final and greatest creation of
Allah, but that we know more than the angels themselves. Furthermore, there are
only two creations of Allah which are able to make decisions for themselves.
While all other creatures simply follow the ways of nature, which is the way
decreed by Allah, human beings and jinns have free will. And here is a clear

warning. To be linked with jinns, usually evil and malicious spirits, shows what dangers there are in having free will. However, those who of their own free will submit (*Islam*) to the known Will of Allah will be rewarded in the life hereafter.

The ethics of Islam rest firmly upon the reality of the Day of Judgment. On that day,

When the Earth is shaken to her utmost convulsion, and the Earth throws up her burdens from within, and man cries distressed: 'What is the matter with her?' On that day will she declare her tidings: for your Lord will have given inspiration. On that day will men proceed in companies sorted out to be shown the deeds that they had done. Then shall anyone, who has done an atom's weight of good, see it! And anyone who has done an atom's weight of evil, shall see it (Sūrah 99:1–8).

Eternal damnation and torment await those who abuse their God-given powers and ability to act for themselves. Again, the linear view of time and history shapes the ethical norms. This is the only life we have. How we make use of it is how we will be judged. Allah cares for and oversees all his creation:

'There is not an animal that lives on the Earth, nor a being that flies on its wings, but forms part of communities like you. We have omitted nothing from the book and they all shall be gathered to their Lord in the end (Sūrah 6:39).

Both in the Qur'ān and in the Shariah, the legal codes of Islam, the rights of the natural world are strongly expressed and the abuse of them by humanity condemned out of hand. The Qur'ān says: 'He set on the Earth, firmly rooted, mountains rising above it, and blessed the Earth and provided sustenance for all, according to their needs.' A modern Islamic commentary on this text draws out its significance for today:

There is hunger, environmental destruction, and civil strife because humanity has broken the laws of Allah, not because it is his Will. Allah has provided enough for the honest needs of all his Creation. Thus, Muslims are forbidden to hoard beyond their genuine needs. To do so is to abuse Allah's Creation.[16]

Notes

1 Janet Martin Soskice, *Metaphor and Religious Language* (Oxford: Clarendon, 1985), 80.
2 International Union for the Conservation of Nature and Natural Resources, *The World Conservation Strategy: Living Resource Conservation for Sustainable Development* (Gland, Switzerland: IUCN, 1980), Section 13.1.
3 Lynn White, Jr, 'The Historical Roots of Our Ecological Crisis', *Science* 155 (1967).
4 *The Upanishads*, trans. Juan Mascaro, (London: Penguin, 1965), 139.
5 *The Assisi Declarations: Messages on Man and Nature from Buddhism, Christianity, Hinduism, Islam and Judaism* (Gland, Switzerland: WWF International, 1986).
6 Quoted in 'Foreword' in Martin Palmer and Esther Bisset, *Worlds of Difference* (Glasgow: Blackie, 1985).
7 *The Assisi Declarations*.
8 Jeffrey McNeely and Paul Wachtel, *Soul of the Tiger: People and Wildlife in Southeast Asia* (New York: Doubleday, 1988).

9 Chatsumarn Kabilsingh, 'How Buddhism Can Help Protect Nature' in Nancy Nash, ed., *Tree of Life: Buddhism and Protection of Nature* (Hong Kong: Buddhist Perception of Nature, 1987), 7.

10 E. Conze, ed., *Buddhist Texts Through the Ages* (London: Luzac, 1954), 131.

11 See Roshi Philip Kapleau, *A Buddhist Case for Vegetarianism* (London: Rider, 1983); and Jo Steward-Smith, *In the Shadows of Fujisan* (London: Viking/Rainbird, 1987).

12 *The Fathers According to Rabbi Nathan*, Yale Judaica Series X, (New Haven, Conn.: Yale University Press, 1955), 60.

13 *The Assisi Declarations*.

14 'Proverbial Sayings and Traditions' in *Hebraic Literature*, trans. Maurice H. Harry (New York: Tudor, 1936), 346.

15 *The Assisi Declarations*.

16 Kerry Brown and Martin Palmer, eds, *The Essential Teachings of Islam* (London: Rider, 1987).

4 Science-based versus traditional ethics

Holmes Rolston, III

In an environmental development ethic, do science-based values occupy a privileged position as criteria against which traditional cultural values are to be tested? Since science-based values are themselves plural, and traditional values even more so, no simple answer is possible. The cases that follow cross a spectrum from conflict through complementarity to criticism. As we travel through them, we will be forced to reorient ourselves repeatedly, ending with an overview suggesting that authentic human life, to be fully developed, must revise both traditional culture and science as presently understood. Our aim is to move beyond instrumentalist models of sustainable development in quest of a global ethic. Respect for the community of life on Earth — ecologically and culturally — is the test of an ethic for the world.

The end of development, the end of ethics, is more life. A development and conservation ethic must be *true to life*. In that sense, *true* development must correspond to the highest human activity that most deeply values life. Humans should be *true to* the Earth, 'their' Earth, in the sense that it is their home, their niche, but not theirs alone. In a traditional biblical phrase, ecumenically and globally applied, humans have to enter the 'promised land', to inherit the Earth. In a scientific phrase, they must know their 'ecology', the logic of their home.

Conflict: Traditional values challenged by science-based values

At one extreme, science-based values clash with values expressed in folklore, or, more pejoratively, in superstition. Ginseng, *Panax quinquefolius*, a once common Appalachian plant, is much sought in the belief that its powdered roots prolong virility and vitality. The Orientals had already eradicated a prized Asian ginseng when a Jesuit priest in Canada in the early 1700s found the American plant. Many tons were shipped to Asia, and ginseng became known as 'Appalachian gold'. Now nearly extinct, ginseng sold in the last decade for about US$70 per pound of roots. The available evidence from scientific investigation suggests that its medical powers belong firmly in the realm of folklore.

A conservation biologist values ginseng for entirely different reasons. It is an unusual plant, a member of the family *Araliaceae*, which has few representatives in the Appalachian forests. With rather precise habitat requirements, ginseng filled a distinctive niche, though its absence has produced no measurable shifts in the ecosystems it once inhabited. Still, it adds diversity, interest, and richness to the woods, for in this species nature has given expression to a modest but noteworthy development not elsewhere attained.

The present trade in roots is nothing more than a catering to mistaken superstition — which conservation biologists deplore. Can there be any compatibility between ginseng as desired in Chinese folklore and *Panax quinquefolius* as a desired component of the Appalachian hardwoods ecosystem? The extinction of the traditional cultural value is preferable to the extinction of the plant. Chinese folk beliefs exploiting ginseng are not true, and those who hold them do not know the biological truth about how to appreciate the world they inhabit.

Rhinoceroses have large horns that are greatly desired for daggers and prized as symbols of masculinity in the Middle East. Black rhinoceroses, which formerly ranged from Kenya to South Africa, are now extensively poached; their horns, worth US$5,000 each, are sawn off and their carcasses left to rot. Just as Europeans came to judge as unconscionable the trade in feathers that took place in the early part of this century (in the single year of 1914 over 20,000 birds of paradise, 40,000 humming birds, and 30,000 other birds were slaughtered to supply London ladies with feathers for fashion), so this deplorable traditional value ought to be replaced with a scientifically based appreciation of the rhinoceros in its ecosystem. What now seems insensitive feminine vanity and unacceptable profit making is parallel to the insensitive masculine vanity that drives a market which contributes to the destruction of the rhinoceros.

Often, however, quite serious human desires — not just vain or superstitious ones — conflict with wildlife. The mountain gorilla, *Gorilla gorilla beringei*, survives in a population of about 240 animals in the Parç National des Volcans, a 30,000 acre national park in Rwanda. This small country has the highest population density in Africa, a population expected to double by the end of the century. About 95 per cent of its people subsist on small farms that average 2.5 acres per family. The park has already been shrunk by 40 per cent to bring land into cultivation, yet there are pressures to reduce it more. Elimination of the park could support perhaps 36,000 persons at subsistence level, only 25 per cent of one year's population growth. Most persons in Rwanda have little interest in wildlife; some poach gorillas to make skulls and hands into souvenirs for tourists or to use the testicles, tongues, and ears for their magical power over enemies.

This third case advances the argument because now we mix folklore with basic subsistence needs. A conservation biologist will deplore the killing of gorillas to make charms of their organs, claiming that superstition ought to be replaced with an appreciation of the zoology and ecology of gorillas. But the conflict of gorillas versus subsistence farmers is more difficult. Surely, by any calculus, the rights and values of 36,000 humans override the rights and values (if such there are) of 240 gorillas. When devising an ethic of appropriate development, one seems torn between enriching the human community by converting the forests to maximum agricultural yield through the use of appropriate technology, and preserving the biotic community — a few gorillas for the price of tens of thousands of impoverished humans.

But an ethic that seeks to sustain life by taking a global view can reverse the presumptions and reply that the lop-sided score in fact favours the gorilla minority, a relict population and the last of an endangered species, against the human majority, of whom there are 3 billion in the world. Further, these 36,000 humans do not now own any rights to this land; the gorillas live there. Indeed, only some of these humans are alive now as subsistence farmers elsewhere; in most cases these humans are as yet unborn. Although humans are individually valuable after they exist, like an additional child in a family, an additional human in a society is not always an appropriate development. Rwandan development pits 240 existing gorillas, the last of their kind, against 36,000 largely potential humans, an excess of their kind. Rwanda already has too many humans, and to sacrifice a species to make place for a quarter of one year's population growth is only to postpone a problem. Such development is not sustainable, and even if technology could make it so, it would not be appropriate because it would not sustain life in the biotic sense. The gorillas would be a casualty of human inability to control cultural development. The global community would be poorer.

Add many negative effects of development — increased erosion from clearing high mountain soil, the loss of revenue from tourism and zoo sales, the unlikelihood of a just distribution of the benefits from clearing the forests — and the trade-offs begin to figure in a different gestalt. Still, saving the gorillas will involve suppressing Rwandan traditional values, their magical folklore, and their desires for new farmland.

Those who advocate preserving gorillas will be genuinely concerned for the good of the Rwandans. But their hidden agenda will be saving the gorillas for reasons that, from the viewpoint of concerned Western scientists, are really science-based. The gorilla will be admired for its biological characteristics, its highly developed social life, its intelligence, its intrinsic value, and as an object of scientific study that can teach humans something about their own evolution.

Tropical forests in the Amazon are being cut at a rate of 5,000 square miles per year, with 125,000 square miles already lost, to make land available for the landless poor. At least so goes the argument — perhaps political rhetoric, since, once it becomes infertile after a few years, the cleared land tends to become grassland suitable mostly for cattle-ranching and is picked up by large ranchers. The landless poor move elsewhere, often to newly cut forests, and the cycle starts again.

Biogeographers believe that certain areas in these forests are 'refugia', historic centres of plant and animal dispersal that continue to restock surrounding areas. Since it seems impossible (and also unwise, given Brazilian needs for development), to save all the rainforests, conservation biologists sometimes argue that it is of special importance to save refugia. Unless this is done, the natural history of the Amazon basin can perhaps never be known. Furthermore, if these are critical areas for restocking fauna and flora, then any tropical forests saved without them will be insecure and subject to catastrophic collapse.

The problem is *how*. How do we combine, honestly and humanely, biologically-based valuations with culturally based valuations? What do peasants care about refugia? The *caboclos*, rural farmers of Indian descent, limit their use of the forests for fear of spirits, and *de facto* biological reserves created as a result of this superstition dot the Amazon landscape. A simple way to protect the forest would be to leave the forest enchanted.[1] This would be false, but effective. Commercial development interests know nothing of refugia; they view the forests simply as natural resources. What care the politicians trying to protect vested interests while saving (in rhetoric or in reality) the plight of the peasant? Even among biogeographers the idea of refugia is debated, and it may prove less important than some advocate.

Perhaps pragmatic conservationists can try to align enlightened Brazilian beliefs and interests so that they coincide with science-based values. We can argue that the rainforest is an ecosystem with nutrients locked into the trees, not the soil, and that the cleared soil, further leached by heavy rains, is too nutrient-poor to support sustained crop agriculture. We can point out the repeated failures of colonization programmes owing to multiple factors: poor land, weak government guidance, and rich, powerful corporate interests anxious to convert the peasants' deforested, defaulted lands into ranchland. We can add that the refugia are likely to be important sources of genetic material for industrial, agricultural, and medical purposes.

In short, we can make the claim that development based on deforestation is not sustainable. An ethic that bases its decisions on the claim of sustainability does not say anything incorrect or insincere to Brazilian citizens. In fact, culturally based values that run contrary to science-based knowledge will not prove sustainable over time. Unprotected, the ginseng and rhinoceroses will soon be gone, and human desires for virility cannot be met in ignorance of what the Appalachian and African ecosystems can support. Those who care nothing about learning how mountain gorillas are specialized to their ecosystems, or about refugia as propagating centres, are likely to modify those ecosystems in misguided ignorance. The Brazilians and the Rwandans will simply lose their gorillas and their soil (as well as their spirits), leaving their social problems unsolved. Even those who only seek to exploit a resource have, sooner or later, to align with the realities of ecosystems. So far as science discovers the way the world is and can be, it constrains human options about what it ought to be.

Further, science uncovers our illusions, and no one is really made worse off after his illusions are removed. If ginseng, rhinoceroses, and Amazon forests are no longer exploited, sellers will lose their already dwindling income, and buyers their fancied increase in sexual virility. Young princes will no longer have their prized daggers, superstitious Africans their charms from gorilla testicles, nor wealthy Europeans ashtrays made from gorilla feet, and forest ogres will no longer serve as supernatural game wardens. But, in a deeper sense, if those involved could come to the truth of the matter — that the ginseng trade is a rip-off, the daggers only a symbol to flatter masculine vanities, the charms worthless, the ashtrays silly, and the ogres fantasy — they would be better off, more excellent persons. They would understand ginseng, rhinoceroses, and Amazon forests for what they are biologically. More truth about the good life on Earth would surely be an authentic development.

Landless Brazilians and Rwandan farmers have illusions about what the future holds, in terms of what both their soil and their societies will support. Eliminating such illusions would be painful, but it cannot be harmful. To care about persons morally is to want them to know the truth about themselves, their society, and their illusions, as well as about the fauna and flora that surround them.

Complementarity: Traditional values reassessed in light of science

Further along a spectrum from conflict to complementarity, consider the belief in karma and reincarnation, widely present in Eastern religions. Karma is a belief in the persistence of moral value, thought to be covertly present as a determinant in animal as well as human life. Animals, with less good karma than human lives and to that extent of less value, are in fact beings that once were and may again be human beings, and so are of high value. All life is kindred. Daisaku Ikeda, a Japanese Buddhist keenly interested in biological conservation, says that the doctrines of karma and reincarnation make all living beings 'blood relations'.[2] The first Buddhist commandment is that one should harm no living thing, that one should practice non-injury, *ahimsa*, reverence for all life.

A conservation biologist will puzzle whether this oriental belief is friend or foe. At first it seems to complement biologically-based values. Darwinians find in evolution evidence that we are all blood relations. If Buddhists can come by this belief from religious sources, then Western science and Eastern metaphysics will simply reinforce one another. Reverence for life, although a feeling known by conservation biologists almost universally, is rather hard to derive from pure biology; natural selection is a competitive struggle, and the survival of the fittest requires the early deaths of most individuals and has resulted in the extinction of 98 per cent of all previously existing species. Deriving from religion a reason for valuing life can only enhance biological conservation.

But conservation biologists are not really interested in valuing zoological lives metaphysically as once-human, transmigrating souls. At least *qua* biologist, a wildlife biologist's admiring respect for a bull snake cannot be based on the religious belief that it has been or might be reincarnated as someone's grandmother. Conservation biologists want to value snakes, bats, and worms as the causal products of evolutionary forces, not as unsolved moral problems of human life. Animals need to be valued intrinsically for what they are, and instrumentally for the roles they play in ecosystems.

Environmental ethicists and conservation biologists regret the loss of vital information when species become extinct; they worry about shutting down the speciation processes that have been so prolific in India and Africa, the cradles of dispersal and creation. They worry about stability and balance, resilience and diversity in ecosystems. They want a valuing system that yields admiring respect for alien life forms, such as jumping spiders and voles, not just a respect for kindred souls trapped in transient animal life. They may want to value gorillas because they are next of kin to humans, but they also want to value rhinoceroses in their wild integrity as forms of life beyond sympathetic ken, with modes of perception and experience remote from that of humans. What is it like to be a sloth or an ostrich? In these life forms nature has explored unique ranges of experience and potential. Is it not an injustice to interpret them as determined by karma imported from previous human lives?

The East's injunction to reverence for life, *ahimsa*, is initially impressive. But when scientists realize the nature of the religious beliefs about the animals which command non-injury, they wonder whether the doctrine of *ahimsa*, disenchanted and demythologized, can remain an effective force in biological conservation. Does it complement or does it conflict with a science-based value theory? If an account is really true to developments in evolutionary natural history and to human development, it will avoid projecting human moral development onto non-human beings. Perhaps there is some account yet to be found that retains a karma metaphysics consistent with and complementary to biological integrity. That discovery could be an authentic development toward a global ethic.

To take another example, when ecologists speak of equilibria, hydrologic cycles, nutrient cycles, food pyramids, homeostasis, recycling, renewable resources, and the like, they frequently find nodding approval from oriental listeners. Western ecological theory seems to match the Eastern law of binary complementarity, the oscillating yang and yin. The way of the Tao, and the concept expressed in the Tao Te Ching (stanza 40), 'in Tao the only motion is returning', parallels scientific insight recently reached in ecological theory.[3]

Paired oppositions are impressively present in nature, and many at everyday levels were noticed by the Chinese Taoists. There is the oscillation of hot and cold, summer and winter, sun and moon, wet and dry, growth and decay, waxing and waning. There are mountains and valleys, males and females. Biologists can add that the male–female dichotomy permeates higher plants as well as cryptogams and algae, and that genes come in pairs. Meteorologists find warm and cold fronts. Ecosystems undergo successions from pioneer to climax communities, recommencing after outbreaks of fire, flood, and disease. It would seem that we have found a fortunate complementarity between Western science and Eastern classical culture. Conservation biologists want to preserve the natural rhythms as much as Taoists, and if the former come to value these cycles from their science and the latter from their religious philosophies, so much the better.

Indeed, scientists have lessons to learn from the East. Taoism is a model of authentic development. True to nature and human nature, it blends yang and yin in its sustainable, steady state. The teaching about the Tao is not merely a description of the way biosystems work; it is a prescription for human behaviour. Huston Smith, born and bred in China and long the resident religious philosopher at the Massachusetts Institute of Technology, finds the root of the ecological crisis in the wild 'yang trip' of Western science and so 'Taoism throws its ounces on the side of yin, but to recover the original wholeness'.[4] The ecological crisis resulted from too much machismo. The West needs a recovery of the feminine; we need to flow with nature in order properly to attune ourselves to its rhythms. The Tao, descriptive of nature, becomes prescriptive for human behaviour.

As before, there are second thoughts. There is nothing particularly binary about long-term evolutionary histories, about the storied developments from protozoans to persons, about biogeographical distribution patterns of plants and animals, about speciation and extinction patterns, or about Mendelian genetics. In ecosystems, returning is not the only motion. Ecosystems irreversibly evolve, and they can be pushed by human development into degenerating spirals. From extinction there is no returning, just as from development there is perhaps no holding back. Taoists find natural systems ever the same; historical science finds them never the same.

The Taoist way is an ethic of minimal intervention, *wu-wei*, action by inaction, in the belief that things will take care of themselves. They may in spontaneous natural systems when uninterrupted by human activities, but in India, China, Japan, and Africa today, if biological conservation is to succeed at all, one needs active environmental managers and wildlife professionals. One needs studies of where the DDT is going in food chains, what the minimum thresholds of viable breeding populations are, what damage is done by exotic parasites and feral animals, how much the water table is falling, and what drought will do to grasslands and ungulate populations.

To plan authentic human development, we need to know about those world markets which force natives to modify their traditional cultures, to know what the potential for tourist income is if the wildlife is preserved as a visitor attraction. We need studies about tolerable pollution levels and rates of soil erosion. The call for more yin may result in doing too little too late because of ignorance of the real causes of the loss of biological diversity. We may fail to exploit possible commercial forces for recovery, blinded by the belief in the resilient powers of spontaneous nature. Taoism may have its contribution to make but, followed uncritically, it is no certain path either to the conservation of nature or authentic human development.

A metaphysically-based, culturally derived value that runs *contrary* to science-based values will not be intellectually sustainable over time. Thus it will not be socially functional either. To survive, values must be made *complementary* to the facts of science. If from biology we learn that the various species are what they are primarily as a result of biological determinants, then those with oriental or native philosophies will have to decide what the operational value of their metaphysics is. How far are their views testable against science? How far are they claims about realms to which science has no access? How far do they yield an ethic for the environment? For authentic development?

Despite the karma belief that moral force is conserved through reincarnations, is not something lost in extinction? Before the extended evolutionary natural history, is the Tao enough explanation? What do we wish to sustain for the future, and how much yang or active intervention is required?

Questioning may yield a revised account of karma, reincarnation, the yang and the yin — a deeper account in which the noumenal metaphysics is clearly distinguished from the empirical, phenomenal claims, yet clearly related to them. Made congruent with science and congenial with conservation biology, those classical views will have become more mature. We do no favour to believers to protect their beliefs from the forces of critical selection, any more than we do species a favour by removing them from the forces of natural selection.

Questioning will compel a clearer account of reincarnation, karma, the Tao, and *ahimsa*, one that can be set beside or beneath science, and if none is forthcoming, then these beliefs are illusory and ought to be abandoned. Where there are illusions or inadequacies of belief, no one will be harmed (though they may be troubled) by such beliefs collapsing or reforming under critical pressures. This is the only path to authentic, true human development.

Criticism: Science-based values challenged through dialogue

There is another possibility. This encounter of science with alien metaphysical systems may expose the metaphysics that drives *science*. Science may need altering. It may have a loaded metaphysical agenda, may focus on some aspects of experience and obscure or distort others. Science may be infected by *hubris*, by desire for power and domination; it may serve a *praxis* that looks to satisfy human thirsts.

Likewise traditional views, elsewhere made light of, may render perceptible something authentic in nature to which science blinds us, and traditional cultures, being sensitive to this, can prove superior to ours. Remember: no one is the worse for having his or her receptive faculties increased — whether by science, religion, art, philosophy, myth, or whatever.

Science comes in two parts: evolutionary ecoscience, which describes the way nature operates; and technological science, which permits humans to prescribe the uses to which nature will be put. The former describes what *is* the case in nature; the latter requires judgments concerning what developments *ought* to be. These are connected. What we believe about the world licenses and constrains our uses of it. The axiology with which we interpret natural history interlocks with the axiology that drives our cultural development.

Science has discovered the community of life on Earth in ways not known to classical cultures — through microscopes, explorations around the globe, fossil evidence, and the labors of taxonomists with their phylogenetic insights. But the same science that, theoretically and descriptively, has revealed the extent of biological diversity has, practically and prescriptively, often pronounced nature to be valueless, except in so far as it can be used instrumentally as a human resource. Knowledge is power, and biological knowledge has fuelled technology, agricultural development, the control of disease organisms, declines in infant mortality, lengthening spans of life, the elimination of predators, and the exploitation of genetic resources. Culture has exploded with escalating demands on ecosystems. The logic at the bottom of all this is that a valueless nature can be put to any cultural use we please; humans are constrained only by prudence and regard for our fellow humans.

The greatest of the science-based values, if we may put it so, is exploitative resource use. This value is based both on applied, technological science and on a theoretical, evolutionary ecoscience that seems to conclude that nature is intrinsically valueless. The believed absence of any intrinsic value and the enormous possibility of instrumental value couple to produce a single conclusion: The only reason for biological conservation is human welfare. In a blunt metaphor, Paul and Anne Ehrlich claim that biological species are important because they are rivets in the aeroplane in which we humans are flying.[5] In the words of Norman Myers, humans care about 'conserving our global stock'.[6] That seems pragmatic, sensible, humane — quite concerned about people in non-Western, lesser-developed countries. It can even seem a global ethic for sustaining life.

But is this the last word? Exploiters do not really live in an environment. They only have resources, something like the way in which slaveholders, as such, do not have friends, only slaves. Even the most enlightened exploiters, *qua* exploiters, do not live as selves in a society; they are not citizens of a world, only consumers of materials. They reduce their environment to food or faeces, to resource and sink. The environment must be this much, of course, but it can be much more, and proportionately, as the instrumentalist development ethic increases, the environment is reduced to little more than resource.

Though traditional cultures do not have ecology as a science, they often have what ecology means etymologically: a logic of a home. They have world views in which they are meaningful residents in a meaningful world. It can hardly be said that science has yet given us a world view in which we readily find ourselves at home. The West with its growth ethic has tended to replace ecology, the logic of a home, with economics, a logic of efficient resource use. That growth will be claimed realistic, and pragmatic, for the poor and hungry must eat, and we need commodities before amenities. The logic can be science-based: does not every creature act as an imperialist, taking over as much of the world as it can? Playing by the same rules, humans maximize their niche in the world.

Such an ethic of dominance in the only moral creature becomes one of arrogance, an Earth-eating mentality that has become consumptive and no longer resides in any place in peace. We begin to wonder whether those who espouse such science-based values have forgotten what traditional cultures know about the intrinsic worth of these neighbouring forms of life, about how culture ought to be of a piece with the whole. In this perspective, the military-industrial-agribusiness nation-states in the modern West, which think themselves so cosmopolitan, can in fact be quite provincial cultures, more so than the tribes and kingdoms of traditional societies.

Compared with the 'traditionalists' who believe that the myriad natural kinds all have a place under the sun, that creation is divinely created and good, that a spiritual integrity places claims on human conduct, we 'moderns' are the ones who seem axiologically naive. Perhaps we are on a wild yang trip. We see more comprehensively than they biologically; but sometimes they see more comprehensively than we axiologically. They have a global ethic that we have not yet attained. Not always, of course, for doctrines about the dominion of man often originated in the same context as those about the goodness of all created things. Teachings about reverence for life mingle with contradictory abuses. Meanwhile, those of us who embrace the modern scientific and technological world view have little to brag about in our untempered anthropocentrism.

The developmental view that triggered the great losses of biological diversity in this century did not arise from traditional cultural values, either classical or primitive. These losses began when science-based models were exported to traditional societies. The damage done within primitive and classical cultures (which was sometimes considerable) pales beside damages done in our own century when these cultures are 'opened up' for development, when they get entangled in world markets and military alliances, when they aspire to Western standards of living, and when they are secularized. The American consumer mentality (that can sacrifice a relict wilderness for molybdenum to make electric carving knives) needs to reform its values as much as do the foolish folk who desire ginseng or rhinoceros horn daggers. In a world without value except by human preference assignments, science-based values are not part of the solution; they are the root of the problem.

At an elevation still to be attained, science can help provide a clearer vision. Humanity cannot return to superstitious folklore; most contemporary men and women do not live in an enchanted world. It is unlikely that we can lift intact from traditional cultures any pre-scientific, mythological way of valuing nature. But partly as a result of our dialogue with these cultures, we might accept our non-human neighbours on Earth for what they are in themselves, not as rivets in spaceship Earth or global stock. Perhaps we can begin to see ourselves not so much as maximizers of human development but as fellow residents in a global community of life. Using traditional values as a catalyst, we might draw our model of Earth from ecology, rather than from physics, chemistry, computing, or mechanics. No model of development can be 'right' in terms of inter-human justice unless it is 'right' in terms of adapted fit to the land. We reach the conclusion that science-based and traditional cultures alike need a revised environmental ethic.

Notes

1 Nigel Smith, 'Enchanted Forest', *Natural History* 92 no. 8 (August 1983): 14–20.
2 Aurelio Peccei and Daisaku Ikeda, *Before It Is Too Late* (Tokyo: Kodansha International, 1984), 65.
3 Arthur Waley, *The Way and its Power* (London: George Allen & Unwin, 1934, 1965).
4 Huston Smith, 'Tao Now' in Ian Barbour, ed., *Earth Might Be Fair* (Englewood Cliffs, New Jersey: Prentice Hall, 1972), 80.
5 Paul R. Ehrlich and Anne H. Ehrlich, *Extinction* (New York: Random House, 1981).
6 Norman Myers, 'Conserving Our Global Stock', *Environment* 21 no. 9 (November 1979): 25–33.

Part Two
International Response

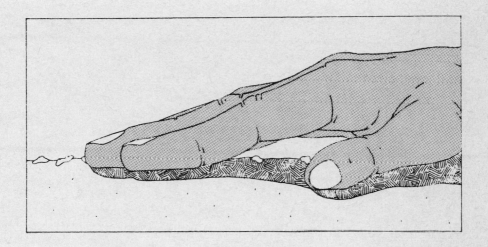

Western Europe and North America

5 Towards an ecological world view

Stephen R. Sterling

How should we live? This ethical question has occupied philosophers and ordinary men and women for thousands of years, but at this juncture in human history it is paramount. The answer that we arrive at collectively will determine not only what sort of future we will have, but whether there will *be* any long-term future.

The most pressing need is for the emergence, clarification, and adoption of a new ecological world view that can create a sustainable culture capable of treating the Earth with gentleness and respect. As Gregory Bateson wrote, 'the world partly becomes — comes to be — how it is imagined'.[1] The new ecological world view, based upon a rising tide of thinking and practice that can be called systemic or holistic, is the only genuine hope for a sustainable future for humankind and the Earth. Its articulation is inherently difficult, however, for it relates to a way of thinking and being which is far deeper and more extensive than any single attempt to express it, and which goes beyond any one individual's interpretation.

Every society is characterized by one or several coexisting traditions, faiths, ideologies, and philosophies which give rise to a world view or set of assumptions about reality and the world. Concomitant with a society's world view is its ethos — an ethical *system* influencing how people should interact in and with the world. The world view and ethos shape institutions, the parameters and character of debate, and the patterns of human interaction with the natural world. Reciprocally, these factors tend to reflect and reinforce each other, thus perpetuating themselves and the total cultural milieu.

Our concern here is primarily with Western culture, which has dominated virtually all other cultures, particularly through science, technology, and economic and political institutions. Western anthropologies looking 'from the outside' have long recognized that 'world view' is the key to understanding a different culture, but it is both more rare and difficult to examine and challenge the Western world view 'from the inside' when its critics are products of its tradition and cannot help but be influenced by it. Furthermore, it is to be expected that most members of a society will not be objectively aware of their cultural milieu. Even those that are cannot intellectually stand fully outside their cultural heritage. Our contemporary paradox is characterized by widespread awareness of the gravity of the global malaise coupled with an inability or unwillingness to recognize in our world view its root causes. This lack of truly radical self-examination, together with an outward-looking, 'pioneering' orientation, perhaps accounts for the dominance of Western culture.

However, a major attack on any world view may drastically change its nature. Such upheavals in Western history are commonly identified with Copernicus, Galileo, and Darwin, who radically challenged their societies' norms on the basis that these no longer provided an adequate construct of reality. Western culture is showing clear signs of a potentially historic transformation towards a sustainable view of development based upon the ecological or systemic/holistic world view and ethos. This represents real hope for the global future of human societies and the biosphere.

The Western world view

The Western world view developed directly from the scientific revolution of the seventeenth and eighteenth centuries. The work of such key figures as Galileo, Bacon, Descartes, and Newton stimulated changes in thought on a scale that eventually eclipsed the earlier world view of medieval Christendom. This new world view was essentially secular and mechanistic, and it introduced key methodologies and principles which were mutually reinforcing. This framework complemented the growth of capitalism and materialism, forming a cultural nexus that has had a determining effect on the mainstream thought and action of individuals, societies, and institutions to the present day. The significance of the scientific world view can hardly be overemphasized because, as Morris Berman says, it is 'our consciousness, in the Western industrial nations — uniquely so'.[2] In addition, there are few non-Western industrial cultures that have not been affected by Western ideas and practices. Science, economics, politics, technology, art, philosophy, health, education — and indeed, even conservation and the current discussions about environmental ethics — all are affected by and reflect the beliefs, values, and methodologies associated with this world view.

Although the Western world view has been spectacularly successful over the last three hundred years, the major crises that now afflict the world must be viewed as evidence of its fundamental weaknesses. Put simply, it no longer constitutes an adequate model of reality.

The critical characteristics of the modern scientific world view are separation and dissociation. Cartesian logic laid the foundation for the scientific paradigm by differentiating mind and body, subject and object, value and fact, spirit and matter. These distinctions were necessary to the liberation and flowering of scientific inquiry as we have come to know it, but the schism implied between these opposites is now at the heart of our contemporary crises. Thus, there is a bias in favour of thought over feeling, reason over emotion, fact over value, intellect over intuition, analysis over synthesis, instrumental over intrinsic goals, and quantitative over qualitative factors. Most importantly, Cartesian duality set human beings apart from and over nature, thus opening the way for a relationship that is primarily exploitative and manipulative. We have faithfully enacted Descartes' belief that humans should be 'the masters and possessors of Nature'.

It is only to be expected that our world view has conditioned our perception of the role of ethics in relation to the environment and conservation. The development of ethical thought in Western societies has been emasculated by the positivist influence of Descartes and others. Positivists hold that, because all value judgments are subjective and unreliable, they do not constitute 'proper knowledge'. By positing the 'naturalistic fallacy' they claim that it is not possible to infer 'ought' from 'is', the *prescriptive* (value) from the *descriptive* (fact). Whether consciously acknowledged or not, these elemental ideas still underlie common attitudes, even in conservation circles, towards the debate on the nature and place of ethics in everyday life.

Thus, discussion about 'right' and 'wrong' with regard to decision-making is largely regarded as irrelevant. Political, economic, commercial, and technological decisions are backed by an appeal to 'objective' facts, evidence, and probabilities which effectively mask the values of justifying evidence. Where a situation demands that the ethical dimensions be more overt, constructive ethical debate can again be undermined by the effects of positivism in the guise of ethical relativism. No ethical position is held to be necessarily better than another, because they are all essentially subjective and, therefore, unprovable. A chasm is opened between public and private values, and any inconsistency between them is regarded as quite normal and acceptable. It is also normal to draw narrow boundaries around an area of responsibility beyond which matters are not 'our concern'. As Michael Polanyi has commented: 'Objectivism seeks to relieve us of all responsibility for the holding of our beliefs . . . the responsibility of the human person is eliminated from the life and society of man.'[3]

At the same time, instrumental values play a predominant yet often unrecognized role in Western and Westernized societies. Instrumental values are concerned with the utility of things as opposed to their intrinsic value. Thus, persons, objects, actions, and all aspects of the natural world tend to be evaluated in terms of their use. It is not uncommon for narrow instrumental values to be cited in support of an ethical position which is, by all other criteria, ethically untenable.

Furthermore, the Western linear view of history and causation affords no underlying sense of 'optimum' or 'enough', or of cyclical effect and change. If something is 'good', then 'more' or 'bigger' must be better. This idea of limitless maximization is a key element behind much of the environmental malpractice which the conservation lobby attempts to halt and reverse. Though this lobby is often effective, the real irony is that since it inhabits the same mental universe as the rest of the Westernized world, it employs arguments based on instrumental values to resist instrumentally-based forces. Thus, the main argument for conserving a species or ecosystem is its present or future scientific value or economic worth. The 'softer' instrumental values of aesthetic or spiritual worth are a poor second, while conservation of nature for its own intrinsic worth rarely receives serious consideration. Although many conservationists are aware of these broader values, they feel constrained by the accepted parameters of debate to advance the instrumental ones only. They operate in a society where ethical considerations are regarded as a worthy but separate criterion, essentially unrelated to political or economic criteria. In a trade-off between 'hard economics' and ethics, the latter is usually dispensable.

The status of ethics in society at large, and in conservation, is thus complicated, and this tangle impedes intellectual and practical progress. Many professional conservationists have an intuitive feeling that ethics is a vital part of conservation thinking, yet are unclear about the how, what, and why involved. This confusion is a direct result of the Western intellectual tradition based on separation and dissociation.

We need then, a world view and ethos which are more complete and better approximations to reality. Most crucially, we need a framework capable of tackling the massively complex problems we have created, and of shaping a fairer, safer, more caring, and sustainable world. A basis already exists in the ecological world view, also called the holistic, systemic, organic view. It is still evolving but it contains the seeds of a cultural transformation equal to or surpassing that of the scientific/industrial revolution of the past three hundred years.

The ecological world view

The lineage of the ecological view can be traced throughout history, and includes a number of modern philosophers and scientists who opposed the mechanistic/objectivist school of thought. However, it is really only in the last thirty years, and especially the last decade, that the various strands of 'holistic thought' have been identified and, more importantly, felt to be aspects of a coherent philosophy. Ironically, developments in physics, popularly regarded as the foundation of the classical scientific world view, provided direct challenges to the basis of that world view. In 1958, Heisenberg, one of the founders of quantum mechanics, wrote:

'by its intervention, science alters and re-fashions the object of investigation, in other words, method and object can no longer be separated. The scientific world view has ceased to be a scientific world view in the true sense of the word.'[4]

In other words, there is no independent observer *of* reality but only a participant *in* that reality. As Fritjof Capra says: 'The patterns scientists observe in nature are intimately connected with the patterns of their minds; with their concepts, thoughts, and values.'[5] The classical disjunction between subject and object, value and fact, is invalid; the knower is implicated in the known and there can only be 'relative objectivity'. *How* facts are investigated, selected, and interpreted depends on one's values, which are coloured by how one sees the world. This does not leave us in a frightening morass of subjectivity but instead is an essential awakening to the interactive character of our relationship with the world. It is an essential element of the ecological world view, a key to rediscovering a participative rather than an exploitative relationship.

A further important basis for the new world view is systems biology. In this conceptual framework, cells, like organisms and groups, are at the same time both units and complexes, individuals and communities. At each level of organization, there is a dynamic balance between self-assertive (independent whole) and integrative (dependent part) tendencies. Conventional reductionist thinking understands phenomena by looking at constituent parts and parts of parts. Systemic thinking maintains that the concept of 'part' as a discrete entity is really an illusion which blinds us to the dynamics of the *relationships* involved in the system. The unit of survival is not the organism, but the organism *and* its environment (the larger whole). If the biosphere is evolving towards the fittest natural system, this implies a degree of cooperation and mutual support which, in turn, implies fewer degrees of freedom for components within the system. These ideas have been most strikingly expressed in Lovelock's Gaia theory which views the planet (Gaia) as a living organism which optimizes conditions for its (her) survival. When an organism

benefits the environment as well as the organism itself, then its spread will be assisted. Eventually, the organism, and the environmental change associated with it, will become global in extent. The reverse is also true: any species that adversely affects the environment is doomed: but life goes on.[6]

This systemic approach points to an altogether more complex, dynamic, and fascinating model of the world than that afforded by the modern scientific world view. Instead of a mechanistic world, we see one characterized by organic, complex, dynamic interrelationships. Instead of linear cause and effect, we see a complex web of often cyclical interconnections across time and geographical space. Instead of a world analysed into discrete parts, we see relative wholes, which, by virtue of their organization, are greater than the sum of their parts. Developments at the leading edges of physics, mathematics, chemistry, biology, and neurophysiology are giving rise to a new holistic science which extends the common idea that 'everything is related' to a degree that stretches comprehension, but one which most certainly includes human consciousness and the existence of mind in nature.[7] These universal relationships may be described in terms of processes of co-definition, synchronism, dynamic balance, and synergism — processes evident alike in the complementarity of sub-atomic particles and the independent/dependent tendencies of biological systems.

Thus, systemic understanding is a new model of reality. It is a key to healing Cartesian duality in human psyche and behaviour, and as such it has immense potential to realize a sustainable world.

By underwriting such concepts as the optimization of multiple variables, cyclical change and balance, homeostasis, stability, and diversity, it harmonizes with the way the world actually works and 'wishes' to work. By contrast, the old scientific paradigm promotes the maximization of single variables, with resultant imbalance, rapid change, instability, and homogeneity. Key elements of these two world views are shown in Table 5.1.

Holistic understanding gives rise directly to an ethical framework. First, it shows that no set of ideas is value-free. But the ecological world view goes further to show that, as the world is based upon systemic processes and relationships, our values and actions should be consistent with systemic reality. If they are not in accord, the results of our actions will nevertheless rebound systemically, and everything will suffer. Philosophically (and completely contrary to the 'naturalistic fallacy'), the ecological world view insists that we must infer prescription *with* description, and that fact and value, far from being discrete, are in close relationship. In other words, there is direct correlation between right

Table 5.1   Mechanistic versus Ecological World Views

Mechanistic/Cartesian	Ecological/holistic
Descriptors	
Mechanistic, reductionist, objectivist, technocentric	Organic, holistic, participative, ecocentric
Primary characteristics	
Fact and value unrelated	Fact and value closely related
Ethics and ordinary life separated	Ethics and ordinary life integrated
Subject and object separate	Subject and object interactive
People and nature separate — relation is one of domination	People and nature inseparable — relation is one of systemic synergy
Knowledge divisible, value-free, empirical, controlling	Knowledge indivisible, value-laden, both empirical and intuitive, empathic
Linear concepts of time and causation	Cyclical concepts of time and causation
Nature understood as being made up of discrete parts; the whole is no more than the sum of its parts	Nature understood as being made up of interrelated wholes which are greater than the sum of their parts
The power of a unit equated with well-being (money, influence, resources)	The quality of interrelationships between systems equated with well-being
Emphasis on the quantitative	Concern with the qualitative
Emphasis on material reality	Concern with physical and metaphysical reality
Analysis key to understanding	Synthesis given greater emphasis
Instrumental values	Instrumental and intrinsic values integrated through systemic values
Few or no technical or ecological limits	Ecological limits determine technical limits
Secondary characteristics	
Centralization of power	Decentralization of power
Specialization	Multidimensional approach
Emphasis on the competitive	Emphasis on the cooperative
Increasing homogeneity and disintegration	Increasing diversity and integration
Undifferentiated economic growth	Steady-state economy or qualitative growth

(accurate description) and right (ethically correct).

The ecological world view recognizes that we are connected to the rest of nature both materially and spiritually far more intimately than the conventional world view permits us to acknowledge. This being so, if we work through and with nature, if we respect and care for it, if we are creative and enhance it, we will benefit both materially and spiritually. This understanding takes us beyond the two competing justifications for conservation — those of instrumental value (utilitarian) and intrinsic value (preservationist). Both have a degree of validity, but neither is an adequate basis for thought or action. While holism does give the intrinsic value of nature much weight, ultimately it stresses that humanity and nature are intimately bound, and that all divisions, no matter how real they may seem, are an illusion.

Conflicts arise where the subtle complexities of systemic relationships are neither perceived nor understood. Systemic logic explains the increasing convergence of the mutually reinforcing problems that we have created, but it also holds out hope for their resolution. Thus, what is conducive to social stability, cultural development, and sustainable economic patterns is also conducive to ecological health, planetary survival, and individual happiness.[8] This gestalt of interlocking and converging imperatives was confirmed by the World Commission on Environment and Development.[9] Our awakening to systemic reality is also an awakening to ecological ethics.

Mechanistic development versus ecodevelopment

The ecological world view simply yet profoundly recognizes that we must act in accordance with the Earth's systems. The direction of evolution appears to be one of diversification and integration as *complementary* processes. But the mechanistic Western world view, while sometimes paying lip service to 'harmony with nature', is in practice fundamentally at odds with the evolutionary process. By underwriting narrowly defined economic and political goals, it rarely encourages attention to the complex patterns of feedback that our actions set in motion. As a result, through the use of political and economic power, and in this century by vastly increasing energy flows and material transfer, we tend to break down both ecological and cultural complexity, particularly at the local level. This reduces the resilience of natural (including human) systems and their ability to self-regulate by increasing their vulnerability to sudden change.

Raymond Dasmann has made the distinction between 'ecosystem people' and 'biosphere people'.[10] The former depend on the local ecosystem for material support and their culture is closely integrated with their bioregion. Virtually all traditional societies are or were ecosystemic. Biosphere people, living under the influence of the mechanistic world view, draw on the entire globe through networks of trade and communication. They feel distanced from and uninvolved with the places that their demand affects, and they often initiate large-scale and inappropriate economic schemes which disrupt and distort local ecosystems. As the component systems are simplified and destabilized, the larger system is itself weakened and endangered. By so destroying the abilities of systems to self-organize and self-regulate — be they non-human, human, or both — we destroy diversity and reduce options for the future. Also, we reap massive managerial problems both locally and globally. These are then addressed through an inadequate single-issue 'techno-fix' approach which may give the appearance of relieving the problem, yet often exacerbates it through unforeseen systemic feedback. We are wreaking massive and historically unprecedented changes at a time when, as Norman Myers says: 'Our ignorance is so vast that we are not aware of it . . . we know next to nothing about the workings of the Earth's ecosystem . . . and have only begun to grasp the nature of planetary life as a whole.'[11]

In the sphere of development strategies, the new ecological world view has given rise to the concept of 'ecodevelopment'. The 1980s have witnessed a growing understanding of the complementarity of conservation and development and the need to enact that complementarity in the practice of sustainable development. There is a growing accord between the development practitioners who see ecodevelopment as a practical and urgent necessity and the ecophilosophers who see it as an ethical imperative. Given the systemic nature of the world, this consensus should be expected; 'ecodevelopment' was waiting to be discovered. Put another way, the growing costs of ignoring natural limits and systemic responses is forcing more and more of us into thinking holistically.

The growing advocacy of such mutually supporting ecodevelopment principles as self-reliance, local needs orientation, ecological soundness and sustainability, pluralism, participation, appropriate technology, and human scale can be viewed as timely Western recognition of a form of human interaction with the environment long practised in many traditional societies. In the industrialized world, the principles of ecodevelopment are being brought home in the concepts of the green movement and bioregionalism. The latter, especially, emphasizes the need for societies to *reinhabit* — as opposed to occupy — their region, and to evolve 'social behaviour that will enrich the life of that place, restore its life-supporting systems, and establish an ecologically and socially sustainable pattern of existence within it.[12] In short, for us to begin to re-establish ourselves as ecosystem people. This is not to advocate parochialism, but rather the reverse. The aim is local rootedness with a planetary vision.

An essential element of ecodevelopment is social and economic justice. Indeed, perhaps the single most effective step that could be taken towards the alleviation of environmental and related crises is the pursuit of social and economic justice within and between nations. Yet our reductionist culture typically regards social ethics and environmental ethics as separate. Meanwhile, the world offers mounting proof that they are not: a disempowered, exploited person often has no option other than to harm his or her environment, and a degraded environment will impoverish those depending on it. But the reverse is also true: the 'whole' person and community and the 'whole' environment can exist in a harmonious symbiotic relationship.

The ecological world view and the whole person

The key concepts of the ecological world view apply no less to the relation of human individuals to themselves as to each other and the environment. There is an inevitable reciprocity between an integrated, fulfilled person and a healthy planetary ecology. Since the global crisis is a projection of the way in which we view the world, our disintegrated world view creates a disintegrating world.

If we consider such pairs as subject/object, value/fact, mind/body, intuition/ reason, spirit/matter, feeling/thought, unconscious/conscious, feminine/ masculine, and synthesis/analysis, it is easy to see that Western culture emphasizes the latter 'hard' half of each. Our personal crisis is that we see these areas as essentially unrelated and often suppress the unwanted halves, while in actuality they interact in a systemic fashion. We are therefore a group of lop-sided, detached, dis-integrated minds trying to impose an incomplete and crude mechanistic sense of order on an essentially holistic complex natural order. Our astonishing psychological ability to segregate areas of life allows us to indulge in behaviour that other parts of ourselves may be saying is unethical.

Becoming more integrated persons depends on achieving a fuller consciousness, and this cannot be acquired purely through intellectual effort since rationality is only one aspect of the mind. Western psychotherapy attempts to get in touch with the non-rational mind in order to develop the self-actualized person. Eastern thought has long recognized the intimate connection between the everyday and the teleological, the microcosm and the macrocosm. The ecological world view concurs. In the words of Barbara Ward, 'what makes our time unique in history is that the immediate and ultimate questions are again bound up together'.[13] We should pursue ecodevelopment principles not only because they are the most sensible course of action, but because, through enhancing the wholeness of human and natural communities, we also enhance our individual wholeness.

As Berman has said:

for more than 99 percent of human history, the world was enchanted and man saw himself as an integral part of it. The complete reversal of this perception in a mere four hundred years or so has destroyed the continuity of the human experience and the integrity of the human psyche.[14]

Indeed, the Western cult of the ego may be seen as an aberration that has alienated us from ourselves and from our environment. It may prove to be terminal. Berman suggests that, although we are unable to return to animism, the holistic paradigm may enable humankind to bridge the lonely alienation of the subject/object dichotomy and achieve a form of 'participating consciousness' with nature — a synergy by which both may be more fulfilled.

Such thinking has been expressed in the literature of ecophilosophy and deep ecology. The degree of closeness between people and nature advocated by deep ecology may not be possible in the short term for a culture which has lost contact with its world, and the language may sound too value-laden for our objectivist norms, but deep ecology (see Arne Naess's chapter in this volume) points the direction in which we should be heading.

It is impossible to predict the outcome of the clash between the rival world views against the background of worsening crises and the need for wholesale change. Our detached, analytical approach and narrowly perceived interests are not conducive to the holistic vision and spirit necessary for full comprehension of the ecological world view. Nevertheless, for increasing numbers of people in the West, pieces of the holistic jigsaw are fitting together and bear the promise of an alternative reality. We are most probably in the first, uncertain stages of a cultural rebirth, and history shows that such change is a long and difficult process. This time, though, the whole future is at stake. A clear exposition of the ecological world view is the vital catalyst for this critical transformation.

How should we live? In human experience, the simplest questions are often also the most profound. The global crisis is a warning; an opportunity for fundamental reappraisal that must not be missed. The problem is that the profoundest questions challenge the security of our accustomed norms. There is no doubt that many individuals and institutions *are* moving towards ecological/ holistic perspectives. The change is taking place. If we *consciously* pursue and enact the ecological world view, the transformation needed may yet be in time.

Notes

1 Quoted in Morris Berman, *The Re-enchantment of the World* (New York: Cornell University Press, 1981).
2 Ibid., 22.
3 Michael Polanyi, *Personal Knowledge* (London: Routledge and Kegan Paul, 1958), 323.
4 Werner Heisenberg, *The Physicist's Conception of Nature* (London: Hutchinson, 1958), 29.
5 Fritjof Capra, *The Turning Point — Science, Society and the Rising Culture* (London: Wildwood House, 1982), 77.
6 James Lovelock, 'Gaia: The World as a Living Organism', *New Scientist* (18 December 1986): 28.
7 John P. Briggs and David Peat, *Looking Glass Universe: The Emerging Science of Wholeness* (London: Fontana, 1985).
8 Stephen Sterling, 'Culture, Ethics and the Environment — Towards the New Synthesis, *The Environmentalist* 5 no. 3 (1985): 203.
9 World Commission on Environment and Development, *Our Common Future* (Oxford: Oxford University Press, 1987).
10 Raymond Dasmann, *Environmental Conservation* (New York: John Wiley, 1984).
11 Norman Myers, *The Gaia Atlas of Planetary Management* (London: Pan, 1985), 258.
12 Raymond Dasmann, quoted in Berman, *The Re-enchantment of the World*, 294.
13 Quoted in Brian Johnson, 'Dedication to Barbara Ward — The Duty to Hope', *The Environmentalist* 1 no.2 (1981): 95.
14 Berman, *The Re-enchantment of the World*, 23.

6 Sustainable development and deep ecology
Arne Naess

Non-industrial cultures insist upon the meaningfulness of life. A large part of their mental and physical energy is devoted to religious and other practices supporting this belief. Behaviour must conform to it. This pressure towards conformity is often immense, and is sometimes resented by the young.

The advent of rich, industrial cultures makes it appear possible to skip the labours that support the meaningfulness of life. What is left of non-industrial cultures today is threatened by the nearly irresistible lure of the 'free', 'unconcerned' ways of life manifested by tourists, economic development experts, and other visitors from rich nations. To the young, these strange beings seem to have been able to get rich while remaining free of onerous social duties. The cultural cost of economic growth within rich nations is rarely considered. The ecological cost is incalcuable.

If one shifts from being an observer of cultures to being a student of the history of ideas, one may trace a line of thinking that roughly suggests a movement from the ideal of 'progress' to that of 'development' and 'economic growth', and from these ideas to that of 'sustainable development'. Some of us hope for a further step along this line, from sustainable development to 'ecological development' to long-range 'ecosophical development' — with an emphasis on the need for wisdom (*sophia*) as much as on the need for science and technology. If this line is to be followed, it will entail our studying the loss of beliefs and cultural identities now happening because of the tremendous impact of the economy and technology of big, powerful, rich industrial societies. As members of these societies we are largely responsible for this impact and the resulting cultural shock. Any model of ecologically sustainable development must suggest ways to avoid furthering the thoughtless destruction of cultures, or the dissemination of the belief in a glorious, meaningless life.

The above goal may be expressed in shorter form by asking for ecosophically sustainable development. Every decision in every country in the world has an ecosophical aspect. The centres of philosophical and religious thinking have to be mobilized as energetically as the centres of ecological, economical, and technological learning.

The term 'developing country' should either be avoided or applied to rich countries as well as to poor, for practically every country today is developing in a way that is ecologically unsustainable. It ought to be a goal of the rich countries to change policies in such a way that they eventually reach a level of sustainability of development.

Because of the wide range of cultures deeply affected by unsustainability, the philosophical and religious underpinning of changes towards sustainability must differ. There must be a marked pluralism of ultimate conceptions of meaningfulness. I place these philosophical and religious conceptions on 'level one' of any development systematization. From this basic level, one should be able to derive ecosophically important views furnishing guidelines for change. The important thing is to recognize that if we hope for rich cultural diversity on Earth in the future, there can be no completely general blueprint for development. Development must differ to assure cultural continuity. Cultures will not be lost along the way, as is occurring today, if we insist on the relevance of level one, and if concrete plans are tried out to ascertain whether the changes allow for the persistence of deep cultural diversity on Earth.

Deep ecology and the world conservation strategy

The ecophilosophically important general views I discuss in what follows are characteristic of a great number of active people from many nations, and are open to different articulations. The set of tentative formulations I shall use, the so-called 'deep ecology platform', comprises eight points:[1]

1. The flourishing of human and non-human living beings has value in itself. The value of non-human beings is independent of their usefulness to humans.
2. Richness of kinds of living beings has value in itself.
3. Humans have no right to reduce this richness except to satisfy vital human needs.
4. The flourishing of human life is compatible with a substantial decrease of the human population. The flourishing of non-human life requires such a decrease.
5. Present human interference with the non-human world is excessive, and the situation is rapidly worsening.
6. Policies must be changed in view of points (1)–(5). These policies affect basic economic, technological, and ideological structures. The resulting state of human affairs will be greatly different from the present.
7. The appreciation of a high quality of life will supersede that of a high standard of life.
8. Those who accept the foregoing points have an obligation to try to contribute directly to the implementation of necessary changes.

Let me compare the deep ecology platform to the view of sustainable development that has been formulated in the World Conservation Strategy (WCS).[2] While it is difficult, and for present purposes unnecessary, to determine exactly the nature of agreements and disagreements between the WCS and the deep ecology platform, this analysis suggests areas of tension. Three quotes from the exceptionally careful formulations in Chapter 1 of the WCS point to an initial difference:

1. The term 'development' is defined in the WCS as 'the modification of the biosphere and the application of human . . . living and non-living resources to satisfy human needs and improve the quality of human life'.
2. Development's close relation to the term 'conservation' is made clear in the definition of conservation as 'the management of human use of the biosphere so that it may yield the greatest sustainable benefit to present generations while maintaining its potential to meet the needs and aspirations of future generations'.
3. The term 'sustainable' is not defined, but that it is meant to imply the *long-term* support of life on Earth is clear from the two opening sentences of Chapter 1 of the WCS: 'Earth is the only place in the universe known to sustain life. Yet human activities are progressively reducing the planet's life-supporting capacity at a time when rising human numbers and consumption are making increasingly heavy demands on it'.

These quotes reveal that a difference between the deep ecology platform and the WCS view of development is in the basis each uses for valuing non-human life. The question arises as to whether non-human life is of intrinsic or of only utilitarian value.

It is true that expressed concern for non-human life *for its own sake* is not completely absent from the WCS. In the third quotation above, 'the planet's life-supporting capacity' is used, not the 'planet's man-supporting capacity', and Chapter 1 of the WCS, where 'a new environmental ethics' is asked for, may plausibly be interpreted as referring to an ethics where non-human life is conserved for its own sake. Furthermore, the title 'World Conservation Strategy' suggests something wider than conservation for the sake solely of humans.

Nevertheless, the WCS leaves little doubt that the ultimate concern is for humans: 'Conservation, like development, is for people.'[3] In the second WCS quotation above, the reference to generations may, taken in isolation, be interpreted so as to cover all living beings, but that is not possible when reading the context.

In contrast, the deep ecology platform makes it clear that non-human life is valued independently of human life. Furthermore, the deep ecology formulation expressly supports a policy of non-interference with continuing evolution, for example, the evolution of mammals demanding vast territory, and of highly different landscapes with their special organisms.

From the narrow definition of development in the WCS it follows that satisfaction of non-human needs and the improvement of the life quality of any nonhuman kind of being cannot possibly be a part of development in a *direct* way. There is, however, at least one possibility of making the three above quotations on development from the WCS compatible with points 1 and 2 of the deep ecology platform. This possibility leans heavily upon two hypotheses: first, that mature human beings believe at least implicitly in the intrinsic value of non-human life, and in the diversity of life, and second, that they accordingly experience a strong need to oppose actions and policies incompatible with these beliefs. If the two hypotheses are accepted, one may assert that there is a human need to protect nature for its own sake. This protection of the full richness and diversity of non-human life on Earth for its own sake acquires the status of usefulness for humans and is fully compatible with important forms of utilitarianism. I personally accept the hypotheses when 'maturity' is taken in the strong sense of all-sided (German *allseitige*) maturity.

This admission of a utilitarianism of sorts may be important for those supporters of the deep ecology movement who tend to conceive of themselves as utilitarians and who don't feel at home with valuations seemingly 'totally independent' of human valuation.

The firm acceptance of the two first points of the deep ecology platform is of considerable social and political importance. As long as major efforts to protect, and to restore, the richness and diversity of life on Earth are supported solely on the basis of human need narrowly defined, they will be piecemeal, not holistic. They will not concern whole ecosystems and will not be carried out with maximal perspective in time and space. Without a respect for the ecosphere as a whole, efforts will continue to be focused on special spectacular items — pandas, wolves, acid rain, ozone layer, carbon dioxide. Respect for the welfare of all facilitates acceptance of long-range efforts including changes within human societies. Ecologically sustainable development will automatically refer to the whole planet and not to ecologically arbitrary boundaries of nations.

Another way of conceptually closing the gap between the two documents is to look at the meaning of 'life' and 'living'. When a campaign with the aim of protecting a river against so-called 'development' is launched, the slogan 'Let the river live' does not concern the water of the river, but a somewhat vaguely conceived ecosystem as a whole — a 'living whole'. In some cases it includes people who live along the river or use the river in an ecologically appropriate way. It is clear that most campaigners for the protection of the river against major interference feel that the interference reduces the meaning of their own lives. People have a vital need for meaning which they try to protect. We are again led to a concept of sustainable development for the satisfaction of human needs which also protects the planet for its own sake. The Gaia hypothesis has shown its value not only as a working hypothesis, but also as a way for people within cultures imbued with Western science to experience the Earth as something living, as alive in a broad sense.

Rights and vital needs

Point 3 of the deep ecology platform, that humans have no right to reduce the richness and diversity of life on Earth except to satisfy vital human needs, engenders controversy about the terms 'rights' and 'needs'. Philosophers who are dubious about the notion of 'right' propose the substitution of the phrase 'humans should not' instead of 'humans do not have the right to'. But the postulation of certain 'human rights' has a positive influence today. As long as the term is used in this connection, it might also be used to refer to non-humans. Some say that humans can have rights because they have obligations. Animals don't have obligations, therefore they have no rights. However, a limitation of the meaning of 'rights' is not found in the everyday use of the term, as when one speaks of the rights of lunatics or of small children.

Indeed, formal 'Declarations of Rights of Animals' are being codified. A

Norwegian version was signed by thousands of people. And a pilot study of answers to questions of whether animals and plants have rights revealed a great majority of positive views.[4] Not included in the eight points, but quite expressive of opinions among supporters of the deep ecology movement, is the following formulation: Every living being has the right to live and flourish.'

However, the acceptance of point 3 does not, strictly speaking, depend upon the acceptance of the existence of rights of humans and non-humans. If a mother says to her son, 'You have no right to prevent your little sister from eating all her birthday cake', this does not imply any doctrine of rights of sisters to eat. There is an important everyday usage of the expression 'no right to' which has to do with injustice and related phenomena, and the same holds of 'no right to' in the formulation of point 3.

In the area of needs, point 3 is not meant to imply that there should be no extravagance. It does not, for instance, condemn the extraordinary richness of occasional feasts within non-industrial cultures. Nor does it necessarily imply that the few people for whom producing a lot of children is a deep and intense joy should be discouraged. But when there is already a vast population of humans, an increase has detrimental consequences for both humans and non-humans.

The intention when using the strong term 'vital need' is to announce a limit of justifiable interference. Not every demand on the market proves that there is a corresponding need. Hundreds of millions of people have unsatisfied vital needs of the most pressing kinds; hundreds of millions of others are wasting the resources of the planet for purposes generally considered trifling and unworthy (although more or less unavoidable as things are). The gigantic gross national product of the rich industrialized states is a measure of pollution and waste, with doubtful gains for human life quality. Already in the 1960s, GNP was called 'Gross National Pollution'. Unfortunately, an increase in GNP does not guarantee an increase in the satisfaction of vital needs, a fact painfully obvious in poor countries where increases so far have had little effect on the desperately poor.

Where to draw the limit between vital and non-vital is a question that must be related to local, regional, and national particularities. Even then a certain area of disagreement must be taken as normal.

The population factor

What is the carrying capacity of the Earth? This question has often been raised within a narrow frame of reference, with certain premises attached:

Premise 1: Nature has no intrinsic value, so we need not have any animals or plants other than those which science or tradition tells us are useful for us. 'Carrying capacity' therefore refers to 'carrying capacity' for humans, not 'carrying capacity for humans and non-humans'.
Premise 2: If there is a conflict between the human urge for space for more human settlements and the urge of other species for more territory, humans have a priority and may even reduce the habitats of the others.

Generally it has also been taken for granted, with some justification, that new technologies will be discovered that will make increases of population manageable, for instance, that there will be new 'green (red, blue) revolutions', relying heavily on chemicals and on a transition from small-scale family agriculture to agribusiness.

Today the old debate on 'carrying capacity' seems rather queer. Now at stake are the freedom, richness, and diversity of life on this planet, including the life quality and cultural diversity of humans. Accordingly, for an increasing number of people, these two goals are not in conflict.

Point 4 of the deep ecology platform contains two rather different propositions. The first, the positive effect of population decrease, is arguable from human history. The history of humanity is of a vast diversity of cultures with rather modest populations. Contemporary destruction of cultures does not proceed because of lack of humans. Admittedly, this point is rather abstract, but it allows for an important long-range, global perspective: the goal of a number of people small enough to avoid gigantic bureaucracies and insufferable crowding, with easy access to free nature and spacious room for every activity consistent with 'live and let live'.

What the first proposition of point 4 does not mention is the transition period — how to go from, let us say, 8000 million to substantially less people than there are today. Perhaps a transition period of a thousand years is needed, or perhaps much less. In any case, the long perspective is liberating for our minds and of practical importance for long-range planning of cities and areas of free nature. Furthermore, the prospect of a period with comparatively few small children should stimulate us to think how to make it possible for all child-loving adults to enjoy all their life in the company and care of small children. The dominance of the nuclear family concept in rich countries largely excludes this.

The presentation of a vision of a stabilization–reduction–stabilization process rarely meets objections among deep ecology supporters, but it cannot be said to be a favourite theme! More old people and less children — unpalatable! And how are people persuaded to limit child production? Cruelty and injustice must by all means be avoided.

Against the second proposition of point 4 — that maintaining (and, I am tempted to add, restoring) the richness and diversity of life on Earth require a significantly smaller population than 5000 million — it may be posited that if ecologically responsible policies were substituted for the present non-responsible ones, human interference would no longer be a problem, and therefore ecologically responsible policies rather than population decrease should be the focus. But it seems to me that this process may prove to have as many obstacles as the reduction of the population. Very large populations create very large problems of freedom and organization, and centralization, giantism, and reduction of cultural diversity seem unavoidable features of life with a population of 5000 million.

Plans for sustainable development often neglect the population issue. For example, this neglect compromises the adequacy of the Brundtland Commission report, *Our Common Future*.[5] The subject is a touchy one. Several assumptions and attitudes make responsible and energetic population policy difficult:

- It is unreasonably assumed that because a humane and otherwise acceptable population reduction will take a long time, perhaps many centuries, it is unimportant to discuss or prepare for it.
- As long as rich nations, which account for a large part of the degradation of life conditions on Earth, try to uphold their present population, they will have little credibility when they try to push poor nations towards rapid stabilization.
- It is unreasonably supposed that the economy, and therefore the life quality, of rich nations will necessarily be adversely affected, at least in the transition period towards lower population.
- Global competition for power and military strength are considered inevitable and are thought to favour big populations.
- It is unreasonably assumed that successful population reduction policies must make it difficult for people who deeply love children (for their own sake) to have four or more of them.

A good meal in the rich countries may require, directly and indirectly, about forty times as much energy as a first-rate dinner in a Third World country. This means that, for instance, in Norway, with about 4 million people, the energy consumed when eating compares to that used by 160 million in a sustainable energy economy. Cleaning operations in a rich country, because of the chemicals used, may result in eighty times as much pollution. Planetary stress would be much more reduced with one million fewer Norwegians that with 1 million fewer people in Calcutta.

A simple conclusion is that sustainable development of populations is a subject of importance in every country, and the greatest responsibility rests with the richest. We must expect an increase of population during most of the next century. Subsequent reduction must be part of the scenario of sustainable future development. Policies based on expectations of great Earth-saving technological revolutions are irresponsible.

From points (1)–(5) of the platform it follows that those who support the deep ecology movement envisage not only deep political, social, and economic changes but also changes in personal lifestyle (point 6 of the platform). This decrease is inevitable if one follows the rule of universalizability: one cannot favour a level of standard of living for oneself which depends upon others not reaching that level.

The term 'standard of living' is preferred to 'material standard of living' because the latter suggests 'spiritual standard of living' as the opposite. Although there need not necessarily be a shift towards spirituality when people attain a higher life quality combined with a stable or lower standard of living, the members of a community with good, intimate inter-personal relations may find that they use more time together in a relaxed way instead of 'going shopping'. As Mother Teresa said privately when receiving the Nobel Prize: 'It is not we but you who are poor.' We, the rich, are poor in deep satisfactions requiring simple means, the means being material, or spiritual, or perhaps beyond those somewhat arbitrary distinctions.

Sustainable development, cultural diversity, and social justice

Any general view inspired by ecology includes reverence for the richness and diversity of human cultures and subcultures. Reverence for life implies it.

Traditional societies before the great cultural shock of the modern industrial era were always in transition, but very slowly. The tremendous speed of change due to the influence of dominating industrial states has severely damaged cultural identity, self-reliance, and even self-respect in many cultures. The introduction of life-saving medicines and life destroying weapons produced in the industrial countries has severely undercut the status of traditional leadership. Development tends to be conceived by the new leaders as a matter of increase in industrial activity and consumption.

Yet the uncritical imitation of Western ways by Third World leaders is now hopefully on the decrease. A growing trend is to look for the assistance of traditional medicines, traditional ways of population stabilization, traditional ecological insights, and in general support of customs which still have some authority and which clearly favour sustainable development, including sustainable cultural identity, and a population proportional to resources.

Modern cultural and anthropological studies show that countries of great material poverty nevertheless maintained extremely rich cultural traditions. For example, the Sherpa village of Beding (Peding), 3700 metres above sea-level in Nepal, had only about 150 people in the 1970s. Statistics show that they were among the world's poorest. But their monastery was beautiful and well kept by their numerous monks and nuns. Much work had an artistic or religious significance. Feasts were sometimes of overwhelming richness and might go on for a week, starting before sunrise with music performed by the monks in honour of their great mountain Tseringma (Gauri Shankar, 7149 metres high). Faced with the question of whether they would prefer the money from foreign expeditions to their unclimbed mountain, or the mountain preserved as it was, all 47 families cast their votes for protection. But the central government of Nepal and the world's mountaineering associations had no sympathy for such a strange idea: protection of a *mountain*? The central government thought of 'progress', the mountaineers of 'conquests', and in the end the cultural needs of the community did not count.[6]

In the 1960s, a new generation of students of social and cultural anthropology and a number of critical researchers described non-industrial cultures in such a way as to indicate that rich industrial societies had as much to learn from the non-industrial as the other way round. Increased respect for non-industrial cultures made itself felt about the same time as the sudden internationalization of the ecological movement with nature as its focus. Aspects of culture were re-examined. While some anthropologists described stone age tribes so as to convey the message that their essential life quality could not be lower, others recognized that within these cultures some fundamental aspects of life quality were at a high level — such as economic security, absence of stressful work, and lots of time for meaningful togetherness bridging the generations.[7]

Among the many aspects of non-industrial cultures which attracted attention were their relations to nature. Their relations to resources were mostly sustainable. One obvious reason was that moderate population and adequate distance between tribes permitted sustainable development. The former view that traditional societies did not develop but were completely inert has been rejected as the result of an explosive increase of knowledge about the history of non-industrial cultures.

Sustainable development today means development along the lines of each culture, not development along a common, centralized line. But faced with hungry children, humanitarian action is a priority whatever its relation to developmental plans and cultural invasion.

As has already been shown, ecology has a social justice side. The degree to which the life conditions of the planet are degraded per capita is highly dependent upon the social lifestyle of the individual. The lifestyle depends upon class, upon social stratification, and upon social services and protection received. The great future effort to reduce per capita degradation of conditions of life will demand discipline and changes of life habits. Moral resentment will attain dangerous intensities if there is not an increase in levels of social justice at local, group, national, and international levels. If their lifestyle does not change, the rich power elites in poor countries will be judged ecological and ethical misfits. Violent reactions must be expected.

A world conservation strategy implies an acceptance of sustainable development. Such development is — or should be — explicit in the programmes of green parties and the visions of green societies. The main relation between the deep ecology movement and the ideals of green societies is simple: the establishment of a green society *presupposes* the implementation of the necessary changes suggested in the deep ecology platform formulation. This declaration remains, however, on a rather abstract conceptual level. If it is posited as a goal that all human societies should be green, it is pertinent to ask: 'What about deep cultural and subcultural diversity?' The blueprints of green societies have so far been the work of industrial Westerners, a rather specialized fragment of humanity. It is to be hoped, but it cannot be taken as a certainty, that development consistent with the guidelines of the deep ecology movement admits and even encourages such a manifold.

From the very beginning, the international deep ecology movement has been non-violent to a high degree, and general Gandhian viewpoints have been common among its supporters. The armament race with all its grave consequences is incompatible with a high level of sustainable development.[8] This has consequences not only for the programmes of green parties, but for all realistic sustainable development plans.

The broadness and deepness of sustainability guidelines demands a global perspective. The rich countries are now rightly expected to see themselves as developing. Their present lack of sustainability is grave, and the challenge is formidable. For the poor countries, the outlook is different. They may avoid the one-sided industrial phase with its consumerism and enter a green post-industrial stage at a higher level of sustainability. For both rich and poor, the obstacles are formidable, and all sorts of conflicts, including wars, may occur along the road. But long-range global sustainability as a central concern may also bring societies together in a more peaceful and joyful endeavour than ever before.

Today there are few or no communities, societies, or cultures which show clear long-range sustainability, which I define as long-range ecological sustainability combined with a satisfactory life quality. A development or general pattern of change within and among communities, societies, or cultures is ecologically sustainable if it is compatible with restoring and maintaining the richness and diversity of planetary life (in the broadest sense). What is 'satisfactory' we scarcely need quarrel about as long as we agree that hundreds of millions of children live at an unsatisfactory level.

Present or future research will not be able to point unambiguously to any one particular way to begin such a development. In practice, we shall have to fight obviously unsustainable kinds of development for a long time while implementing changes that lead towards sustainable development. The industrial countries will be developing countries during this phase, but unsustainable to a diminishing degree. Yet, from the point of view of the deep ecology movement, the victory of the notion of 'sustainable development' over the post-war notion of 'economic development', 'economic growth', and the simplistic 'development' is itself the sign of an awakening from ecological slumber and should be greeted with joy and expectation.

Notes

1 On the so-called 'deep ecology movement' see Bill Devall and George Sessions, *Deep Ecology* (G.M. Smith, Salt Lake City, Utah, 1985), and Arne Naess, *Ecology, Community and Life Style* (Cambridge: Cambridge University Press, 1989).
2 International Union for the Conservation of Nature and Natural Resources, *World Conservation Strategy: Living Resource Conservation for Sustainable Development* (Gland, Switzerland: IUCN, 1980).
3 Ibid., Chapter 1.
4 *Ekspertenes syn på naturens egenverdi* (Trondheim, Norway: Tapir Forlay, 1987).
5 World Commission on Environment and Development, *Our Common Future* (Oxford: Oxford University Press, 1987).
6 Arne Naess, 'Modesty and the Conquest of Mountains' in Michael C. Tobias and H. Drasdo, eds, *The Mountain Spirit*, (New York: The Overlook Press, 1979), 13–16.
7 See Marshall Sahlins, *Stone Age Economics* (Chicago: University of Chicago Press, 1972).
8 For an ecologically-inspired proposal for unilateral disarmament, see Arne Naess, 'Consequences of an Absolute No to Nuclear War' in Avner Cohen and Steven Lee, eds, *Nuclear Weapons and the Future of Humanity: The Fundamental Questions* (Totowa, New Jersey: Rouman and Allanheld, 1986), 425–436.

7 Reverence for life
Henryk Skolimowski

What kind of values do I uphold? What kind of universe do I live in? What kind of destiny do I pursue? These are questions which are of importance to all of us. These are the questions which are at the heart of our existential malaise — whether we are intellectuals or ordinary workers. Because we have not resolved these questions, we cannot find the key to harmony, we cannot resolve the problem of the meaningfulness of our individual lives; and, at yet another level, we cannot find satisfactory solutions to large scale environmental problems. All are connected. When the overall harmony, cohesion, and meaning evade us, we are at a loss as to how to deal with particular problems.

In brief, I will try to argue that the resolution of our environmental dilemmas lies in the matrix of our values. Unless we are able to see in depth what values we hold and how they control our behaviour, unless we are able to establish a new, sound, sane, and sustainable value basis, all the dazzling expertise (based on limited and fragmented vision), all the technological fixes, will be acts full of sound and fury, signifying nothing.

Foundation values

Ethics is not engineering. It asks not 'how to' but 'why'. While developing ethics, we do not search for tools to fix things; we rather search for ultimate foundations which alone can justify our being in this universe. It is very important to bear this in mind in our instrumental age, when we are inclined to reduce everything to a technique. If ethics is a technique, then it is a technique of the soul, following quite a different route from that of present technologies.

We are impatient with general principles. We are impatient with philosophy. We want guides for action now. But that is the attitude of a technician. Ethics, on the other hand, tries to understand a deeper nature of things, and especially why we should behave in this way and not another way. Asking 'why' questions sooner or later leads to foundations, and to foundation values. Foundation values are a rock on which the whole ethical system rests — whatever its nature. If we do not accept some foundation values, nothing follows. For foundation values give us a *raison d'être* for the whole system, its specific subvalues and its specific modes of action.

I call foundation values first-order values. I call the consequences of foundation values second-order values. I call specific tactics and strategies for the implementation of the second-order values, third-order values. Let us use some examples to illustrate the point.

We should persuade legislators to pass appropriate bills to save environments. Our political action (to persuade the legislators) is in the realm of third-order values.

The justification for third-order values is in the second order. Why should we work on legislators? Because we value environments. This is in the realm of second-order values. What is the justification of this one? A still deeper first-order or foundation value. In the system of ecoethics which I propose, this foundation value is rooted in the idea of the sanctity of life. The acceptance of the sanctity of life prompts us to protect other forms of life and threatened habitats, as well as human environments in which life is in peril.

All conservation work, all environmental protection activities, are ultimately based on this deeper conviction of the sanctity of life. Let us be quite clear that if the premise of the sanctity of life is questioned or rejected, the whole design of conservation strategies, and all specific actions for saving environments, hangs in thin air. There is no reason why we should engage in conservation strategies and ecological ethics.

Thus the denial of foundation values leads to the annihilation of the values of specific actions. This point has to be stressed over and over again. We are so intoxicated with action that we often think that it is the only thing of value. But action has meaning only . . . if it has meaning. The meaning of action is determined by the deeper principle this action serves.

The important ethical systems of our times are those which clearly spell out their foundation values and build on those values. Thus, for Gandhi, the foundation value was *ahimsa*, or non-violence. For Schweitzer, it was reverence for life. For Aldo Leopold, it was the sacredness of the land.

Ecological ethics, to my mind, is based on the idea of the sanctity of life. From this idea follows the ethical imperative of reverence for life, which is another formulation of the idea of the sanctity of life.

Ultimate ethical principles underlie and justify our rational strategies and practical choices. Such has been the story of the great ethical systems of humanity. We shall do well to follow the wisdom of past ethical systems without necessarily embracing their specific principles.

Intrinsic values

In this context, we have to see clearly that moral relativism represents not a value position but an abdication from holding a value position. You cannot build anything on moral relativism. You cannot establish any programme of conservation on it; you cannot establish any long-range policies for sustainable development.

To postulate intrinsic values does not mean to postulate either absolute values or objective values, but values that bind us — a species endowed with certain attributes, propensities, and common imperatives — to one another. Because of analytical difficulties, the notion of intrinsic values has been abandoned by many philosophers. This I consider a mistake. We need intrinsic values for the backbone of our conservation strategies, as the ethical basis for right development. I will propose ecoethics as a set of new intrinsic values. But first let me attempt to clarify the status of intrinsic values. In this endeavour, I will build on the proposition that intellectual insight and moral insight are two distinct entities, and that we must therefore not attempt to subsume the moral under the intellectual one, because then we deprive ethical values of what is *sui generis* in them.

Our intellectual consciousness can declare some things of intrinsic value only after it is informed by the axiological level, by the values which we cherish in the depths of our hearts and souls. The fact that it is our value, or axiological, consciousness that informs and guides our cognitive consciousness regarding values is of great importance, for it leads to a new clarification of intrinsic value. There are no intrinsic values beyond our consciousness as a species and independent of it. It is our consciousness that makes things valuable. This is not an expression of subjectivism. Our intrinsic values are species-specific; in this sense they are intersubjective. Indeed, intrinsic values cannot be subjective because they are transpersonal. But intrinsic values are not objective either, except for a Platonist.[1]

Between the Scylla of subjectivism and Charybdis of objectivism there lies an intersubjective justification of intrinsic values as assessed by our axiological consciousness, which is species-specific and therefore *transsubjective*. Hence, there can be no attribution of intrinsic value as ontological claims independent of our valuing *as a species*. Hence, all values properly expressed must result in ethical imperatives and our willingness to act upon these values.

Thus, we can uphold intrinsic values and justify them without slipping into Platonism, subjectivism, or relativism. But a new justification of intrinsic values requires a new moral insight. This new moral insight, for me and many others in our times, is the recognition that nature is not an object to be trampled upon and that all other beings were not created for our use, but that nature is alive and we are a part of it, and that all other beings are our fellow creatures in creation. This insight leads (on the ethical level) to the enunciation of the principle of the sanctity of life or reverence for life — from which an ecological ethics is derived.

Reverence for life and other ecological values

Every new ethical insight spells out a new perception, which usually leads to an articulation of a new relationship between humans and their cosmos. These new perceptions spell out, or at least indicate, our new responsibilities and new obligations, which sometimes are formulated as commandments. An example of a new ethical insight is Aldo Leopold's land ethic:

A land ethic, then, reflects the existence of an ecological conscience, and this in turn reflects a conviction of individual responsibility for the health of the land. Health is the capacity for self-renewal. Conservation is our effort to understand and preserve this capacity.[2]

Leopold is one of the champions of ecological awareness. Leopold's perceptions spell out clearly new values which bind human beings to the land.

The responsibility for the health of the land is one of the essential obligations that we undertake — living on the land, with the land, off the land.

For Leopold, human responsibility for the land is an obligation which does not need any further justification. We are it; it is us. It is a good thing in itself to take care of the land. We must do it because it is our responsibility, irrespective of the yields. Ecovalues are an extension and continuation of two insights: of Leopold's land ethic and of Schweitzer's reverence for life.

Among the intrinsic values for our times, this *reverence for life* is the most important, born of a vision and conviction of the sanctity of all life. This vision is actually easy to accept — that is, before we become influenced and really corrupted by scientific or, to be more precise, by mechanistic thinking. This vision is entertained and accepted in the world view of native Americans, and is natural to small children in our own civilization. We must learn again to appreciate the beauty of this vision.

Yet, the scientific/rational mind finds it hard to entertain anything that is sacred. The very term 'reverence' is difficult to accommodate within the rational frame of discourse. Even such an innocent concept as vision makes some feel uncomfortable. We are told that we do not live in the world of visions but in the world of 'harsh' realities. But we are told wrongly. The mechanistic conception of the universe (and the harsh realities accompanying it) is no less a vision than the reverential conception of the universe. Nature can be viewed in so many different ways. We invent our metaphors, and then find in nature what these metaphors assume.

Responsibility is another intrinsic value of ecological ethics. You cannot exercise reverence without responsibility; ultimately, responsibility becomes reverence. Responsibility is part of the meaning of reverence. The two codefine each other. There is a whole negative historical connotation attached to the notion of responsibility within Protestant ethics. This negativism is baggage which we must throw out so that we can see the concept in its true light: as a radiant principle which enables us to revere the world and appreciate its transphysical dimensions. Responsibility is an ethical principle in the sense that, if you understand the unity of life, and the fact that you are a part of it, and one with it, then you must take responsibility for life, for all life; there is no other way. Thus, the right understanding of the world, and in particular, the understanding of the sanctity of life, implies responsibility for it. It is just that simple. Responsibility is the connecting link between ethics and rationality. Rationality without responsibility is monstrous. Ethics without responsibility is empty — as is the case with formal ethical systems. Responsibility is the spiritual bridge which makes of rationality human rationality, and of ethics a nourishing river for the meaning of our lives.

The larger the scope of responsibility you assume, the larger you become as a human being. Escape from responsibility, which the indulgent society perpetuates, is an escape from your own humanity. If you want to shun *all* responsibility, there are only two ways: to live as a complete hermit, away from everybody (but this is not possible, for you will be in the company of birds, plants, Mother Earth, and Father Sun); or, more radically, to commit suicide (and this is the last thing which responsible people should do). The truly great lives, like Gandhi's and Mother Teresa's, are lives pregnant with immense responsibilities.

Another intrinsic value of ecological ethics is *frugality*. Frugality is not to be confused with abnegation or destitution. Frugality is an altogether positive value, a form of richness, not of poverty. It is a vehicle of responsibility, a mode of being that makes responsibility possible and tangible in a world in which we recognize natural constraints and symbiotic relationships. To understand the right of others to live is to limit our unnecessary wants. The motto in one of the Franciscan retreat houses reads: 'Anything we have that is more than we need is stolen from the person who has less than he needs'. Is this too strongly expressed? Poor people will not think so.

On yet another level, frugality is a precondition of inner beauty. We are frugal not only for the sake of others but also for our own sake. Frugality is an optimal mode of living *vis-à-vis* other beings. A true awareness of frugality and its right enactment is born out of the conviction that things of the greatest value are free: friendship, love, inner joy, the freedom to develop within. Indeed, to buy these things is surely to destroy their inherent worth.

On a higher level still, frugality is grace without waste. The greatest works of art are frugal in this sense. Grace without waste shines through them. Thus, we must cultivate meaningful and elegant frugality. To do so, we will need to develop a new language so that we are not constrained by past connotations which attribute to frugality dreary and tiresome characteristics. Let us therefore be supremely conscious that frugality is not a negative commandment (be frugal or be doomed) but a positive precept (be frugal and shine with health and grace). You cannot live in grace when you live in poverty. On the other hand, you cannot live in grace when you wallow in spurious luxury. Grace is the dividing middle. Aristotle was aware of the beauty of frugality when he wrote: 'The rich person is not only the one who owns much but also the one who needs little.'

The true image of frugality is Gandhi, whose life was slender in means but incomparably rich in ends, woven into the tapestry of others, confirming the unity of all, and affirming justice for all. An impossible dream? But Gandhi made this dream a reality.

Frugality is an aspect of reverence. You cannot be truly reverential toward life unless you are frugal in this present world of ours in which the balances are so delicate and so easy to strain. The three basic ecological values — reverence, responsibility, and frugality — are so interwoven that the meaning of each presupposes the existence of the other two. These precepts — be reverential, be responsible, be frugal — are ethical commands following from our deeper insight into the connectedness of life, the unity of life, and life's essential fragility.

Ecojustice is another value specific to ecological cosmology. Ecojustice means justice for all. Justice is a venerable, ancient concept. We are all familiar with it, particularly as it applies to ourselves. Nearly all past ethical codes accept justice as an integral part of moral behaviour. Yet, in traditional moral codes, justice is limited to the human universe. Sometimes it is limited to a particular religion. Then 'infidels' can be mistreated — they are not the children of *our* God.

Ecojustice as justice for all is a consequence of our ecological cosmology, of the idea of responsibility for all, and of the perception of the interconnectedness of all. If the cosmic web embraces us all, if it is woven of the strands of which we are part, then justice to the cosmic web means justice to all its elements — to all brothers and sisters of creation, as native Americans would say. It is difficult to render justice to all in this complex and contingent world of ours; this we know. But it is our moral duty to attempt to do so. Moral principles can be enunciated even if it is difficult to live by them.

Conservation is a modus through which we express our responsibility to nature. Conservation is a very special kind of activity. It expresses care, pietism, love, attention — and a lot of hard work to save what we deem worth preserving. In one sense, conservation may be considered an ethical act in itself: an act of caring to the point of fighting for what you consider important to preserve. On a deeper level, conservation is a set of strategies for implementing primary values. We design various tactics and stratagems to save what is worthy and necessary of protection, be it our individual life, our family life, our social and civil life, or ecohabitats because we value life as such, and we uphold the principle of the sanctity of life. Strategies come after the primary values are established and accepted.

Reverence, responsibility, frugality, and ecojustice form the minimal core of intrinsic values for right conservation and sustainable development. Ecological values are exactly like other traditional values: they are ideal signposts and imperatives for action. The fact that they may be difficult to implement in practice in no way negates their importance and desirability. Great value systems of the past were established not because they were easy to practise but because they expressed the imperatives for action whose purpose it was to safeguard life, meaning, and human dignity. Ecovalues, like all values, serve life and the quest of human dignity.

Ecological values are only a core. Their application will differ in specific circumstances and they will need a creative extension in various walks of life. But before there can be a set of specific strategies — how to deal with conservation and development in this or that region, and with regard to this or that problem — there must be an underlying matrix of values to guide us in our attempt to establish right relationships with the Earth, nature, and other cultures so that we may secure a meaningful future for ourselves and for the generations to come.

Reverential development

How should we conserve sustainable development in light of the foundational values of sustainable development? To develop or not to develop is not the question. But *how* to develop is the question. The central question is: what are the aims, goals, purposes, and ends of development?

The ultimate end of all development is life. Development serves life and positively contributes to life. Furthermore, it is not merely life that we value, but quality living for all creatures. What is at the kernel of development is not just biological life, but life with meaning, dignity, and fulfilment. Unless we respect this conception of life, we need not bother about development.

Thus, when carefully examined and unpacked, the idea of development presupposes that life has meaning, dignity, fulfilment, self-actualization. If we look perceptively, we shall see that those concepts of development which are truly comprehensive assume that development serves the variety of life, not just economic ends.

We may approach the issue from the other end: accepting the notion of reverence for life enables us to see immediately that development is not only an economic phenomenon, but that it is also a vehicle for betterment of human life on all its levels. While reverence for life does not deny the importance of the economic factor, the satisfaction of basic wants is only part of the life of dignity.

At this point I wish to propose a new concept, that of *reverential development*. 'Reverential' is not merely a nice adjective which I have attached to traditional, economically defined development. Reverence for life and development are intricately connected in the framework of thinking and action in which the meaning of human life prevails, and in which respect for nature is part of our conscious and compassionate interaction with all there is. ·

Ecological ethics as based on reverence for life is universal in the sense that, in all cultures and major religions, there is a latent premise of the worth of life, and indeed of its sanctity. In most traditional religions this sanctity derives from God. What is important for our consideration is not the source of the sanctity of life but its recognition. The fact that reverence for life is an implicit premise of most traditional religions and ethical systems should only reassure us that there is an underlying core of ethical values common to all people and most religions. Ecological ethics represents a new articulation of traditional intrinsic values. It represents the search for meaning, dignity, health, and sanity at the time when the planet is seriously threatened by inappropriate development.

In proposing a new form of development, reverential development based on ecological values, I wish simultaneously to bring about sustainability to the planet, dignity to its diverse peoples, and unity to humankind now fractured by inappropriate development. Reverential development is unitary in the broadest and deepest sense: it combines the economic with the ethical and reverential; it combines contemporary ethical imperatives with traditional ethical codes; it attempts to serve all the people of all cultures; and it promises to bring about a peace between humankind and nature.

Notes

1 Henryk Skolimowski, 'In Defense of Ecophilosophy and of Intrinsic Values: A Call for Conceptual Clarity', *The Trumpeter* 3 (Fall 1986).
2 Aldo Leopold, *A Sand Country Almanac* (London: Oxford University Press, 1979), 236.

8 A new Christian reformation
Robert J. Moore

Long before Prime Minister Gro Harlem Bruntland assumed the leadership of the World Commission on Environment and Development, Barbara Ward and her colleagues at the 1972 Stockholm Conference on the Human Environment had begun warning us of the catastrophic consequences of our philosophical, theological, and technological perspectives on nature. They saw nothing short of a collapse of the planet in the face of the continuing battering to which humankind was subjecting it. Barbara Ward, in particular, challenged her fellow Christians to re-examine their theologies and practices in the light of global environmental degradation and literally to reread their scriptures with fresh eyes:

When we confront the ethical and the natural context of our daily living, are we not brought back to what is absolutely basic in our religious faith? On the one hand, we are faced with the stewardship of this beautiful, subtle, incredibly delicate, and fragile planet. On the other, we confront the destiny of our fellow man, our brothers. How can we say that we are followers of Christ if this dual responsibility does not seem to us the essence and heart of our religion?[1]

The domination of nature

'I am come in very truth leading you to Nature with all her children to bind her to your service and make her your slave.'[2] Those words were written by Francis Bacon in the seventeenth century. They epitomize an attitude and a set of assumptions that became the common stock in trade of Western scientific and industrial culture. The imagery Bacon used is significant: the master–slave relationship. In the slave societies of the Western world, societies that reached their apogee in the Caribbean, Brazil, and the United States, the crucial question about the slave was not *who* he or she was but *whose* he or she was. Slaves were objects of other people's purposes, not subjects of their own. Their value lay in being units of production; their merit lay in their capacity to be both used and used up. Applying that sort of thinking to the natural world reinforced the conviction that it was an object to be exploited for our rational curiosity, our aesthetic enjoyment, or our economic utilization. In short, nature was a vast piece of real estate, awaiting its destiny to be appropriated for human enterprise.

Those who required scriptural support for that assumption thought they found it conveniently and succinctly expressed in Genesis 1:28, which said: 'Be fruitful and multiply, and fill the earth and subdue it; and have dominion over the fish of the sea and over the birds of the air and over every living thing that moves upon the face of the earth.' That certainly sounds like a charter for imperialistic human behaviour — a divinely granted mandate for us to do as we please with nature. Furthermore, a previous verse, Genesis 1:26, said that we were made in the image of God. Did this not mean that our, admittedly finite, sovereignty over nature on this planet mirrored God's transcendent sovereignty over the cosmos?

The root of this interpretation lay in some of the most powerful traditions in Christendom, especially the traditions of the Latin West. The distrust of the body which appeared early in Christian experience, and which was crystallized by Saint Augustine in the fourth century, went along with an equally powerful distrust of nature, for the body was humankind's most intimate experience of nature.[3] The soul's proper aim was to master the body and in so doing distance itself from it as much as possible. Men were considered to be better equipped to do this than women who, because of their reproductive cycle, were deemed to be more immersed in the natural world and more controlled by its rhythms. Hence the necessity for women to be dominated by men.

The contrast between the attitude enshrined in Latin Christianity and the attitude characteristic of Eastern Christianity has been vividly portrayed by Lynn White, Jr. Surveying the iconography of Genesis 1:28 in the two traditions, he notes: 'In Byzantine manuscripts Adam is shown at repose in his Garden; the animals are dispersed at random; sometimes God's hand appears from a cloud blessing the situation. The mood is relaxed, idyllic.'[4] But the scene in the Western manuscripts is one of impatient patriarchy:

With his left hand God has seized Adam's wrist, and he is shaking his index finger at Adam with great earnestness, giving him detailed instructions as to his ruling of the life that has been given him. There is a mood of imminent action, urgency. At one side the animals are huddled, looking a bit frightened.[5]

Clearly, it is in terms of the latter imagery that Genesis 1:28 has been interpreted in the West.

It is no wonder that for the heirs of Latin Christianity, for example, the strict Puritans of the Calvinist Reformation in the succeeding centuries, nature was the domain of the demonic, the source of corruption in men and women. Even to Roman Catholics and Protestants of less sin-soaked theologies, nature represented a downward gravitational pull against which both the soul and the mind had to struggle constantly — the soul in order to achieve purity of life, the mind in order to achieve clarity of thought. All agreed that nature was 'fallen', that is, afflicted with some aboriginal depravity. It should not therefore be left to itself but should be redeemed by being forced into submission, obedience and compliance with human purposes.

It was during the Enlightenment era that this interpretation of Christian existence became fully secularized and the process grew to full bloom. God, the Supreme Clockmaker, had created a universe that obeyed calculable laws with no room for eccentric variations. Human beings were essentially rational (when freed from clerical and superstitious encumbrances) and their business was to uncover those laws of nature. Increased knowledge inevitably meant increased power over the natural world, for as we could predict, so we could control and direct. The consequent mastery which this entailed would ensure human progress on a grand scale.

This view of the human–nature relationship involved a clear separation between the knower and the thing known. The knower is the subject; the thing known is the object. The business of the subject is to break the components of the object down to its final irreducible particles. Then it can be reconstituted for the use of the subject. Nature is the object of our investigations and we humans the subjects conducting those investigations. As the quotation from Francis Bacon indicates, the relationship was unabashedly viewed as a relationship of dominance and control. Not surprisingly, this conception of human knowledge and power reached its zenith in a period of Western history when empires were at their zenith, when Euro-Americans saw themselves as the lords of humankind, and when ancient cultures, with far sager concepts of nature, were being threatened with extinction.

Restoring theological foundations

Western theologies, whether Catholic or Protestant, have been at pains to make a clear distinction between God and his creation. God, the Creator, stands over against the world he has created; deeply loving it, to be sure; ever sustaining it, certainly; nevertheless absolutely demarcated from it. Indeed, in some theologies he is referred to as 'the Absolute Other'. In one respect this is perfectly understandable. It was important for God not to be *equated* with nature. Therefore, it seemed to follow logically that God must be taken completely out of nature.

Now, under the threat of ecological catastrophe, Western theology is rediscovering the Holy Spirit. The third Person of the Trinity, the Giver of gifts, is not only responsible for the creative genius of humankind, but is also the Spirit of the universe. He interpenetrates the creation. It is his abode, the place of his indwelling. This point was well articulated by Jürgen Moltman in the Gifford Lectures for 1984–5:

Through the powers and potentialities of the Spirit, the Creator in-dwells the creatures he has made, animates them, holds them in life, leads them into the future of his Kingdom. In this sense the history of creation is the history of the efficacy of the divine Spirit. So even when we consider the original biblical traditions, it is one-sided to view creation only as the world of 'God's hands' and, as his 'work', something that has simply and solely to be distinguished from God himself. Creation is also the differentiated presence of God the Spirit, the presence of the One *in* the many.[6]

Indeed, in Moltmann's reconception, the Holy Spirit is the power that not only sustains the creation but has propelled the evolutionary process through the billions of years it has taken to move our planet from a molten star to the intricate ecosystem that now constitutes its being. From the time when the first amoeba-like animal moved about in the waters until the time when humankind eventually emerged, it was the Holy Spirit that directed the process.

God, in short, is immanent as well as transcendent. We are accustomed to thinking of the great one-sided relationships between God and Creation — the relationship of making, preserving, maintaining, and perfecting. But God as the Holy Spirit relates to creation in such a way as to bring into being a cosmic community of all created beings — through the relationships of in-dwelling, sympathizing, participating, accompanying, enduring, delighting, and glorifying. Behind this reconceptualization of the God–creation relationship lies, of course, the foundational Christian doctrine of the Trinity. God the Father is the Creator, for it is his will that there should be a creation at all. But he created through the operation of the Holy Spirit and participates in the creation through the same Spirit. In God the Son, the history of creation and the history of humankind are seen to be parts of the same whole. For in the Incarnation, God enters both the rhythms of nature and the political, social, and economic configurations of human history and by being a complete human person he demonstrates that those two orders of being are inextricably interwoven. That, too, is a fundamental reminder for our times: we have tended to regard nature as simply a backdrop or stage set for human history and not as an integral part of the historical process. Our ecological blunders, together with our more mature theological insights, are helping restore our understanding of their essential unity.

If the relation of God to his creation is one of governance, in-dwelling, and immersion, and if our planet's non-human and human life are alike manifestations of the creative power of the Holy Spirit, then the relationship between humankind and nature cannot be one of domination, exploitation, or master and slave. It has to be one of solicitude, of reciprocal respect, and of creative intervention.

In the light of a more mature understanding of the meaning of creation, the powers given humankind are not those of a sovereign but of a steward. And if humankind was created, as Genesis states, in the image of God, then our exploitative, battering, and polluting behaviour towards nature is a corruption of our own status and an affront to the Holy Spirit. As stewards of creation, human beings have a special position within it. But the basis of that position is the fact that through us the universe reflects upon itself and its Creator. Consciousness is the key to the privilege we possess. It confers immense powers — powers that should be used to create a balanced relationship between ourselves and nature.

Retrieving symbols

It must be remembered, too, that Genesis 1:28 is neatly balanced by Genesis 2:50, which states: 'And the Lord God took the man and put him into the Garden of Eden to dress it and keep it.' There is no hint of domination in this passage. What is explicit here is humankind's work of protection and cultivation. A gardener is, after all, a creative interventionist whose empathy with nature is the basis of his or her vocation. Accepting nature as intrinsically valuable, awe-inspiring, delicate, and of equal significance to humans, the gardener seeks to marry the human imagination to the rhythms of creation in order to bring about an epiphany in which the glory of the natural order and the artistry of the human order are both revealed in heightened magnificence.

The symbolism of the garden reappears in the New Testament stories of the crucifixion and the resurrection. The last hours that Jesus spends in prayer before going to his trial are spent in a garden — Gethsemane. The crucifixion stands in stark contrast to that lovely garden. A dead man on a dead tree symbolizes, in the most shocking and ultimate way, the effect of evil on God, on humankind, and on nature. But we return to a garden on the morning of the resurrection. This is one of the most overlooked but genuinely revealing symbols in the New Testament. And according to the Gospel of John, when Mary Magdalene sees the risen Lord, she instantly assumes that he is the gardener. On a superficial level, Mary Magdalene made a mistake; but on a deeper level, she had a profound recognition of the nature of him who once said: 'Consider the lilies of the field, how they grow; they toil not, but neither do they spin; but Solomon in all his glory was not arrayed like one of these' (Matthew 6:28).

But whether as gardener, steward, manager, or Justice of the Peace, humankind in the biblical tradition is not the crown of creation. That is reserved for the Sabbath. For on the Sabbath, God the creator rested and celebrated his creation. If the creation is seen as a six day project, then God is conceived of as merely a working deity. But according to Genesis, the creation was not complete until the Sabbath when God rested, and in resting rejoiced in his creation, and in rejoicing hallowed and blessed the seventh day.

God is not just a labouring God. He is a God who can stop to appreciate the work of his hands and let his creation express its being. The Sabbath, therefore, represents his glory and it was to participate in that glory that the world was made. Accordingly, the Jewish Sabbath was intended to remind human beings that nature does not exist primarily for their purposes but for God's. That is why on the Sabbath the soil was not tilled; the animals were not worked. They were simply allowed to *be* — not dominated, not coerced by humankind.

The Psalter takes up this theme when it asserts that the non-human members of creation are perfectly capable of expressing their joy in their Creator: 'The heavens declare the glory of God' (Psalms 19:1). The same conviction is articulated in the well-known canticle 'Benedicite omnia opera' (Daniel 3:28–68 in the Apocrypha). It is an exuberant invitation to all creatures to glorify their maker and it knows no hierarchy of being: the sun and the moon, the showers and dew, wind, winter and summer, plants, animals, angels, the souls of the dead, men and women, are all juxtaposed and all are 'to bless the Lord, praise Him and magnify Him forever'. Saint Francis of Assisi, that gentle revolutionary of the twelfth century, lived his life in the spirit of the 'Benedicite'. For him, humanity was no monarch set over the rest of creation, but rather *primus inter pares* in a democratic brotherhood and sisterhood of all God's creatures. Lynn White, Jr, has provided us with a lucid distillation of the saint's theology:

His view of nature and of man rested on a unique sort of pan-psychism of all things animate and inanimate, designed for the glorification of their transcendent Creator, who, in the ultimate gesture of cosmic humility, assumed flesh, lay helpless in a manger and hung dying on a scaffold.[7]

In his understanding of the mutual relationship between humankind and nature, Saint Francis was not a contemporary of his own times. But he is very much a contemporary of our age as we painfully come to conclusions that he joyously divined long ago.

The significance of these oft-neglected symbols is crucial. They disclose the fact that our special position in the cosmos gives us the chance consciously to appreciate ourselves as members of the community of creation. We are expected to show respect for the other members of the community and to practise a loving reciprocity, recognizing the interdependence of the community and the mutual vulnerability of each of the members in regard to the others.

Renewing the covenant

Modern technology has given human beings the power to annihilate the world by nuclear war. It has also emboldened us to be so reckless in our treatment of the planet's environment that we risk ecological collapse. But that collapse can also be achieved by the crippling poverty of the Third World peoples. Poverty, in the late twentieth century, is as great a destroyer of our fragile environment as is resource-intensive industry. An international economic system in which immense poverty exists side by side with immense wealth is a recipe for planetary apocalypse.

Christians are not alone in wanting to prevent such an outcome. Convinced, as many increasingly are, that a wanton disregard of the 'rights' of the non-human members of creation is a sin not only against the Holy Spirit, but against the Holy Trinity, they have begun to devote their intellects and imaginations to the preservation of our earthly home. And again they are discovering messages and meanings in their scriptures which hitherto had eluded them. As they look anew at the message of the prophets of the Old Testament, for example, they discern an interesting connection between justice in the human sphere and harmony in the relations between themselves and the natural order.

For the Hebrew prophets, the most important feature in the life of the Jewish people was their covenant with God. That is what gave them their sense of history and their sense of community. It also meant certain prescriptions about the way they ran their society. Fidelity to the covenant required justice between the various groups and classes in their polity. And the inevitable consequence of observing the principle of justice was a harmonious relationship between humankind and nature.

Whenever the covenant was broken, it was because groups or individuals put their own self-interest above the claims of justice. That in turn entailed the domination of the weak by the strong, the exploitation of the poor by the rich, a decline in compassionate interpersonal relationships and corruption in high places. It also usually meant that the people of Israel were deserting the worship of Yahweh for the gods of the nature religions of their neighbours. For those gods did not demand higher standards of justice and 'a preferential option for the poor' but rather the preservation of a lop-sided status quo which favoured the rich.

In the prophetic perspective, it was at such times that catastrophes — both natural and historical — occurred. Either the Jewish people were overrun by their much stronger neighbours; or the Earth shook with tremors; or pestilence, drought, and famine invaded the land. On the other hand, whenever the prophets portrayed the reign of the Messiah whose coming would restore the covenant, they described the liberation of the poor from their bondage to the rich, an era of peace and equity between groups and individuals, and a return by the Jews to a sense of history as ordered by the moral law of God. Most significant for our purposes, the vision of a coming reign of goodness, justice, and peace always included vivid images of harmony between humankind and nature. In the time of the Messiah, the land would be restored to its fecundity, the dried-up rivers would flow again, the valleys would grow fat with crops as the animals would grow fat with offspring, and there would be a notable absence of sickness and hostility within society. Perhaps best known of all such prophetic utterances is that of Isaiah 11:6: 'The lion shall lie down with the lamb, and the little child shall lead them' — a perfect image of harmony within nature and between nature and humans.

The extraordinary fact about the prophetic utterances is how contemporary they sound. Faced, as we presently are, with four great interlocking crises — the arms crisis, the debt crisis, the population crisis, and the ecological crisis — we are discovering that in order to address any one of them we have to address all of them. In particular, we are learning that in order to find global solutions to the ecological crisis, we must also find global solutions to the rampant poverty of the Third World societies. That involves changing both our values and our lifestyles in the wealthy West, which in turn implies reassessing the need to spend millions of dollars every day on armaments. As the prophets saw it, if we wish to prevent the environmental deterioration of the Earth, we have to develop a strategy for empowering the poor to overcome their poverty and thus cease the assault on the environment which poverty compels. The prophets would have felt completely at home with the conclusion to which we are being rapidly driven: that we can no longer afford, ecologically or morally, the poverty of the poor.

Shaping history

Christians like to refer to their faith as a historical religion. By that they mean not only that Christianity was born out of certain historical events in the land of Palestine in the first century, but also that Christians feel, or ought to feel, responsibility for helping to shape the course and configuration of events which we call history. Acknowledging God as the Lord of history, they see themselves as God's instruments, agents, or even colleagues, in shaping the way institutions, developments, and events turn out. That places a heavy responsibility on their shoulders and they often invoke as a justification for this responsibility a favourite quotation from Saint Augustine: 'Without Him we cannot do it, without us He will not do it.'

Christians recognize two contradictory conditions in human beings which affect their approach to the shaping of historical forces: the first is our 'fallen' nature and the second is our immense creativity. The second condition gives human beings the capacity to create reasonably habitable societies in which staggering contrasts between wealth and poverty do not obtain. But our 'fallen' condition prevents us from ever creating in the historical realm a society which could be described as utopian. The most that Christians can say is that while they do not believe in the possibility of a perfect society, they refuse to accept as incurable the imperfections of their present societies. They recognize that each historical era faces a number of challenges which require solution if human societies or clusters of human societies are not to dissolve into Hobbesian chaos. But in the nature of things, each time humans respond successfully to some of the challenges facing them and work out acceptable and even reasonably just solutions, they also ignore other challenges and create anomalies and distortions in the process. Those anomalies and those unmet challenges are left for the next historical era to address. Realistically, therefore, Christians cannot believe in a doctrine of inevitable progress to higher and better forms of society. The furthest most of them will go is to accept the dictum of the nineteenth century German historian, Leopold von Ranke, that every generation is equidistant from eternity.[7]

Christianity, like all the great religions, is accustomed to the passing of historical eras and the coming of new ones. But even Christians have to admit, as the twentieth century draws to its close, that the condition of the planet is unprecedented in the long march of human history. Never before has it been possible for humankind to destroy the planet by detonation or to cause it to collapse by environmental recklessness. Never before has the planet itself sent such direct messages of impending disaster as it does now. Those messages constitute the challenges of a new era. They are unambiguous and leave no doubt about the need for political will to respond to them.

As they come to a more profound understanding of creation and of the place of human beings in it, Christians are beginning to feel empowered to approach the ecological crisis with theologies and methodologies relevant to the task in hand. But they have also learned that they must cooperate with the people of other religions and with people of no religion to save the planet. Many Christians are also willing to acknowledge the debt they owe to other religions in helping them to rediscover a genuinely biblical doctrine of creation and the significance of the prophets. They have lived by rather inadequate interpretations of both for some centuries now.

Christians are also beginning to see the founder of their religion in a broader and deeper perspective. In particular, they are rediscovering the extent to which he was concerned for the poor and the oppressed as well as his profound knowledge of and love for nature as God's creation — a knowledge and love amply evidenced in the parables he told. But most of all, they are beginning to understand the significance of his messianic message: the coming reintegration of all the scattered, fragmented, and alienated constituents of God's creation. For as that great architect of early Christian thinking, Saint Paul, realized, Jesus of Nazareth came not only to redeem humankind from its bondage to selfishness, narrowness, greed, and the lust for power, but also with a promise to redeem the natural world from the pain of transience so that it could more amply fulfil its manifest destiny and express the glory of its Creator:

yet always there was hope, because the universe itself is to be freed from the shackles of mortality and enter upon the liberty and splendor of the children of God. Up to the present, we know, the whole created universe groans in all its parts as if in the pangs of childbirth (Romans 8:21–23).

Hence the increasing determination among Christians to help shape a new historical era in which our economics will possess ecological sanity. That determination is cogently expressed in the Pastoral Letter 'What is Happening to Our Beautiful Land?' issued by the Roman Catholic bishops of the Philippines early in 1988. The letter refers to environmental concerns as 'the ultimate pro-life issue'[9] and it calls for a Filipino theology of creation which will be sensitive to the unique living world, the diverse cultures, and the religious heritage of the Philippines. With ecumenical sensitivity, the bishops commend the tribal, often animist, Filipinos as exemplars of ecological wholesomeness, commenting that 'they see the Divine Spirit in the living world and show their respect through prayers and offerings'.

With accuracy, the bishops highlight the fact that women have been at the forefront of the ecological movement in many countries. But the most compelling passages in the document are those in which the bishops emphasize the indivisibility of worship and politics. At the same time as calling for eucharistic celebrations of the beauty of the natural world, the umbilical closeness between humankind and the natural world *and* the ongoing struggle for social justice, they gave advice to their fellow Roman Catholics on how to mount campaigns at all levels of society for the protection of the environment. Wisely observing that programmes never implement themselves, they recommend education in the politics of creating organizations robust enough to withstand official or corporate resistance, astute enough to devise compelling strategies and tactics, and vigilant enough to act as watchdogs whenever public bodies violate environmental ethics.

At the heart of the bishops' passion for all Filipino creatures, animate and inanimate, is their theology of Christ.

Our faith tells us that Christ is the central point of human history and creation. All the rich unfolding of the Universe and the emergence and flowering of life on Earth are centered on Him . . . The destruction of any part of creation, especially the extinction of species, defaces the image of Christ which is etched in creation.

That kind of theology — and the acute sense of political process which accompanies it — is one among many signs that Christians are, at last, giving a wholly new and totally healthy meaning to the doctrine of human dominion and will therefore have something to contribute to the survival both of our home, the Earth, and our species, humankind.

Notes

1 Barbara Ward, 'Justice in a Human Environment', *IDOC International/North American Edition* 53 (May 1973): 36.
2 Quoted in William Leiss, *The Domination of Nature* (New York: Braziller, 1972), 55.
3 Augustine, *Soliloquies*, in Philip Schaff, ed., *A Select Library of the Nicene and Post-Nicene Fathers of the Christian Church* VII (New York: The Christian Literature Co., 1888), 540.

4 Lynn White, Jr, 'Continuing the Conversation' in Ian G. Barbour, ed, *Western Man and Environmental Ethics* (Reading, Mass: Addison-Wesley, 1973), 60.

5 Ibid.

6 Jürgen Moltman, *God in Creation: A New Theology of Creation and the Spirit of God,* (London: Harper & Row, 1985), 14.

7 Lynn White, Jr, 'The Historical Roots of our Ecological Crisis' in Barbour, *Western Man and Environmental Ethics,* 29.

8 Quoted in Herbert Butterfield, *Christianity and History* (London: Collins, 1949), 89.

9 Catholic Bishops of the Philippines, *What is happening to our beautiful land? SEDOS* Bulletin 4 (April 15, 1988): 112–115.

Eastern Europe and
the Soviet Union

9 Raising the biosphere to the noosphere
I. Laptev

Today, we must take a hard look at the history of civilization and at the traces left by social progress on the face of our planet. The dialectical process by which human beings and nature mutually transform one another has involved the entire planet in ways no one would have dared to predict even a short while ago. Nor, for all our pride in the advances and power of world science, can we predict the results of our present activity.

In the words of the great Russian scientist, V. I. Vernadski: 'Mankind as a whole is becoming a powerful geological force.'[1] Indeed, what we are doing on the surface of the Earth has no parallels in the history of the planet. By such activities as mining out ores, constructing dams, digging channels, and disposing of metallurgical slags, we are annually moving many cubic kilometres of rock up onto the planet's surface, successfully 'competing' with volcanic processes. A year's ploughing moves three times the mass brought from the planet's core by all the volcanic eruptions in the same period. By dispersing and concentrating the natural resources from the Earth we have greatly accelerated the transfer of atoms in the biosphere. Industrial and agricultural products have spread all over the world and found their way back into the soil at the sites of consumption, and we have thus created chemical combinations never before found in nature.

We have also broken out of the constrictions of our environment to take hold of an extrabiospheric source of energy — nuclear energy. In so doing, we have acquired such control over the forces of nature that only a slight effort of the muscles — pushing a button — is sufficient to trigger off processes of catastrophic proportions. Virtually cancelled is the notion of world distances, for our various means of transport can easily take us to any spot on the planet. There is no longer a corner in the world too hostile for us to live and work in, and our hand-made, 'second nature' aircraft, ships, railways, machines, and buildings greatly increase our independence of primary nature.

Consequently, the limelight of science is shifting to a new fundamental fact: the pressure constantly exerted by the expanding, all-encompassing, and all-permeating, high-tech world of human beings acting on the world of nature, a phenomenon become so great that the response of nature is beginning to check the growth of economies and to threaten the human being as a biological entity.

Society–nature conflicts

This chaotic and short-sighted exploitation of nature has given rise to a whole set of society–nature conflicts. Though some of these conflicts can be traced far back into the history of the human species, the unprecedented advances and operations of productive forces under the conditions of market competition, unplanned economy, and lack of knowledge about nature have dangerously aggravated them and allowed them to assume global proportions.

Recent developments in the interaction between the world of human beings and the world of nature create situations that can be called the situations of *economic conflict*. Estimates show that if present day rates of development remain unchanged, the depletion of the biosphere to the point of instability will occur in the second half of the next century. For example, today the energy extracted from fossil fuels is used to maintain and augment present consumption levels. But energy and labour will be needed to stabilize the environment if the biosphere can no longer cope on its own. In that case, most energy and labour will go into the effort to stabilize the environment, leaving very little for the maintenance and development of civilization.

We need always to bear in mind that to single out this or that aspect, this or that situation, is merely to highlight certain aspects of a connected process; interdependent and mutually determined natural phenomena become abstractions if considered separately. Thus, when taking up the issue of soil reserves as the basis of agricultural production, it is essential not to neglect their importance, first, as the habitable space for people, and second, as a major factor in sustaining the proper functioning of the entire biosphere of the Earth, for people are by no means unique in needing the shadow of forests and the grass of meadows.

Considering the fact that the human population is daily increasing by between 280,000 and 300,000 (which means that the pressure on the environment is growing on a global scale) and that we are constantly polluting the soil, ocean, and atmosphere with great amounts of radioactive and poisonous substances, one may view the present situation from a global perspective and define situations of *geological conflict*.

We are presently spending the potential energy of the biosphere at ten times the rate it is being accumulated by living organisms that can absorb sunlight, while the green areas are dwindling. Farming areas are growing at the expense of forests. In the course of the history of civilization, at least 60 per cent of the forests of the planet have been lost. The carbon tied up in the forestial biomass is rapidly burned to carbon dioxide and discharged into the atmosphere. Thus, the impact of human activity on the productivity of the biosphere is of truly geological proportions.

Young Karl Marx called the natural environment our 'inorganic body'.[2] The truth of these words has been fully revealed only in our time under conditions of growing ecological stress. It is becoming increasingly clear that our existence depends, in a multitude of ways, on the conditions of our 'inorganic body', on how rich and healthy it stays. This dependence is evidenced indirectly through industry and agriculture, through the life cycles and development of animals, fish, and birds; but it is explicit in our use of food, air, and water as well as in the joy of being close to nature.

Today it is evident that the equilibrium of biospheric processes is threatened, for many of the 'accommodation mechanisms' of the biosphere are functioning dangerously close to their full capacity. This stress is the root cause of the profound negative shifts that have occurred, and are still occurring, in the biosphere as well as in the human physical condition, for example, in our defences against various diseases.

No one will deny that as a result of the development of civilization and the splendid victories of the human mind, many diseases have been eradicated and there has been a tremendous improvement in sanitary and hygienic conditions at work and at home. That is not, however, the whole story. Industrialization and urbanization, new ways of life and work, the mechanization and automation of production, strides in chemistry, ecological shifts, fast-paced change, and intensified psychoemotional life, can and do give rise to new disorders and alter the old 'classic' pathologies. The last hundred years have seen the emergence of whole families of previously unknown diseases: new infections, genetic disorders that frustrate any attempts at prevention, endocrine disorders, allergies, toxic diseases, including the radiation and toxic-allergic sicknesses gaining momentum with the growing mass of synthetic material totally alien to natural human environment; the notorious AIDS is but the latest addition to the list.

In other words, among the major effects of human activity, many of which are neither entirely predictable nor desirable, is the creation of a new environment which differs from the natural environment in many of its material, technical, chemical, radiological, and psychological parameters. This new environment is, in its turn, affecting human beings in ways quite different from the natural one, thus establishing new feedbacks and other interactions in the human–nature system.

In the foregoing discussion we have not even touched upon the issues raised by the IUCN *Red Data Book* litany of endangered species, the problems created by the all-permeating pesticide contamination, the psychological pressure of large human masses made manifest in the nervous exhaustion of city-dwellers, information satiation, the altered behaviour of some animal species, mutations, etc.[3] Nevertheless, what little has been elaborated gives a clear notion of a situation of *biological conflict*.

Society–nature dependencies

Humankind has always consumed vital natural resources. But only recently has it become evident that consuming any particular resource sets off a complex environmental reaction; the breaking of one or a number of links entails the restructuring of the entire system on a new level. For, in the words of Friedrich Engels, nature delivers the first fruits we were expecting, then serves a second and third unforeseen course which is likely to render the primary success meaningless.[4] Man has become like Hercules in that he is able to move mountains, but . . . aren't some of the challenges humans have to face as a result of their deeds Hercules' foes incarnate?

These changes, the herculean labour, intensity, and complexity of life, conceal from us the crucial fact that humankind is an integral part of the biosphere. It is often argued that forays into space, robots working on the Moon, synthetic materials and products, and the prospect of producing all we need from primary elements of matter prove that humans can become independent of nature. Yet, when people are exploring space, what is the environment they work and live in? Terrestrial, of course. They breathe the same air, eat the same food, and drink the same water as on the Earth; in their spacecraft and suits they recreate the pressure of their home planet. Their bodies go on with the old physiological functions. People bring with them a 'pocket of biosphere' and carry on in its well-known conditions. Vernadski said: 'As living matter, humanity is inseparably tied to the material and energy processes of a certain geological envelope of the Earth — bound to its biosphere. Man cannot be physically independent of it, not for a minute.'[5]

Thus, we have to face a paradox: even settling on other planets cannot make humans forsake their terrestrial conditions unless they find a twin sister to the Earth or cease to be a terrestrial species by adapting to a new environment. The latter possibility is highly unlikely, for the adaptation of a complex creature to a fundamentally strange environment takes a very long time. Therefore, our biosphere will in all probability remain with us forever, will remain our Earth on all the star paths we may choose.

I believe that such concepts as 'power over nature' or 'man's independence of nature' that sometimes are taken so far as to suggest the possibility of an eventual weaning of the human organism from the biosphere are all a fallacy. Conquering nature, holding sway over it, and gaining independence from it are all possible only on the condition that in conquering nature we submit to it; wielding power over nature, we play by its rules; and striving for independence from it, we fall into utter subservience to its forces.

As for the conviction that technology is remaking nature in the best way possible, 'regulating' it and adapting it to human needs, it is nothing else than an illusion of present-day polytechnicism. Such a conviction gives birth to concepts of transforming the biosphere, or designing an artificial biosphere and regulating the environment by technical means. The important thing about these concepts is that the properties, qualities, and functions of the biosphere are being projected, as it were, onto means created by humans to serve as an intermediary between society and nature; thus, the future of both humanity and nature is regarded from that angle. This leads to the emergence of a neo-Cartesianism of sorts and to attempts at interpreting the biosphere as some giant machine which is as easy to operate as a car. It is not accidental, therefore, that one comes across semi-fantastic proposals for a technical reconstruction of the human organism itself.

Concepts of 'technicalizing' the biosphere call for a very guarded and cautious approach. It is essential to assess each of them carefully from the standpoint of the future and from the position of morality; and not only because these concepts are fraught with the threat of putting the biosphere, by means of technical transformations, beyond the parameters essential to the normal functioning of the human organism. It is also because their planning, even in theory, becomes a serious obstacle to harmonizing the relationship between society and nature. They prod human beings to 'deprive' nature unnecessarily of some function or other, convinced that technical systems will be able to perform that function better than nature itself. More often than not, they lead to serious complications in nature management, for nature is then perceived as separate from the human organism, whereas the possibilities for transforming the environment can be assessed objectively only if one takes due account of the biological requirements of human beings and the ability of the biosphere to adapt. Willingly or unwillingly, such concepts suggest that technology is paramount to humankind. To suggest this is not only immoral; it is basically at variance with the principal aim of our society — raising harmonious and comprehensively developed people. To transform the environment from the standpoint of technology means to subordinate humans to technology in one way or another.

Somehow, we are inclined to overestimate the reliability and longevity of what is created by our intellect and our hands; we forget how much nature had to work on those wonders in the first place. To build, say, an artificial satellite of the Earth, one has to cram into it virtually all the Periodic Table, every element to be found in the core of a mountain, on a river bank, and in the vent of an extinct volcano. To manufacture the necessary plastics, trees have to be felled; lumber processed; oil, gas, and coal mined and burned. And how much water and energy has to be taken from nature and nature alone! Let one of the elements or resources disappear and the edifice will be severely shaken from top to bottom, and the more sophisticated, the more perfected its construction, the closer will it come to tumbling down.

The way to harmony

The growing domination of human beings over nature and their increasing powerfulness should be regarded as another stage in the mutually transformative interaction between society and nature, a development resulting in qualitative changes on both sides. It is this two-way effect, the interdependent character of changes, that should be kept in mind when considering the future progress of the biosphere as determined by the new geological force of human activity. Our conception of this progress is that of the 'noosphere' which offers probably the only way to a harmony between the world of human beings and the world of nature.

The term 'noosphere', which today has come into wide use and will most probably become a household word, is Greek for 'sphere of mind'. Both the Russian scientist, V. I. Vernadski, and the French scientist, Pierre Teilhard de Chardin borrowed the term from the French Bergsonian, Edouard le Roy, but each interpreted it in his own way and imparted to it a different meaning.

Teilhard de Chardin, a Jesuit priest, prominent palaeontologist, and anthropologist, understood the noosphere as an ideal formation, an 'envelope of thought' around the planet Earth. The first sparkle of reflecting consciousness started a fire around itself; the burning spot expanded; the fire spread far and wide; finally, the entire planet was in mental flames. There is but one understanding of and but one name to this transcendent phenomenon, and that is the noosphere. It is as embracing as, but as we shall see, much more integrated than all preceding shrouds, for it is a new shroud, indeed, a 'thinking layer' which, once it emerged at the end of the tertiary period, has ever since been unfolding over the world of plants and animals — beyond and over the biosphere.[6]

What an interesting and-elegant attempt at describing the biosphere blessed with the ability to reason! But what does 'beyond and outside the biosphere' mean? Reason and consciousness existing outside of their material carriers? A flow of information, as some scholars later interpreted the noosphere to be? If it is consciousness 'outside ourselves', information 'above the world of plants and animals', we have little grounds for optimism about the future. Teilhard de Chardin himself speculated that all future human evolution will converge on 'point Omega', in some new deity.

Vernadski filled the concept of the 'noosphere' with a fundamentally different content. For him, the noosphere is a material envelope of the Earth changing under human influence.

Humanity as a whole becomes a powerful geological force. The challenge for man, his thought and work, is the restructuring of the biosphere in the interests of free thinking mankind as a whole . . . The noosphere is a new geological phenomenon on our planet.[7]

For Vernadski, the noosphere is not a 'thinking layer' that exists over the planet and outside the biosphere. It is a stage in the development of the planet itself — a development that is changing everything and is showing itself very vividly in the most dynamic and 'youngest' envelope of the Earth, its biosphere. Becoming 'an agent of a unique kind' in the biosphere, human society is changing the very structure of the biosphere with increasing speed, ensuring and determining its transition into the noosphere. This transition does not occur outside the bounds of the biosphere, nor is it a transformation of one planetary envelope into another as is sometimes perceived; it occurs within the biosphere as a transition from one of its states to another, from a certain level of tension to a higher one. Vernadski repeatedly emphasized this and noted that the noosphere is a 'new state of the biosphere', the 'last of many states of the biosphere's evolution'. This means that the noosphere is the biosphere in a certain state, at a certain level of its progress. In other words, the noosphere is the only *possible* state, the natural, physical foundation of a new society built on principles that are the most felicitous for human life and activity. It will be a new stage in humanity's command and management of the environment, but command and management within new social forms through which alone this goal can be achieved. Marx foretold such a future state in the history of society and the history of nature when he wrote that 'for the socialist man the entire so-called history of the world is nothing but the emergence of nature for man', and that communism 'is the genuine resolution of the conflict between man and nature and between man and man'.[8] His view of history, and of the entire nàtural historical process of society's emergence as an objective process, found its remarkable corroboration in Vernadski's conclusion that the unity of all humanity is a law of nature. 'I'm using the notion "law of nature"', Vernadski pointed out, 'the way it is showing itself more and more forcefully in our life in the sphere of physical and chemical sciences; as an accurate empiric generalization.'[9]

Vernadski noted:

Until now historians and the Humanitarians in general conscientiously disregarded the laws of nature that apply to the biosphere, the only sphere where life can exist . . . In reality not a single living organism can be found on Earth in a free state.

He did not read the *Economic and Philosophical Manuscripts of 1884* where Karl Marx arrived at the same conclusion, not via the sciences, but via philosophy and history: 'That man's physical and spiritual life is linked to nature means simply that nature is linked to itself, for man is a part of nature'.[10]

The biosphere is raised to the noosphere by humanity. For Vernadski, human society 'is unique in changing in a new way and at an ever-increasing pace the structure of the very foundations of the biosphere'. How strange — humankind playing the role of the main driving force of a natural process, of 'a great geological, perhaps even cosmic force!'[11] By influencing its environment and changing it, humanity has been changing itself; its *own* nature. These changes in turn have enhanced the impact of the human world on the world at large, and from them have arisen hitherto latent forces both in human beings and in nature that enforce the rules of reason on the interplay of these forces. By this process, human intrusion is transformed into a qualitatively new driving force on the development of nature, a force that leads to the biosphere–noosphere transition, and that occurs within the biosphere and is a transition from one of its states to another or from one level of tension to a higher one.

Let us reiterate that this transition is a result of human activity, and can be regarded by the naturalist as 'nothing else but a natural process on a par with any other geological phenomenon'.[12] Consequently, the interaction between human society and nature, understood as *mutual development*, manifests itself as an objective phenomenon, a process in natural history. Indeed, the unity of human society and nature, as well as their mutual opposition, is revealed to be in process, in daily and hourly acts. In human society, via society, nature gains a capacity for unlimited development. We are convinced that Vernadski was absolutely right when he said that

the laws of the cultural development of man are intimately related to the tremendous process of nature and cannot be regarded as incidental. This development — directed at the further subjugation of natural forces, and their transformation by consciousness, by thought — is determined by the flow of the geological history of our planet. It will not halt at our will.[13]

True, human beings cannot interrupt the 'work' aimed at transforming the biosphere into the noosphere.

This impossibility is particularly apparent when one does not consider human activity as something in opposition to nature — that is, nature regarded as a life-support medium, and human activity as a process of using, remaking, and consuming it — but recognizes the unity of the two worlds of humanity and nature. Seen in this light, human activity reveals itself as an interaction between a part and the whole which determines the development of the latter. The activity of a social being is seen as the progress of nature, as the superior form of motion in nature, which is a mode of existence of matter and thus of nature. It is through humanity and its development in labour that nature comes in its eternal path to the horizons of perfection, and the human being has no power to stop this process short of ceasing to be human. Teilhard wrote: 'the more human man becomes, the less ready will he be to accept anything short of the infinite and inextinguishable movement to what is new. The very course of his action embraces something absolute'.[14] Contrary to Teilhard, we believe that the 'absolute' resides not in man, but in nature, in its perpetual and indestructible movement, its continuous development and ascent from inferior to superior. Only in the light of this interminable development, and taking into account its acceleration by human society, should one understand humanity as a geological force that is forever on the rise. It is in this sense that human society becomes 'the only agent of its kind' in the biosphere.[15]

The ethics of creating the noosphere

We believe it essential to emphasize the ethics of the process of the formation of the noosphere. Vernadski wrote that 'in the geological history of the biosphere man is on the threshold of a magnificent future open to him *provided he sees it and abstains from using his mind and labor for self-destruction*'.[16] It is evident that humanity can satisfy these demands which call for decisions of the highest ethical order only within a society of 'free-thinking' people living in social justice. If this condition is met, and moral principles are victorious all over the world, it will be proof of the high level of the productive forces of humanity, and also of its unity and collective reason. Satisfying this most essential social and ethical requisite for human activity will bring the biosphere into that state which is characterized by human control over natural processes for the sake of universal interests — the state of the noosphere.

Nature, in its entire complexity and in the diversity of its ties with space and not with some unknown miracle, has achieved the height of social relations through humanity. It is safe to assume that human beings are beginning to get used to that height, are still only adapting to it, formulating rules of behaviour, seeking forms of the intellect's manifestation, and working out norms of relations with others. This effort is nearing a logical point where, more and more often, the human organism begins to look back at the path traversed, and more and more often ponders over the results achieved, as well as the future road.

By building a new world, uncovering great mysteries of the 'inorganic body', and turning knowledge into a real productive force, human beings gradually rid themselves of the infantile desire to remake and 'conquer' nature and learn how to use its forces precisely as natural forces, and not as some conquered and transformed forces. Production based on such an attitude towards the outside world enables us to look at ourselves not as 'creatures on two legs and without feathers', not as 'animals which can produce implements' with whose help we could conquer nature and reign over it, but as nature's crown of creation and, by virtue of that, its real creator; as the summit of nature's history; and as the summit of a pyramid whose foundation we should always protect and strengthen, if we are ever to scale new heights and develop further. The problem of the relationship between society and nature is more and more often perceived as a human problem.

It is therefore safe to conclude that the current period is not only a period when society is increasing its consumption of nature, but also a period of increasing human unity with nature, implying all the social consequences arising from this fact. Human activity is seriously transforming the environment, and this transformation will be adequate to human nature only on the condition of a 'human' understanding and knowledge of nature. For this to happen, people must grasp the mysteries of their social existence so that they can organize it in ways that develop the interaction between society and nature, and thus create a society that corresponds to the fullest power and prospects of humanity. Herein lies the source of historical optimism in charting prospects for the development of 'the world of people — world of nature' system. Only such a society will enable men and women to give due regard to the limits of what is possible in nature, and not to their personal objectives alone. Vernadski pointed out that the emergence of the noosphere comes as a natural substratum of the historical process. One may evidently presume the contrary as well: social progress is a social substratum of the noosphere; its emergence presupposes that society achieves a degree of perfection which enables human beings to define and follow a genuinely reasonable attitude to nature.

The quest for the good in relations between people, and the affirmation of such traits of the human personality as kindness, the desire to help the weak, and compassion should show themselves in the nature-forming activities of human society. It is not an accident, therefore, that the collective intellect has always been opposed to senseless cruelty and a predatory attitude toward nature and has tried to affirm love toward nature. Nor has the feeling of sheer compassion been its only motive force. Cruelty displayed outside the limits of human relations always has a chance of invading the human sphere as well.

Such an approach is all the more indispensable today in this time of scientific and technological revolution and the social renewal of humankind. The unprecedented increase of humanity's essential forces, the disruption of the normal course of natural processes as a result of production, and the depletion of certain natural resources — all this makes humans aware of the horizon of morality involved in their attitudes to nature, and makes humanity responsible not only for its own 'back yard' but also for the planet as a whole. It encourages them to think not only of today, but also of a day that is still to come. To paraphrase the great humanist Albert Schweitzer: today, the responsibility for and to the future should be considered boundless.

Notes

1 V. I. Vernadski, *The Chemical Structure of the Earth's Biosphere and Its Surroundings* (Moscow: Navka 1965), 328. (In Russian).
2 Karl Marx and Frederick Engels, *Collected Works* 3 (Moscow: Progress, 1976), 276. (In Russian).
3 Warren B. King and Jane Thornback, *Endangered Birds of the World: IUCN Red Data Book* (Gland: IUCN, 1981); Martin Jenkins, *The IUCN Mammal Red Data Book* (Gland: IUCN, 1982); Brian Groombridge, *The IUCN Amphibia-Reptile Red Data Book* (Gland: IUCN, 1982); Susan M. Wells, Robert M. Pyle, and N. Mark Collins, *The Invertebrate Red Data Book* (Gland: IUCN, 1983); Phyllis Lee and Jane Thornback, *Threatened*

Primates of Africa: The IUCN Red Data Book (Gland: IUCN, 1989).

4 Frederick Engels, *Dialectics of Nature* (Moscow: Progress, 1978), 180. (In Russian).

5 Vernadski, *The Chemical Structure of the Earth's Biosphere*, 324.

6 Pierre Teilhard de Chardin, *The Phenomenon of Man* (New York: Harper & Row, 1965), 182.

7 Vernadski, *The Chemical Structure of the Earth's Biosphere*, 328.

8 Marx and Engels, *Collected Works*, 296–7.

9 Vernadski, *The Chemical Structure of the Earth's Biosphere*, 328.

10 Marx and Engels, *Collected Works*, 276.

11 V.I. Vernadski, *Biogeochemical Essays* (Moscow and Leningrad:Navka, 1940), 47. (In Russian).

12 Ibid., 44.

13 Ibid.

14 Teilhard de Chardin, *The Phenomenon of Man*, 227.

15 Vernadski, *Biogeochemical Essays*, 47.

16 Vernadski, *The Chemical Structure of the Earth's Biosphere*, 327.

10 The development vision of socialist humanism
Mihailo Marković

An epoch of extraordinary social development was made possible by the use of fast-growing scientific knowledge, by the creation of ever more efficient technologies, and by the emergence of a lay culture that liberated individual energies for the exploration of the world in every conceivable direction: for increasing mastery over nature; for unlimited self-assertion; and for the enrichment of life. A concept invented by the seventeenth century summarized best the basic meaning of this modern development — progress. In modernity, progress became steady, relentless, accelerated, and exponential. Marx, whose view of progress differed from that of Mill or Spencer in that it included periods of crisis, disintegration, and discontinuous change, did not differ from them in believing that, in the new society, productive forces would continue to grow and human domination over nature increase.

It was hardly controversial — until recently — that progress was good, indeed that it was one of the highest values. Unpalatable social practices, such as firing people from their jobs when machines arrived, breaking up extended families, turning creative work into mechanical drudgery, flooding entire villages and destroying traditional cultures in order to build hydroelectric plants, and replacing rifles with nuclear missiles, were legitimated by progress. As late as 1967, Charles Frankel could write: 'the idea of progress in its most important aspect is itself a regulative moral idea, not simply a belief about history'.[1]

Urgent moral questions

It is still possible to accept progress as a moral ideal if we take it to mean 'increase of freedom' as in Hegel, 'dealienation' and a 'growing wealth of human needs' as in Marx, or even as the regulative principle that all 'inquiry should be kept open and critical, and that no bounds can legitimately be set to the authority of such free inquiry' as in Frankel. However, the prevalent meaning of 'progress' in modern culture is material growth, expansion of production, increasingly comfortable life, and the spread of civilization all over the globe. This concept of progress is now under attack. For the first time in history it is exposed to moral questioning which does not merely challenge some of its particular aspects, but the quantitative, expansionist idea of progress in its totality. For example:

- Is not constant striving for greater wealth and power counterproductive and immoral? Counterproductive, because if the ultimate purpose is a higher quality of human life, the very opposite of it will be reached in this one-sided way. Immoral, because interests in material wealth and power are intrinsically exclusive and restrictive, eventually destroying human relationships in any community.
- Is it moral that a few generations consume natural resources which needed billions of years to be generated, and which are indispensable for the survival of all coming generations?
- Is it permissible that our natural environment is irreversibly polluted for the benefit of a minority of people in developed countries?
- Is it right to have a social development that reinforces the hierarchical organization of society and increases the gap between rich and poor?
- Is it justifiable to reduce scientific knowledge to quantitative, material growth; to put increasingly powerful scientific technology in the service of greater efficiency and profitability — goals achieved by producing nicely packaged goods of deliberately reduced durability, contaminated, and dangerous to our health?
- May we continue in good conscience to use science for, ultimately, global self-destructive purposes; to produce global weaponry?
- Is it just to continue to promote the speed of quantitative progress to the entire world when (a) the developed part of the world, owing to its control of capital, international markets, advanced technology, and communication networks will effectively prevent this happening; and (b) if this does ever conceivably come true, it will rapidly lead to a breakdown of the world's entire ecological system? How can quantitative progress be a goal for some if it means the utter injustice of a hopeless, lasting, irreversible split of humankind into the classes of haves and have-nots.

Moral questions of this kind come from a variety of social groups, scholarly circles, and new social movements: humanist critics of science, democratic socialists, ecologists, peace activists, feminists. They challenge different dimensions of the prevailing paradigm of world development. That paradigm originated in Western Europe and Northern America but spread all over the world during the last few decades.

Poverty stricken people throughout the so-called Third World who needed social development have accepted it readily. There did not seem to exist any alternative to it. When socialism came into existence, the Third World also accepted some of its basic premises, since, after all, the original socialist idea was the child of Western Enlightenment, of modernity and industrialism. In the twentieth century, the Western model triumphed in India, Japan, Korea, and most other Asian countries as well.

Criticism of philosophical foundations

These urgent moral questions reveal the need for a thorough critique of the philosophical presuppositions of the dominant Western paradigm of development.

One of the most fundamental premises of the prevailing paradigm of world development is the concept that human nature is immoral. Nearly all great liberal philosophers construe human nature as essentially acquisitive, egoistic, possessive, aggressive, and individualist — with conservative philosophers adding belligerent, brutal, and destructive. This can hardly be accepted as a realistic description of human nature. Sheer egoism without creativity, freedom, and rationality cannot account for the impressive historical development of the human species. Thus, the view is not factual, but *normative*. It is, of course, possible for a philosopher to arrive at a sceptical view of human nature and yet conclude that for there to be progress in history, there must also be a progressive development of human nature made possible by the creation of conditions for human betterment. That would characterize an *ethical* approach to social development. An ethically *neutral* approach would have to start with an ethically neutral conception of human nature, seeing both its good and bad features. Its theory of social development would have to dispose of the value-laden concept of progress and construe 'development' as a neutral concept that maintains a neutral view of human nature.

The philosophers who contributed to the Western paradigm of development acted neither as ethical thinkers nor as neutral observers. They made two obviously ideological steps. One was construing their pessimistic, value-laden image of humanity as true human nature. Another was presenting a factual process of growth — complete with all kinds of unfairness, brutality, and injustice — as progress, the best thing that can happen to human beings in history. Both ideological steps, presenting a biased image as the true one, were necessary: the former in order to be able to justify competition, greed, and lust for power by reference to human nature; the latter in order to legitimate industrialization, urbanization, and modernization as not only a necessary pattern of history but also as something good and desirable. There is, of course, a hidden contradiction in this construction: how are bad human beings (greedy, envious, selfish, possessive) able to create an essentially good history? Here an element of mystification enters the picture. An 'invisible hand', a 'logos' of history, or a 'divine providence' takes care that the mess created by people turns inexorably into a better future.

A philosophical position that presents humans as worse than they are in order to rationalize vicious social practices, which does not give humans any credit for social improvements, which divorces social improvement from the concept of developing moral virtues, and which ends up declaring that what is good for rich and powerful elites is good for humanity — such a philosophical position cannot be characterized as anything but ideological and non-ethical.

Another philosophical premise of the prevalent paradigm of development is the concept that the relation between humans and nature is a permanent state of war. In pre-modern societies humans were the inferior party, exposed to overwhelming, threatening natural forces; suffering from both scarcity and fear.

Armed with weapons forged by modernity — scientific knowledge, machinery, natural powers tamed and used against the rest of nature — humans have turned into masters. That has been praised as the greatest victory in history. That we dominate and plunder nature is not just a fact, it has been considered a value, a state of affairs that ought to be maintained indefinitely. Marx himself writes about conquering and mastering nature in the same approving, jubilant way as any other philosopher of the Enlightenment and the Industrial Revolution. That that epochal victory contained also a seed of ultimate defeat was discovered rather late, in the second half of the twentieth century. Nowadays, we have begun to understand that the object of our ruthless exploitation is not infinite, inexhaustible cosmic matter but just a tiny planet with very limited resources.

All basic economic constituents of the prevalent paradigm of development presuppose the unlimited exploitation of nature. Any capitalist corporation and any socialist enterprise strives toward maximal expansion of material production. The interest in expansion is understandable and ethically valid as long as, and to the extent to which, it serves to produce goods and services that are necessary to overcome material poverty and to meet the basic needs of all people. However, this self-limitation is entirely missing in the Western paradigm of development. In the absence of any built-in criteria for the just distribution of goods, this paradigm generates material wealth that becomes the monopoly of particular social groups and turns into dominating social power. Even at its best, when it incorporates the idea of a welfare state and recognizes socioeconomic (in addition to civil) human rights, it is committed to producing surplus wealth which knows no limit; therefore, there is no limit to the wasting of natural and human resources.

In the Western paradigm the mediating link between the production of goods and expanding power is consumption. Goods *must* be sold and spent before they bring forth revenue and power. Therefore, once the primary hunger for goods, stemming from poverty, is satisfied, a secondary hunger, stemming from a false perception of needs, must be produced. For an ever expanding supply of goods, demand is artificially created by manipulating human minds to produce a false awareness of needs. Thus, a consumerist lifestyle emerges with its endless improvements of material comforts, its rapidly changing fashion, and its inevitable piling up of useless, expendable things. A hedonistic culture replaces the early Protestant culture which was characterized by saving and frugality.

This model of development requires a strong state. It generates so much polarization, friction, and conflict that an authoritative agency becomes indispensable to mediate among parties, protect property, and secure a minimum of necessary coordination. All of these become roles of the state. Citizens busy with production and consumption have no time or energy for genuine political life and participation in democratic decision-making. Therefore, this paradigm of development requires a more or less bureaucratic and centralized political system which only to a limited degree depends on citizen consensus. The Western paradigm of development is incompatible with true political and economic democracy.

The alternative humanist ethic

The preceding critique of the prevalent paradigm of social development presupposes an implicit ethical point of view. Now is the moment to state it explicitly.[2]

Kant's 'categorical imperative' expresses a necessary but not a sufficient condition of any morality. Indeed, unless human beings are treated as ends, not as means, and unless rules that govern our conduct permit universalization, a view of social development does not have moral character. And yet this approach can be interpreted in different ways. The fact that the advocates of some abusive and destructive practices accept the universalization of the rules governing those practices does not make them moral. Marx provides some essential content when he says:

The criticism of religion ends with the doctrine that man is the supreme being for man. It ends, therefore, with the categorical imperative to overthrow all those conditions in which man is an abased, enslaved, abandoned, contemptible being.[3]

This is the negative formulation of the basic content of a humanist ethics. It sums up the ethical principles of a revolutionary social change. Obviously, a positive formulation is needed, especially with respect to social development in general. It can be expressed in the following way. *Create social conditions under which all human individuals would equally be able to bring freely to life their potential creative powers.* This fundamental ethical principle of social development can be called the 'principle of equal self-realization'.

The ethical standpoint presented here is explicitly humanist. It grounds ethics in a normative conception of human nature which includes those characteristics which are specifically human and responsible for an impressive historical development. Such characteristics include: symbolic communication, rationality, creativity, capacity for autonomous choice, cultivation of the senses, and harmonization of social relationships. All these are inherent in each human individual, but, under unfavourable social conditions, they may be thwarted and wasted. Therefore, the basic moral requirement is not pleasure or material comfort, but free self-development and self-realization.

The concept of human nature presupposed here refers to an objectively given structure of possibilities in each person. Some of the latent dispositions which are present already in the genetic make-up of human beings have universal character; some, such as special talents, are uniquely individual. They are objective both in the sense that they exist independently of our knowledge of them, and also that they can be tested by producing the conditions under which they will be manifest.

An ethical point of view with such an objective ground is clearly superior to the ethical subjectivism cultivated in modern philosophy.[4] It is very convenient for an advocate of the Western paradigm of development to be able to say that opposite moral judgments about dumping toxic wastes into rivers and air are 'merely ejaculations' of different feelings of approval or disapproval.

The humanist point of view overcomes the dichotomy of individualism versus collectivism. Any living person is both a unique individual and a communal being. Unique in the sense that he has a unique potential, developed by a unique interaction of genetic make-up and social influences; therefore, he has a unique identity. Communal in the sense that only in the process of socialization (by learning a language and developing capacities of conceptual thinking, by being exposed to culture, and by internalizing rules of social behaviour) does a human organism become a truly human being. That is why some of the basic needs of each individual are to belong to a community, to be recognized, to share, to care, and to be cared for. Consequently, 'self-realization' does not mean 'doing one's own thing', in the spirit of 'possessive individualism'. It means self-development and self-affirmation which are responsible and concerned with the needs of other people.

Equality is here compatible with freedom. The former does not mean equality of opportunity, treatment, or remuneration as commonly understood. It recognizes inequality of strength, talent, individual needs, and aspirations. Unequal people in that sense must be treated unequally in order to acquire true equality of conditions for self-realization. And this coincides with freedom. To be free means, first, to be aware of the existing plurality of possibilities; second, to make an autonomous choice among them and to act accordingly; and third, to be able to control the situation to such an extent that one's actions will not be blocked and produce entirely unexpected consequences. This concept of freedom unifies the ideas of positive and negative freedom, of the freedom of will and the freedom of action. It could be in conflict with the concept of equality only if the practical activity in question were a struggle for wealth and dominating power. These are exclusive assets. Possession by some means exclusion of all others. However, learning, communication, creative action, enjoyment of the beauties of nature or of the arts, joys of friendship and love, participation in communal festivities — these are *not* exclusive in that sense. Far from eliminating others, most of these activities presuppose sharing with others. That the conditions to enjoy them should be equally opened to all does not in any way constrain the freedom of each individual.

The alternative humanist paradigm of development

What then, from this standpoint, should be the alternative to the prevalent paradigm of development? First, concerning the idea of progress, the emphasis should be shifted from reckless quantitative growth to sustainable qualitative development. True progress should no longer be conceived as an accelerated and endless accumulation of material goods and services, but as the enrichment of human life through the satisfaction of a variety of increasingly articulated and refined human needs. The former is 'quantitative' since it amounts to having more and more of one and the same dimension of life — more and more material comfort. The latter is 'qualitative' since it involves diversified being in a number of dimensions and spaces of life. A reasonable level of material comfort goes together with a wealth of cultural and spiritual needs; with a growing depth, intensity, and subtlety of personal relationship; with a variety of expressions of one's creative potential; and with a vivid, joyful sense of belonging to the larger wholes of community, humankind, and nature. Two opposite conceptions of the purpose of life underlie these two concepts of progress: dominating power and consumption in one case, creative power and self-realization in the other.

Quantitative progress is reckless and destructive since it inevitably brings human beings into confrontation with the natural environment. It presupposes an infinity of material resources, whereas the resources of our tiny planet are limited, scarce, and to a large extent, non-renewable. Qualitative progress, on the other hand, is sustainable since it depends on scarce resources only to a limited degree.

Second, in contrast to popular views concerning 'limits to growth', there should be no limit to the development of science, humanities, or culture in general. The growth of reliable, scientific knowledge should not suffer as a result of the misuse of knowledge. Truth will always remain both an end in itself and a necessary means to any sustainable development.

It is, however, necessary to overcome the present gap between knowledge and morality, science and ethics. We should relearn what we forgot: Greek *theoria* included an awareness of moral values, of virtue. In modern science this union was broken; morality was excluded from scholarship and relocated in the sphere of religion, or interpreted as wholly subjective. The time has come to redevelop a concept of a critical, ethically engaged social science. This approach presupposes that morality can be objectively grounded and clearly distinguished from religion and ideology. Its practical consequence is a greater sense of responsibility on the part of intellectuals and scholars for ideological, militaristic, and other misuses of their work.

Third, there should also be no limit to the development of various alternative technologies that increase the productivity and efficiency of human labour. Those ecologists who advise giving up industrial civilization and returning to agricultural and cattle-raising communities lack any sense of history, and tend to compromise any ecological critique of modern society. Humankind cannot voluntarily go back to its past impotence, drudgery, and poverty. What could and should be done is to use increasing productivity for purposes other than the expansion of material output.

Fourth, once the basic needs of all people are met, our primary concern should be the creation of necessary conditions for the satisfaction of higher-level cultural, communal, political, and psychological needs. This will not lead to the abolition of work but definitely is a historical step in the process of transcending alienated labour. One of the greatest tragedies of humankind is the discrepancy between potential being and miserable toiling existence. Neither long daily drudgery nor simple mechanical work satisfies the capacity to talk, to reason, to imagine, to have a sense of beauty, or to create new objects.

For the first time in history, technology can replace the human labourer's most routine operations. The tasks which remain, if equally distributed to all members of society according to their competence and skills (a preferable solution to throwing people out of their jobs, as is the case within the current, strongly competitive paradigm of social development), will lead to an overall decrease in working hours.

Free time is an important value within the alternative paradigm. However, there are those who oppose any reduction of obligatory working time on the grounds that free time will be filled by watching TV. The satisfying use of free time depends on education. A society that saves natural and human resources that are today insanely wasted on over-consumption and armaments can afford to make immense improvements to education. Once young people are prepared in educational institutions not only for a specific role in the professional division of labour, but also for an active life in their leisure time, time will become the single most important scarcity in human life. It will continue to be filled by a great deal of work. Only, for a change, this will be a freely chosen activity, a need and an end in itself.

Fifth, the development rate of different areas of production in this model is the inverse of that presently prevailing. Those enterprises that supply conventional industrial goods should slow down their production. People should learn to appreciate goods for their aesthetic qualities — their durability and their compatibility with environmental concerns. This will give a tremendous impetus to the development of traditional arts, to the revival of crafts, and, in general, to the production of unique, hand-made objects and services. Consequently, the most rapidly developing social area will be cultural production, including an active interest in art, philosophy, science, politics, free communication, and meaningful communal gatherings.

Sixth, once humankind finds a way to live better with less waste of material resources, it becomes possible to reduce and reverse the suicidal trend of growing pollutions and the depletion of natural surroundings. This is where a humanistic socialism has a better chance than other social systems: it need not continue the brutal exploitation of nature that is practised in those societies in which maximization of output and of profit is the very ground of their identity.

Where the paradigms under consideration mostly differ is not so much in the goals and values to which they are committed, as in their hierarchy. All contemporary societies aspire to material growth, to emancipation in some sense, to social justice, and to the well-being of their citizens. It is in situations where these values conflict, and where one is given priority over the other, that the true identity of a system is revealed.

A humanist socialist society, confronted with ecological problems, must and can give priority to social well-being over the maximization of material output. As in market-orientated systems, economic efficiency and high productivity of work rank as an important value, other conditions being equal. But when other conditions are not equal, when the highest productivity can be reached only at the expense of considerable destruction of the natural environment and long-term damage to the population, in a humanist socialist society economic profitability must, to a certain degree, be sacrificed.

For example, while building nuclear plants could be an economically rational way of producing energy for a country that owns its own resources of uranium and which could earn scarce convertible currency by exporting a surplus of produced electricity, the impossibility of a permanent solution to the problem of depositing nuclear wastes must be a single sufficient reason to give up nuclear energy altogether. Installing pollution control equipment increases production costs and can put an enterprise in a unfavourable market position. However, where markets are regulated within the framework of a national policy of economic development, a variety of economic instruments can compensate the installer of ecological equipment. In this way society as a whole pays the price for the health of its citizens.

Heavy air pollution in cities can be avoided if industries are transferred out of urban areas, if heating systems are centralized, and if the burning of cheap gasoline containing lead is prohibited. That is exactly what must be done, regardless of the expense. It will not be done, however, if material growth is the primary goal, even though in the long run the medical expenses incurred by the victims of heavily polluted air will be considerably higher than the costs of a direct attack on the problem.

Finally, considerable energy could be saved by the insulation of houses, the use of superconductors for the transmission of energy, and by the development of miniature equipment. Private corporations will make the necessary investments only if they are profitable. In humanistic socialist societies, on the other hand, those investments would be a matter of a reasonable national policy.

Seventh, liberation from constant labour and a greatly improved general education open up space for a true flourishing of democracy. However, the most essential precondition of democracy is the abolition of any monopoly of power. In politics, such monopoly can be overcome through free elections, political pluralism, and the deprofessionalization of leadership. In economics, it is necessary to socialize the means of production or at least to separate ownership rights from economic decision-making power. In both areas, as well as in culture, the principle should be followed that as an individual, as a citizen, as a producer, and as a consumer, one has the right to take part in decision-making in the communities where one lives and works; furthermore, one has the right to delegate power to a representative and the right to keep that representative responsible to oneself.

Thus the principle of democracy should be extended from the sphere of politics to economy and culture. Direct participation should be combined with responsible representation. In contrast to the present day bureaucratic state, this new form of social organization should be constituted by activists who are freely elected, rotatable, recallable, and devoid of any material privileges and of any claim to lasting power.

This new humanist paradigm of social development solves some of the most urgent problems of our time better than the prevalent growth paradigm. Even if it has only a utopian character, it can be of considerable intellectual and moral importance, for utopias are repositories of forgotten and neglected values and may be essential for reorientating our strivings at a time of crisis. However, in this case, actual historical tendencies make the new paradigm viable.

Owing particularly to the work of the Club of Rome, the United Nations University macro-project, 'Goals, Processes, Indicators', directed by Johan Galtung, the Argentinean Bariloche project, the World Federation of Future Studies, and other scholarly groups and communities, an increasingly negative view of quantitative development has developed in recent years. That the world must find a way to live better with less waste of natural and human resources has now become common wisdom.

That technological progress should not be used exclusively for the increase of material output but should also generate more free time is not only a theoretical view expressed by many social scholars, but also a practical demand formulated by many trade unions in the world.

A significant change of attitude toward the natural environment is one of the most important features of social life in most advanced countries today. Laws oblige industrial enterprises to install equipment for the protection of air, water and soil. Under growing pressures from ecological groups, the building of nuclear plants is being abandoned. Industrial plants have been moved out of big cities and the air and waters are already cleaner than a century ago. Energy-saving policies and technological innovations have stabilized the overall consumption of energy for the first time in recent history.

The new humanistic paradigm of social development can prevail only if there is a process of radical democratization of social life. A new political culture is emerging both in the East and the West, the basic components of which are: a critique of the bureaucratic state; a concern about the full realization of human rights, both political and socioeconomic; and demands for direct participation and self-government by citizen and producer.

Naturally, we are not able to see, beyond the horizon of our epoch, what conflicts and malformations might emerge on this new ground. We cannot even know for sure if social development will continue, and if humankind has any future. In that sense we are parting our ways with the dogmatism of modernity. We have to make choices and act on the ground of the possible.

Notes

1 Paul Edwards, ed, *Encyclopedia of Philosophy* VI (New York: Macmillan, 1976), 487.
2 See Mihailo Marković, *Democratic Socialism: Theory and Practice* (Hassocks, Sussex: Harvester Press, 1982); 'Historical Praxis as the Ground of Morality' in N. Storer, *Humanist Ethics*, ed., (Buffalo, NY: Prometheus Books, 1980), 36–51; 'The Principle of Equal Self-determination as a Basis for Jurisprudence', *Archiv für Rechts- und Sozial-Philosophie* 13 (Wiesbaden: F. Steiner Verlag, 1979), 181–93; and 'Philosophical Foundations of Human Rights', *Praxis International* 4 (Oxford: Basil Blackwell, 1982): 386–401.
3 Karl Marx, 'Contribution to the Critique of Hegel's Philosophy of Right' in R. C. Tucker, *The Marx–Engels Reader*, ed., 2nd ed (New York: W. W. Norton, 1978), 60.
4 Ethical subjectivism in modernity was well criticized in Alasdair MacIntyre, *After Virtue* (Notre Dame Ind.: University of Notre Dame Press, 1981).

South and Central America

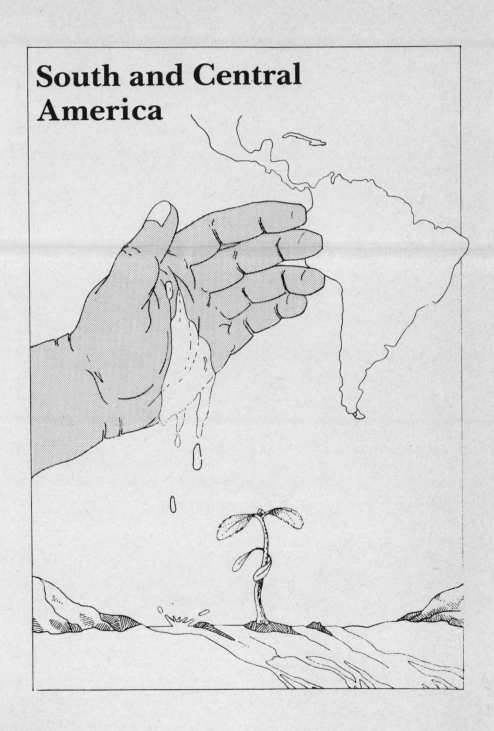

11 The search for an ethic of sustainable development in Latin America
Eduardo Gudynas

Latin America is a region of the world where the close relationship between predatory natural resource and development strategies is very clear. It is also a place where many of the oldest and some of the newest ideas which link ethical and environmental concerns are being developed. Latin America is illustrative of the failure of these ideas to take hold in the modern consciousness, but its failures signal the steps which must be taken in order to develop a new ethical understanding of sustainable development.

The value crisis in Latin America

Spanish colonization and domination of Latin America rested on the extraction of natural resources. Beginning in 1542, the bloody search for *el dorado* and mining of Potosí, Zacatecas, and Guanajuato sustained the Spanish crown and stimulated European development.[1] Since then, the moral problem of natural resource management has been closely related to the moral problem of creating just relationships between persons and societies.

Drastic reductions of native populations accompanied the extraction of minerals, as the colonial economy made use of overt or covert slavery to grow. While the Spanish profited from the metallurgy and mining techniques of traditional aboriginal cultures, they otherwise regarded the natives as inferior, culturally backward, and unworthy of Christian salvation. Today it is recognized that aboriginal cultures had complex knowledge systems and used their vast natural resources wisely. The Maya developed agricultural techniques requiring a deep knowledge of forest structure and phenology. The Andean agricultural empires maintained complex civilizations on mountain slopes. Their ingenious constructions were based on a normative understanding of the relationship of humans to the land, which was conceived as sacred and living.[2]

Amerindians could help a lot in developing sustainable development programmes, but today they are disappearing together with their forests. Most of the ethical wisdom and ecological knowledge of native peoples was lost during

European colonization. Western culture, now predominant in Latin America, has disseminated a different ethical attitude, and whatever remnants of aboriginal sensibility have surfaced in recent years, along with new concerns about environmental problems, have done so within a climate dominated by Western neoclassical economic theory.

In this dominant 'market' paradigm the good life is obtained by the buying of commodities; the environment is fragmented; its holistic properties are ignored; and the costs of environmental disruption are externalized.

In Latin America this paradigm has resulted in a generalized development style that, since World War II, has been related to peripheric capitalism, and is directed toward increased industrialization.[3] Nevertheless, two development systems may be recognized; capitalist and socialist. Although their objectives are different, environmental problems transcend this dichotomy.[4]

Whether originating from the left or right, the reigning development style is anthropocentric in the worse sense. It exalts success and production, views nature as humanity's servant and without rights, assumes that growth should be maintained at any price, and that technological progress is both end and means of social, political, and cultural life. It acknowledges no material obstacles to development, in part because Latin America is imagined as an enormous region with unlimited resources and large distress buffer capacities. Finally, all factors and data that reveal the potentially dangerous consequences of these attitudes are minimized or ignored. Under this paradigm, underdevelopment has been conceived as something humiliating, and all efforts are directed to reaching the development level of highly industrialized and urbanized countries. Development is a race and to lag behind is to die.

With regard to the relationship of science and ethics, this development paradigm presents the following characteristics: ethical values are separate from science; scientists do not evaluate the moral context of their actions; there is an absence of ethical judgments regarding development and its consequences; and the initial scientific question of how the universe can be understood is transformed to the question of how the universe can be dominated. Paradoxically, some of these characteristics are also found in some of the so-called 'alternative' technological strategies, and it is difficult to imagine that alternative technologies alone would be enough to transform present society.

These postures are accepted uncritically and are not subject to discussion at most levels. Thus they approach Kuhn's concept of a paradigm. This development paradigm has ancient roots, and is deeply implanted in present day culture. It is supported by non-rational feelings. H.C.F. Mansilla developed the concept of 'collective pre-conscious' for this non-rational paradigm, and referred to its origin in cultures of the centre.[5] As the anthropological studies of D. Ribeiro show, many Latin American cultural groups, including ruling elites in most countries, can be understood as 'transplanted nations'. They have resulted from the expansion of European nations and follow their 'mother' ideology.[6] In these groups are found the non-rational bases of the present development paradigm.

The ethical issues of sustainable development

Sustainable development has been one of the primary purposes of environmental groups and governments in Latin America trying to change the present non-rational development paradigm. Sustainable development emerged on the continent during the mid-1970s along with the new concepts of 'development styles', 'ecodevelopment', and 'alternative development'. Many of these ideas originated from work in the area itself, notably by the Centro del Desarrallo (CENDES), Venezuela, and the Economic Commission for Latin America (CEPAL).

Various attempts to define the meaning of sustainable development have disclosed a series of moral conflicts. Beneath varied definitions of the meaning of the term itself lie questions concerning the nature and end of growth, the desirability of industrialization, the stance to take on population reduction, and questions related to the place of environmental problems in social and political arenas.

Authors use the term 'sustainable development' in different ways, and no theoretical body of thought yet exists to stabilize the term. The World Conservation Strategy (WCS) defined sustainable development as 'the modification of the biosphere and the application of human, financial, living and non-living resources to satisfy human needs and improve the quality of human life'.[7] The WCS definition is invoked by mainline conservationist groups including the Brazilian Association for the Conservation of Nature; the Fundación Vida Silvestre, Argentina; and Natura, Ecuador.

No mention is made in this definition of either economic or social growth. However, the WCS has been perceived as a complement of the United Nations International Development Strategy, and the latter does look for economic and social growth. A.W. Clausen, president of the World Bank, states that sustainable development must allow for continued economic growth, especially in the Third World.[8] Clausen stresses that poverty imposes strains on the natural environment, and that at survival levels people exploit their environment too intensively. I attach much significance to this position, as it reflects the posture of a large financial agency related to development aid in Latin America.

Along with the question of growth comes the question of how much, if any, industrialization is needed for sustainable development. It has been observed by Mansilla, among others, that most Latin American groups have not adequately dealt with the validity of the need for industrialization.[9] A non-rational position with regard to the need for industrialization and growth has often been maintained by groups critical of the dominant development paradigm. For example, Brazilian delegates voted for United Nations Resolution 2849 (a resolution the United States and United Kingdom voted against) which condemned the industrial countries for contaminating the world, yet Brazil also supported (but soon abandoned) development 'at any price'.

The ethics of population growth is a major source of disagreement within the concept of sustainable development. The WCS does not mention population growth, although it is considered in a major recent paper on sustainable development by the Global Tomorrow Coalition in North America. The Global Tomorrow Coalition's executive statement reads: 'In many nations, rapid population growth is already exerting unsustainable processes on the resource base and frustrating efforts to meet human needs.'[10] The ideology of industrial development and the theory of Latin American dependence both oppose any population decrease. Many Latin Americans consider high population figures as a way to reach an industrialized state. M. Max-Neef's concept of 'ecological person' or 'eco-son', which measures the resources needed by a person in order to attain a good quality of life, is relevant here.[11] Because a person from an industrialized country requires far more resources than a person from a poor one, it follows that reduction in population growth in Latin America should be accompanied by a reduction of consumption levels in the First World.

Probably the most relevant moral issue has to do with the reconception of environmental problems as social problems. At the time of the Stockholm conference, delegates from less developed countries stressed that 'environment' includes human beings, human artefacts, and, indeed, society itself. This implies the ethical position stated by Josué de Castro, among others, that poverty is the major environmental problem in Latin America. But there is pollution due to industrialization and there is pollution due to extreme poverty. Both must be recognized. Recent examples of concern for the social dimension of environmental problems include Rodriguez Arana's 1986 report on environmental disruptions in Guatemala; the 1987 report by the newly founded Central American Environmental NGOs Network for Sustainable Development; Nicaragua's environmental programmes accompanied by educational support; and even the paradox of CEPAL, which from an initial strictly economics posture, moved first to the social, and then to the environmental dimension.[12]

The recent meeting of United Nations Environment Programme's government representatives on environmental problems in Latin America and the Caribbean (April 1987) pointed out the relationship of economic and social issues to environmental policy and concluded that foreign debt pressures in some countries threaten the environment and quality of life of its people, and that wars have severe repercussions on the environment — a clear reference to Central American conflicts. Peace is being considered an essential condition for quality of life and environment. Pérez points out that in El Salvador's civil war the intensive bombing and use of chemicals have drastically affected not only human beings, but also soils, forests, and wildlife.[13]

Another example of how environmental problems are rooted in problems of social morality comes from rural development in tropical forests. Small peasant landowners have been blamed for environmental disruption which has resulted in the loss of extensive areas of tropical forests and the extinction of many species. Many of these sell their products to transnational agroindustrial companies; others pursue exploitative techniques as an inevitable result of their small size lands. Land ownership is the complex result of historical and socioeconomic conditions. Present inequalities in land access are supported by governments ranging from dictatorships following 'national security' ethics to democracies. Any ecologist dealing with environmental disruption in Latin America will have to deal with this social-ethical dimension of the problem.

Movements for sustainable development

One source of dissatisfaction with the dominant development paradigm originated in concern for Latin America's environmental problems. Workers in several fields — biologists, naturalists, wildlifers, public health service workers — with poor knowledge of each other, and with little interest at first in economic and social problems, initiated activities in the environmental field. The Latin Americans who contributed to *Only One Earth*, the 1972 Ward and Dubos' report, were primarily concerned with exhausting natural resources, the need to slow population increase, and the problems of waste management, points much influenced by the first Club of Rome report.[14]

Environmental concern led to discontent with existing development pathways and the discovery of the social dimensions of environmental problems. Discontent grew very quickly in the late 1960s but still with limited connection among those involved. Then in 1975 criticism of development concepts reached its highest point with, on the one hand, a search for a new theoretical background, and on the other, an acknowledgment of an ethical crisis.

I have identified two main scenarios within the Latin American environmental movement, which is surely an oversimplification, but perhaps useful for analysing the steps now taking place toward sustainable development. One scenario is made up of 'environmental managers', who look for better management of present day development, and who hope to reduce environmental disruption to a minimum. Their approach is that of technicians with short term policies. They do not present different ethical principles nor do they question present ones. I include in this category both ecocapitalists and ecosocialists.

However, in the present climate, even environmental management groups have been invaded by the search for 'another development'. One of the leading voices has been that of CEPAL. Osvaldo Sunkel, for example, exemplifies the changing posture of Latin American economists searching for a new development which includes the environmental dimension. He has called for a range of changes in energy consumption which includes suggestions for new administrative systems based on decentralization and local community autonomy.[15]

It must be pointed out that management groups are doing a most important job, ranging from public education to the ownership of protected areas. Most of these efforts are done by foundations and associations closely related to middle and upper social classes, with representation in both private and state areas, and thus with economic possibilities to develop important projects. Their actions will not change the dominant development paradigm, but they provide indispensable aid in some areas of environmental problems.

A second scenario is composed of 'antihegemonic' groups, mostly small and diverse movements at the grassroots level, with a deep but poorly elaborated ethical concern. They share a common questioning of the development paradigm itself, and a great concern to accompany their ethical premises with their everyday practice. They include diverse groups ranging from Latin American minority groups (anarchists and feminists) to Catholic grassroots groups and others fighting for structural change.

The countries of Latin America with extensive industrial development present the most diverse range of groups. Brazil is a good example. Early concern in Brazil was clearly directed to its exuberant wildlife, and the leading voice was the Brazilian Association for the Conservation of Nature. Since the 1970s, the environmental issue has broadened. The Brazilian environmental groups have been concerned with large dam projects, intensive industrial complexes such as Tucurui, and the nuclear agreement with the Federal Republic of Germany, which has led them to enter the social field. Leading voices include both natural and social scientists, backed by an explosive growth in non-governmental organizations (NGOs). The southern Brazil NGO, AGAPAN, has directed intense public campaigns aimed at social transformation at every level — 'attack today and ever, at the small and large scale, defending life!'[16] Since the early 1980s several persons have entered the political field and state green parties have been founded.

Venezuela also has many distinct environmental groups, many important institutions working in the environmental area, a national network (FORJA), and also a large official body (Ministry of the Environment) where the state plays the role of protagonist. Surprisingly, the best expression of the political dimension is found in an alternative labour union movement, the 'R-cause' movement, which is searching for a new paradigm for a better quality of life.

'Ecodevelopment' has been actively promoted in Latin America by I. Sachs.[17] Although still a limited movement in Latin America, ecodevelopment seeks to link the environmental managers with the antihegemonic groups. First presented as a development strategy to avoid economic growth and depletion of natural resources, ecodevelopment is also part of an ethical movement stressing the development of the human being over material objectives. It supports the recreation of locally-based communities with better utilization of resources specific to ecozones, increasing the quality of life through the satisfaction of basic human needs, appropriate technology, and solidarity with future generations. Human beings are recognized as the most valued resource, and ecodevelopment is a contribution to their fulfilment. This implies horizontal authority and decision-making, and requires a new education to change the attitude of dominance over nature, or, in the case of some aboriginal groups, to preserve and reinforce a respectful attitude towards nature.

One of the most notorious absences at the beginning of the environmental movement was the Catholic Church. It is noteworthy that most of the early environmentalists in Latin America were secular people who found in the environmental movement an alternative or complement to their religious faiths. Since the Medellín meeting, the Church has moved towards a greater concern with social problems. And within this current concern with social problems there seems to be emerging a concern for the ethics of the environment. Theology of liberation was born of a consciousness of dependence and oppression. While traditional theology is non-historical, theology of liberation is a practice that looks for a change in the historical process, particularly one affecting the poorest and most oppressed. Thus its perspective has no particular theoretical context, but proceeds from an analysis of reality with a particular criticism of the dependent capitalism of Latin America. Today environmental issues are being examined from the standpoint of liberation theology. J. Peixoto in Uruguay links human rights and ecological rights and compares the domination of human over human to the domination of human over nature. Bormida in Brazil speaks in a parable of paper-gathering in Buenos Aires about the Third World dying as a result of being fed technological debris from the First World, debris which is part of the system of domination.

Franciscans have long been associated with an environmental perspective. In an early paper, L. Boff suggests that a way of recovering from the environmental crisis is through a recovery of Franciscan spirituality.[18] He recognizes two existential life categories: the present way of being-above-things; and the ancient (and hopefully future) way of being-with-things. Boff suggests that the solution to our present problems lies not in specific measures but in a return to a mystic relation with nature.

Other Christian writers deal with the necessity of human stewardship for nature. J.C.R. de la Peña favours anthropocentric ethics over 'natural-animist' ethics. God has not authorized the pillage of nature, but requires human beings to manage creation.[19] In the same way, Pope John Paul II, in his first 1979 encyclical, stated that the environment must be the object of wise management. These postures do not acknowledge, as do Boff and the Franciscans, intrinsic values in other living beings and nature. Thus, they are only revisions of traditional anthropocentric perspectives.

Today, environmental religious postures continue to diversify. Recently the Episcopal Conference of the Dominican Republic presented a pastoral letter on environmental relations. It refers to soils, forests, and fauna and to the inadmissible inequalities of land access, wealth, and wasteful consumption of natural resources by the rich. The letter asks for an ecological catechism and for religious celebrations of natural events.

Prospects for an ethic of sustainable development

My initial conclusions are pessimistic. I must confess that whichever postures are considered, the morally committed environmental movement in Latin America is limited. We are still a minority and a divided force.

Since the 1970s, there have been a series of declarations and reports about the need for sustainable development, mostly by qualified scientists, — but the environmental situation has not improved, and is in fact worse in many respects. This discourse has been particularly impelled by NGOs. But it is of interest to note that many Latin American governments have also reproduced it while continuing with their exploitive tactics and growth-mania strategies.

While international and national groups call for a new ethics and drastic changes, in the actual world the situation remains unchanged. The reports mentioned are more or less diffuse requests for 'another development' to bring about the wise use of the environment. They can be named 'committee utopias'. In action they have been little more than passive voices, unable to show the path to transform our societies.

Thus, it turns out that neither the enthusiastic denunciations by NGOs, nor the quiet declarations by governmental agencies, have gone beyond solving a few particular problems. In this situation, countries with environmental management policies should be considered but one step beyond countries with no policies at all. We are at the level of diagnosing disease symptoms, far away from recovery. The 1970s have passed away, and many opportunities for change are gone. Even in countries that reached high industrialization in those years, like Mexico and Brazil, the final result seems to be higher poverty levels for the majority at the cost of greater environmental impact. Furthermore, we lost confidence in social scientists, for they were not only unable to promote actual changes but also unable to foresee the present multidimensional crisis.

Some conceive the core of these problems to be in the exploitation of majorities by some minorities, in both socialist and capitalist countries. But this is still an incomplete approach, as similar hierarchical situations are reproduced within most social groups, even among the poorest. The actual problem is the logic of domination shared by most of us, the domination of one person over the other, and of human beings over nature. This logic is firmly rooted in our spirits, and is of ancient origin.

If we are actually working for a change we must develop a new ethical setting. We know that in this century utopia is materially possible, but the challenge is to promote deep moral changes that reach and modify the roots of our hierarchical behaviour. NGOs are being asked to participate actively in a change that would be so drastic that we would hardly recognize even these organizations in the future. The challenge is to go one step further than just another committee utopia. I can advance some points in this path.

First, and most basic, we must change our position from an anthropocentric to a biocentric posture by avoiding all hierarchical postures, by being-with-things, and not above things. To achieve a holistic perspective on the world, we need to acknowledge the tight ecological relationships between all living and non-living elements, and to recognize that all living beings and living systems have the right to fulfilment. Each living being, either animal or plant, possesses rights, and thus the living system also has rights. We should understand that any action taken will strengthen or weaken the health of the ecosystem. In other words, we should seek to maintain synergy in the ecosystem, and to extend it to human social groupings and all human–environment relations.

Second, this change is only possible through freedom, democratic practice, and a new social order. Nature and humanity will be liberated together or not at all, for every step in environmental destruction has the effect of increasing social injustice, and every act of social injustice has the effect of increasing environmental destruction.

In Latin America, Mallmann and Max-Neef, continuing the work of North American Abraham Maslow, provide important clues for a humanistic basis of an ethical alternative development paradigm.[20] According to these thinkers, the creation of 'development on a human scale' depends upon the following premises: development should refer to persons, not objects; the best development process permits an increase in the quality of life of persons; quality of life depends on adequately satisfying human needs; human needs constitute a finite (contra Maslow) non-hierarchical system, and are satisfied through 'satisfiers'. There are no 'basic needs' since all needs are important and at the same level. M. Hopenhayn shows that in the strict sense needs are not satisfied (which implies a lack), but are lived, as they are at the same time a lack and a search of the self.[21] Human needs are the same in all cultures and in all times; the satisfiers change from culture to culture and time to time.

C.A. Mallmann has shown the relationship between human needs, satisfiers and alternative development by replacing the concept of developed and underdeveloped societies with the concept of eutopic and distopic societies.

Distopic societies are equitable in their distribution of satisfiers but still do not promote a high quality of life. This is seen in advanced industrial societies where most satisfiers are distributed in the same way and in much the same amounts for the mass of persons. Yet different persons need different satisfiers to meet the same need. A uniformity of satisfiers implies a uniformity of wishes, which is not true.

In eutopic societies, it is the satisfaction of needs that is equitable. There each person receives the particular satisfiers that he or she uniquely needs, and everyone reaches their personal goals in such a way as to reinforce the goals of the society as a whole; there is an ecological or synergistic relationship between persons and with the environment. This requires free access to the necessary satisfiers at all three levels of basic human need (psychosomatic, psychosocial, and extra-human or environmental) and open participation at all levels of communal decision-making. A high quality of life is attained when all these relationships work together.

Third, to reach the deep roots of our ethical beliefs we must develop a new education and a new science to nurture it. It must be recognized that:

- there cannot be an environmental study without an interrelated social study — social and natural sciences cannot be separated;
- the vital facts are processes and not static relationships — study of the historical components of human and natural systems should be reciprocal;
- Scientific work also requires social work that promotes good human–environment relations;
- Social-environmental work is with the people, and not for the people.

This direction rejects one-way techniques which in the past have been mostly sustained by scientists and technicians who 'tell' the common people what must be done. It recovers co-participative work. The objective is to share with common people perceptions and knowledge of the world, and recognize their problems, which most of the time are not identical with scientific inquiry. Present day dialogue between local communities and technicians is poor, the former being mere recipients of information by the latter. This must be changed to shared participative research where all learn.

Modern development is entangled in an ideological web. Not only environmentalists, but other social thinkers as well, have protested the dominant cultural ideology. The guidelines offered here for a moral vision of sustainable development should help further expose this underlying ideology. But once we acknowledge that this is the situation, we can no longer hope to produce a new kind of development by responding to issues on a fragmented basis. We must go back to the roots of the ideology and produce a new one. This is possible only through a deeper ethical analysis — a deep ethics — that can give birth to such new thinking.

I contrast deep ethics to present day ethics, which seems more a consequence of the dominant ideology than a challenge to it, and is largely irrelevant to science, economics, and politics. If deep ethics were the primary source of thinking and action, development would be conceived as a process of continued satisfaction of human needs at all levels. Before any action, we would ask ourselves how this act would affect ourselves, other humans, and other living beings. Deep ethics requires a new paradigm of freedom and calls for a new model of development. As a fundamental, inclusive ethical concept, freedom is not only a personal reality, something achieved by the individual, but also a collective reality. Individual fulfilment is possible only within the context of social fulfilment. But freedom is still more than this, as it also includes an environmental dimension. There can be no true freedom where domination over nature entails the domination of our interior nature and the nature of other human beings. We must face the challenge of responsibly building a new history, one that empowers humans and other living things together.

Notes

1 E. Galeano, *Las venas abiertas de América Latina* (Montevideo: Dpto. Publicaciones, Universidad de la República, 1972).
2 L. Vitale, *Hacia una historia del ambiente en América Latina* (Mexico City: Neuva Sociedad, Nueva Imagen, 1983).
3 Raul Prebisch, *Capitalismo periférico: Crisis y transformación* (Mexico: Fondo Cultura Ecónomica, 1981).
4 A. Pinto, 'Notas sobre estilos de desarrollo en América Latina', *Revista CEPAL* 1 (1978): 97–128.
5 H.C.F. Mansilla, 'Metas de desarrollo y problemas ecológicos en América Latina', *Cuadernos Sociedad Venezolana Planificación* (1981): 150–2.
6 D. Riberio, *Configuraciones histórico-culturales Americanos* (Montevideo: Centro Estudios Latinoamericanos, 1972).
7 International Union for the Conservation of Nature, *World Conservation Strategy* (Gland, Switzerland: IUCN, 1980).
8 A. W. Clausen, *Sustainable Development: The Global Imperative* (Washington, DC: Fairfield Memorial Lecture, 1981).
9 Mansilla, 'Metas de desarrollo y problemas ecológicos en América Latina'.
10 Global Tomorrow Coalition, *Sustainable Development and How to Achieve It* (Washington, DC: Global Tomorrow Coalition 1986), Es-5.
11 M. Max-Neef, *Economía descalza: Señales desde el mundo invisible* (Stockholm: Nordan, 1986).
12 Red Regional de Organizaciones Conservacionistas no Gubernamentales para el desarrollo sostenido de Centro América (REDES), *Declaración de los participantes a la primera Conferencia Centroamericana de Acción Ambiental* (Managua, Nicaragua: REDES, 1987); G. Rodriguez Arana, *La interacción de los sistemas y el deterioro ambiental en Guatemala* (Guatemala: APROFAM, 1986).
13 O. A. Pérez, 'El silencioso dolor de una guerra escandalosa: Efectos de la guerra en el ecosistema salvadoreño', *Nueva Sociedad* Caracas 87 (1987): 139–48.
14 B. Ward and R. Dubos, *Una sola tierra: Informe no oficial encargado por el Secretario General de la Conferencia de las Naciones Unidas sobre el Medio Ambiente Humano* (Mexico City: Fondo Cultura Económica, 1972).
15 Osvaldo Sunkel, 'Introducción: La interacción entre los estilos de desarrrollo y el medio ambiente an América Latina', *Estilos de desarrollo y medio ambiente en la América Latina* 1, Lecturas 36 (Mexico City: Fondo Cultura Económica, 1980): 9–64.
16 G. Schinke, *Ecología politica* (Porto Alegre: Tche!, 1986).
17 I. Sachs, *Ecodesenvolvimento, Crescer sem des fruir* (São Paulo: Vértice, 1986).
18 L. Boff, 'La espiritualidad Franciscana frente al desafio del desequilibrio ecológio',

Vida Espiritual 50 (1976): 50–61; *Saint Francis: A Model of Human Liberation* (New York: Orbis, 1982).

19 J.C.R. de la Peña, *Teología de la creación* (Santander: Sal Terrae Ed., 1986).

20 C. A. Mallmann, *Calidad de vida y desarrollo* (Santiago, Chile: Instituto Chileno de Estudios Humanísticos, 1977); Max-Neef, *Economía descalza*.

21 M. Hopenhayn, 'Las necesidades humanas y la aventura del desarrollo', Dag Hammarskjöld Foundation, FIDE XII and CEPAUR (1985).

12 The hope for just, participatory ecodevelopment in Costa Rica
David A. Crocker

President Oscar Arias has expressed the hope that Costa Rica is on the way to becoming 'the first developed country in Latin America'.[1] But there is much disagreement about what 'development' should mean. Costa Ricans are no longer making development decisions within a generally accepted paradigm. Rather, they are groping for a 'new development path' and debating various proposals for social change. 'The future', says social analyst Manual Rojas Bolaños, 'is being decided today.'[2]

My aim in this chapter is to articulate and defend the ethical principles of a model of development that is emerging in Costa Rica. This model, which can be called 'just, participatory ecodevelopment', gives highest priority not to economic growth as such, or even to 'growth with equity', but to a sustainable development whose fundamental values are the satisfaction of basic human needs, participatory democracy, environmental respect, and equal opportunity for personal development.

This alternative development paradigm, while also anticipated elsewhere, is not an alien import to Costa Rica. Some of its elements have already been articulated intellectually and realized institutionally in this small Central American country. Costa Rican philosophers Luis Comacho, Manuel Formoso, and E. Roy Ramírez have been treating ethical issues in Costa Rican development.[3] Theoretical work on Costa Rican development that points in the direction of my approach is being done by economists Helio Fallas and Leonardo Garnier, sociologist Luis Vega Carballo, conservationists Gerardo Budowski and Alvaro Umaña, columnist and labour expert Francisco Morales, and Manuel Rojas Bolaños and others at Centro de Estudios para la Acción Social (CEPAS).[4]

The sort of 'participatory democracy' that I advocate is approximated by some aspects of the cooperative, self-management (*autogestión*), comanagement (*cogestión*), and solidarity (*solidarismo*) movements. Innovative and promising development ideas and practices are occurring in some of the projects funded by the Costa Rican government, the United States Agency for International Development (USAID), the Interamerican Foundation, the Canadian-Costa Rican Housing Corporation, and the European Economic Community. Especially noteworthy in this regard are the New Alchemy Group in Talamanca, the community of Estrella de Guarco, and the 'Experimental Workshop for Alternative Agricultural Production and Commercialization' (Teproca-Cot).

Prevailing theoretical and institutional structures, however, have limited the systematic expression, let alone the full practical implementation, of this vision of 'just, participatory ecodevelopment'. By explicitly clarifying and defending this perspective, I hope to contribute to its presentation as a compelling alternative for Costa Rica's future.

The current options

The worn out model

The development style that largely structured Costa Rican life and thought from 1948 to 1980 is a 'growth and equity' model.[5] In this model, implemented by the Partido Liberación Nacional (PLN), development is conceived as occurring if everyone materially benefits and the gap between the haves and have-nots does not widen. The PLN also advocated an 'interventionist' or 'benefactor' state. In order to avoid external dependency, the state intervened in the economy to promote import substitution, some diversification in both agriculture and industry, and regional trade. In order to raise income as a means both to strengthen the domestic market and to secure 'social peace', the government implemented various social measures such as social security and health care. Helped by Costa Rica's abolition of its army in 1948, this model accomplished much, but today it is rejected by almost everyone. It was the economic crisis of 1980–82 that revealed serious *structural* problems. The country was wracked by a precipitous decline in production, devaluation of the colón, triple-digit inflation, high unemployment and underemployment, huge international indebtedness, poor balance of payments (coffee prices dropped and oil prices doubled), a new dependence on foreign investment and technology, and a swelling, notoriously inefficient bureaucracy that employed a third of the labour force. While the old style is being condemned as worn out (*agotado*), different analysts describe the nature, causes and solution of the *agotamiento* in different ways. The two most important current alternatives are free market liberalism and a renovated social-democratic paradigm.

Free market liberalism

The leading candidate to replace the traditional model is free market liberalism or neoliberalism. This outlook is enormously powerful and popular in Costa Rica today. It is on the offensive, setting the terms of the development debate, and forcing other positions onto the defensive. A comprehensive economic-social-political paradigm for development, Costa Rican liberalism is a return to classical, free market liberalism and a democratic state with a minimal role to play. It is not to be confused with Keynesian, New Deal, or welfare liberalism. The central development goal of Costa Rican liberalism is economic growth to be generated and distributed by a free market. Its normative foundation is an antipaternalistic conception of human work and free activity. An interventionist or 'impresarial' (managerial) state is rejected in favour of private entrepreneurial activity and minimal state involvement in economic life, with resources allocated by a market that respects consumer sovereignty and property rights. It is assumed that the economic growth produced by this 'economic liberty' will finally trickle down so as to benefit everyone.

The source of all evil, and certainly of the crisis of 1980, is seen to be the bloated, corrupt, protectionist, and interventionist state. The source of all good is a free market peopled by risk-taking, energetic entrepreneurs seeking their own material gain. An immediate goal is the privatization of Costa Rican society, especially of state enterprises such as the Costa Rican Development Corporation (CODESA), in which the *agotado* model climaxed in the late 1970s. 'Democracy', as Bolaños puts it, 'is reduced to the existence of a complex of more or less formal rules for the election of leaders', and its defence is 'equated with the defence of free market values'.[6]

Liberalism has numerous exponents. It dominates the opposition party, the Partido de Unidad Social Cristiano (PUSC), but also has representatives in the party in power, the PLN. Aided by a Costa Rican press that accentuates the difference between 'Marxist-Leninist' Nicaragua and democratic Costa Rica, free market liberals have succeeded in 'shifting clearly to the right . . . the ideological spectrum of Costa Rican economic policy'.[7] In this, they are reinforced by ideological tendencies within USAID the World Bank, and the International Monetary Fund.

Updated social democracy

Although liberalism sets the terms of the Costa Rican debate, this does not mean that social democracy is dead. Factions in both of the leading political parties are attempting to update the traditional Costa Rican social-democratic 'growth with equity' model. Representative advocates are Germán Serrano Pinto of the PUSC and Ennio Rodríguez Céspades of the PLN.[8]

While granting the market an important role, the new social democrats have struggled to renovate the idea of an interventionist state that selectively stimulates export-led production and ensures that the gap between rich and poor does not widen. Aware that the traditional social-democratic model favoured the middle classes at the expense of the lowest, the new social democrats seek social peace (and political support) by measures such as new houses and jobs designed to ensure that the poor do not lose more ground. Social democrats disagree over the relative weight to give to competition in the international market and to the use of higher wages to stimulate demand for the domestic and/or regional market. But all agree that there should be significant efforts to avoid the social costs of the rapid structural change that liberalism advocates.

Three constraints help explain social-democratic policies, especially in the PLN. First, social democrats are aware that US and international aid comes with free market strings attached. Second, given the liberal climate of Costa Rican opinion, it makes political sense to accept the liberal agenda and come up with alternative answers to the 'size' of the state rather than wrestle with the more fundamental question of 'what is the type of state necessary to confront the challenges of the future'.[9] Third, for social democrats, social problems call more for technical solutions than for ethical reflection. Economic cost-benefit analysis is defended as the instrument by which economic experts can determine social goals. One explanation of this fact is that the advocates of social democracy are often economists whose professional training either absolutizes the value of economic efficiency or makes it difficult to transcend the dogma of value neutrality. In either case, updated social democracy is conceptually hampered from considering fair economic change in relation to good political and social change.

Indeed, the development paradigm of the updated social democrats amounts to a strategy in search of a vision. In comparison with liberalism, social democracy leaves what normative assumptions it does have both unclarified and undefended. Hence, it lacks the power of a more comprehensive and inspiring outlook. Moreover, for some Costa Ricans the accomplishments and implicit ideals of social democracy are 'insufficient' due to continuing poverty, inequality of power, and external dependency.

Brazilian theorist Roberto Unger criticizes the political and economic assumptions of social democracy and argues that 'a detailed alternative to social democracy', a 'radical project', is both feasible and morally desirable. What is more, not only must we 'be realists in order to become visionaries', but, 'our normative commitments' and new vision must help us understand what is really possible.[10] It is to the ethical principles of such an alternative model that we now turn.

Just, participatory ecodevelopment

At least four fundamental normative principles inform just, participatory ecodevelopment: the satisfaction of basic human needs; democratic self-determination; environmental respect; and the equal opportunity for personal self-realization.

Satisfaction of basic human needs

A developed society should be conceived as a society in which the majority of individuals can satisfy their basic needs. If one has insufficient or very low quality air, water, food, clothing, shelter, education, or medical care, one cannot realize one's higher capacities. This is the *moral minimum* of defensible development ethics. Success and failure of development policies, programmes, and projects must be judged by how well they solve such basic-needs problems as hunger, malnutrition, illiteracy, infant mortality, disease, and housing.

A crucial difference exists between filling basic human needs and satisfying mere human preferences. This difference is decisive because it helps distinguish the perspective advocated here from both liberalism and social democracy. In liberalism, trickle-down growth is the fundamental goal: development occurs if most people experience an increase in real income, whether or not basic needs are satisfied. A free market and minimal state allegedly will benefit everyone in this way. Higher income allegedly enables everyone to satisfy better his or her preferences, *whatever they are*. Crucial tenets of liberalism include that a person is the best judge of his or her own needs; that no preferences are intrinsically better than others; and that state power never should be used to impose the preferences of some on others.

A damaging defect of liberalism is that some of the things people want — things that satisfy their preferences and on which they spend their income — do not contribute to their human development and may bring them great harm. Liberals are right (within limits) in their antipaternalism. A free society should not prescribe what adults should prefer. But antipaternalism runs amok when it ignores the crucial moral difference between *basic* needs and other sorts of needs and wants. The liberal's moral neutrality towards all preferences (consumer sovereignty) prevents him or her from distinguishing in principle the rich person's preference for a Mercedes from the poor child's preference for food that will save it from starvation or brain-damaging malnutrition. Liberalism can only make a distinction based on monetary costs and benefits, with the likely result that the preference for the Mercedes comes out ahead.

A basic-needs approach to development yields different sorts of policy than occur in either a trickle-down or equitable economic growth paradigm. Ends are not neutral; they engender or are associated with appropriate means. While trickle-down liberalism stresses the highest market rates of return with no direct regard for equity or basic needs, the equitable growth perspective of the PLN and the new social democrats, is characterized by policies designed not only to achieve economic growth but also to ensure that everyone benefits. Consequently, there is a focus on income generation, the distribution of productive assets (governmental titling of land to squatters), investment in human capital (public education), and better access to resources (credit programmes for small businessmen and farmers).

In contrast to both of these, the basic-needs perspective explicitly targets groups and individuals who suffer basic-needs deprivation. The results are policies designed directly to satisfy these needs, for example, housing, primary education, and basic health care in the poorest sections, food crops for the poor rather than dessert crops for the rich. Basic-needs policies are morally superior to liberal policies because persons presently suffering are not sacrificed for a trickle-down pay-off that may or may not occur sometime in the future. Basic-needs policies are morally more basic than equitable growth, for to exist above the subsistence line is more urgent, morally speaking, than the gap between rich and poor.

When we look at Costa Rica from a basic-needs perspective, we are distressed by how many people remain in absolute poverty. Frequent protest marches and demonstrations are held in the streets of San José by poor farmers who challenge the government's new agricultural strategy, 'the agriculture of change'. This policy aims to 'modernize' Costa Rican agriculture by giving priority to 'efficient' agro-exporters rather than 'inefficient' producers of basic grains. According to CEPAS, the result of this strategy is that 'the impoverishment of the small farmers has accelerated', since they 'have not been able to finance technological innovations on their plots'.[11] State institutions that formally helped poor farmers, such as the Institute of Agrarian Development (IDA), are victims of the liberal reorientation of Costa Rican social democracy. In addition, CEPAS submits strong evidence that a 'sanitation chaos' besets Costa Rica and significantly contributes to lower class deprivation.[12]

With respect to these facts, some remarks are in order. To implement the basic-needs paradigm we need to be able to indicate the number and proportion of those who fall below the lines for survival and a decent minimum standard. Per capita GNP and other aggregate measures such as life expectancy and potable water are not sufficient; for a country can be doing very well on such measures at the same time as increasing numbers and proportions of people are unable to satisfy their basic needs. Also, it very well may be the case that the most efficient way to achieve either trickle-down or equitable economic growth is to adopt a basic-needs perspective as a means or strategy. Perhaps Costa Ricans are more likely as a whole to improve materially and/or the gap between the rich and poor is less likely to widen if the basic needs of the worst-off are targeted and satisfied.

Two more general remarks conclude this treatment of the basic-needs development principle. First, this principle is an integral component in a comprehensive theory of social justice.[13] Social justice requires a social floor in which everyone is socially guaranteed adequate opportunity for the satisfaction of basic needs. A comprehensive theory of justice also includes other elements, for example, a ceiling on income and wealth, set so as to reduce exploitation of the least advantaged by the dominant classes.

Second, the present vision avoids the market/state dichotomy. Because different means work best in different circumstances, this approach assumes that the most effective means for filling basic needs will be efforts that creatively surmount such disjunctions. We must avoid neoliberalism's uncritical and utopian commitment to the market as well as social democracy's assumption that the interventionistic state will always save us. We must not only seek a balance between state and market; we must also invent institutions that do not fit either conception. One of these will be democratically owned and controlled productive enterprises competing in the market.

Democratic self-determination

Free market liberals are correct in advocating liberty. They are wrong in misunderstanding its nature. Liberty is not just an absence of state coercion and constraint; it is also choice and action in the presence of an abundance of real possibilities. Freedom is decreased not only by bayonets, but also by lack of food, employment, and education. Freedom is enlarged when basic needs are met. Consequently, freedom as self-determination requires the satisfaction of basic needs.

Freedom, however, involves something more. It is the right and responsibility of groups as well as individuals to determine their own affairs. Domination happens when some individuals or social groups control the options and make the decisions for others. The 'formally' free contract — a contract signed for meager wages by a poor economic agent with little or no choice — masks real social coercion based on radically unequal bargaining power. This point suggests that a development philosophy needs to add an ethical principle of self-determination. A society is not developed if basic needs are satisfied but people have little freedom of choice and action.

It is good that individuals and groups make their own decisions. Not only are domination and coercion evil, but free decisions realize some of our highest capacities. To have a say is to have the right to complain about the bad and forge the good in our life together. A top-down development philosophy, one in which the experts, whether local, national, or foreign, make the decisions for the recipient, is undesirable. One version occurs when the recipients of development assistance receive that assistance with strings attached. However, we must be careful here because the commitment to self-determination has to be balanced with a basic-needs approach. If attaching some strings to a development proposal can promote basic-needs satisfaction for hitherto neglected groups, such as women or the rural poor, a good reason exists to do so. If a floor of social security requires a ceiling on income, it is justifiable to reduce the freedom of a few to fill the basic needs (and enlarge the freedom) of the many. Consequently, the moral weight of basic needs requires some limitation on freedom. Likewise, our basic-needs principle must be complemented by the principle of self-determination. One reason for this is that basic needs are more likely to be filled in the long run when people, especially the poor, have an essential role in forming the policies that affect them. Another reason is that it is better to be an active, choosing agent than a passive, dominated recipient.

Two implications of the self-determination principle should be spelled out. Authentic development occurs only when the members of the community, region, or nation in question *have* — and do not merely *feel* that they have — an effective say about the basic policies that govern them. A developed society is one in which individuals and groups participate in determining their fundamental ends and means.

Too many decisions in Costa Rica are made by a largely impersonal central government or an even less personal market. Relatively high political participation does occur in Costa Rica if measured by such things as voting percentages (85 per cent), party membership, and political parades.[14] But neither the state nor the market distributes much social power to the poorest of the poor. What is needed is a third sector of democratically self-determining associations that enter into 'scaled-up' relations with each other and interact with, and eventually transform, both the market and the state. Of relevance here is the vision of a self-governing society composed of a 'Chinese box' network of self-managing communities grounded in basic units where individuals live and work.[15] Some popular Costa Rican movements — for example, those of cooperatives, the Sector de Economía Laboral (SEL), solidarity (*solidarismo*), self-management (*autogestión*), and comanagement (*cogestón* are taking theoretical or institutional steps in this direction. These steps, however, are faltering due to a lack of coherent vision and an inability both to compete in the market and contribute to state policy formation. Without congenial or at least non-hostile governmental and economic environments, promising grassroots projects and communities often fail; and showcase projects succeed but contribute to the deterioration of neighbouring communities.

A second implication of self-determination concerns 'economic democracy'. For Costa Ricans, 'economic democracy' often means either equitable growth or more equitable distribution of property: it is a frequent litany that there should be 'more owners (*proprietarios*) and fewer workers (*trabajadores*)'. The implication of democratic self-determination is somewhat different. It means that workers or farmers *own* and, thereby, *democratically control* their cooperative enterprises. Gone is the implicit domination involved in the owner–worker, leader–follower relation. Present are communities in which adult individuals have relatively equal decision-making power and participate together in satisfying their basic needs, producing and marketing goods and services. This *social* property is neither private nor statist. Ideally self-managing groups interact with both market and state without being dominated by either. They could transform Costa Rica's largely centralized and representative democracy into a more decentralized and participatory democracy.

Respect for nature

It is not enough to have a development philosophy that gives priority to basic human needs and the self-determination of human individuals and groups, since people and their communities are part of a natural world to which they owe respect. Hence, a third development principle enjoins us to respect the stability, diversity, integrity, and beauty of the natural world and to live harmoniously with it.

It must be stressed that Costa Rica has made exemplary strides in conservation. The Arias administration, led by Alvaro Umaña, Minister of Natural Resources, Energy, and Mines, has adopted the goal of 'sustainable development'. In the last few years Costa Rica has set up national parks and forest preserves on more than 20 per cent of the country's land. In 1987, President Arias signed a long-awaited Forestry Emergency Decree designed to halt the current deforestation in Costa Rica as well as establish a rational forest and land-use policy for the country. In 1988, Costa Rica followed Bolivia in agreeing to a 'debt-for-nature' swap. Conservation International, the World Wildlife Fund, and the Nature Conservancy are purchasing at a discount a portion of Costa Rica's huge $4 billion indebtedness to private banks. With the money generated, private Costa Rican conservation organizations are engaged in land acquisition, park management, and educational programmes.

But Costa Rica's environmental problems remain enormous. Deforestation outstrips reforestation and conservation. It is estimated that by 1995 Costa Rica will run out of hardwoods, and by 2000 it will have no wildlands outside its parks. The Costa Rican National Parks Service has an inadequate budget, low morale, and remains suspect in the eyes of local communities who see parks as preserves for rich urbanites and foreigners.[16]

Moreover, the currently popular Costa Rican development models all uncritically assume that accelerated economic growth is worthwhile and that an exploitative use of the environment is a means to the good life North American style. As the Bolivian H.C.F. Mansilla argues in relation to Latin America and the entire Third World, informing development models, whether conservative, social-democratic, or socialist, is a 'conviction of progress based on material terms and centered around a concept of accelerated growth . . . growth is infinitely better than stagnation, the new better than the old, the fast preferable to the slow'.[17] What is needed is a new model that integrates the right kind of development and the right kind of conservation. At stake is the viability not only of the Third World but also of the whole world.

The principle of 'respect for nature' will help us articulate a moral vision of 'sustainable development' or 'ecodevelopment' for Costa Rica and other nations. Respect for nature enjoins us to appreciate, conserve, and use nature with restraint. One reason, of course, for this moral imperative is that continual exploitation of nature in the service of economic growth and high consumption most probably will mean human misery when our limited planetary resources are depleted. In the interest of meeting the basic human needs and respecting the self-determination of future generations, we should limit our material needs, and refrain from environmental degradation and depletion of non-renewable resources.

But a less anthropocentric and more 'ecocentric' basis for ecological respect is also possible. We need to approach nature not just as a resource to be used by future generations, but also as an object of our respect. As integral parts of the evolving and surrounding natural world, humans and their various communities owe their existence and their well-being to this natural matrix. Nature and natural places are not enemies to be conquered or objects to be merely dominated. They are our home, the context in which we live and move and have our being. As such, we owe respect based on a debt of gratitude.

To respect nature is not to prevent humans from using and enjoying it. To respect Costa Rica's tropical forests of Monteverde, Santa Rosa, and Tortuguero is not to remove them from human interaction; nor is it to restrict them to the use of foreign scientists, tourists, and rich tarpon fishermen. Respect for nature means a variety of limited, restrained, frugal uses. It also means the conservation and promotion of biotic diversity, stability, integrity, and beauty.[18] Sometimes this can be accomplished best through selective and prudent human intervention.

Conflict of moral principles

Sometimes there are direct and disturbing conflicts between respect for nature and other ethical principles. To prohibit the killing of turtles and the taking of their eggs is to eliminate one source of livelihood and basic-needs satisfaction for the turtle hunters and their families along Costa Rica's coasts. To limit, let alone call a halt to, Costa Rica's incredible rate of deforestation is to destroy one source of profit for small farmers as well as large cattle ranchers. To expand the Corcovado National Park, the Costa Rican government in March 1986 forcibly expelled hundreds of gold panners (*oreros*) who for years had been living in and working on the new park lands. When people directly affected in such situations have their say, they often choose short-term economic gain instead of environmental preservation. So respect for nature can, and sometimes does, clash with individual and communal self-determination as well as with basic-needs satisfaction.

While we should not expect to eliminate conflict in moral principles altogether, it is possible to avoid or reduce conflict in various ways. One way to avoid the conflict between 'respect for nature' and our other two development principles is to weigh the moral considerations in each situation and judge where the most moral weight lies. Establishing a national park that preserves enormous species diversity at the cost of relocating very few persons clearly means that respect for nature trumps our other two principles. But our moral intuitions go in the opposite direction when selective 'harvesting' of forest trees will enable other flora to flourish, not weaken the ecosystem, and generate capital for establishing tropical nurseries that in turn will contribute to both basic-needs satisfaction and reforestation.

We have to avoid the view that there is always what Unger calls the 'tragedy of incompatible ideals'.[19] Many cases exist in which environmental destruction and social injustice either cause each other or are brought about by a common third factor. For example, it is arguable that the following are among the causes of the environmentally devastating clearing and farming of Costa Rican tropical forests and steep mountain land: an unjust land tenure system; an unjust distribution of burdens on the lowest classes during the 1980–2 economic crisis; and government agricultural policies that favour large farmers.[20] Deprived of environmentally respectful modes of access to land and credit, small farmers are forced to farm in ways that contribute to Costa Rica's environmental crisis. Social injustice causes environmental injustice. Likewise, environmental injustice can promote social injustice when the export of exotic woods to international markets makes Costa Rica unfairly vulnerable to international price fluctuations.

Sometimes the imperatives to respect nature, satisfy basic needs, and participate in self-government point in the same direction. Establishing a more just system of land tenure, pricing, credit, and technical assistance for small and poor farmers could reduce deforestation and environmentally unsound farming practices, as well as be a source of basic-needs satisfaction and communal self-determination. Santa Rosa National Park rightly prides itself on integrating the restoration of its dry tropical forest with the education and employment of local residents as 'eco-tour' guides, foresters, educators, and researchers. A proposed Peace Park on the Costa Rican–Nicaraguan border can protect the fragile regional peace as well as an endangered tropical ecosystem.

The general point is that governments and other development agencies can and should seek ways simultaneously to fulfil all of the requirements of ecodevelopment ethics. It is not that the struggle for social justice and the struggle for ecological integrity are always complementary but that we are morally obliged to make them so when possible. This, of course, is easier said than done, for such comprehensive solutions often require resources or commitment that are in short supply. However, as Unger argues, 'the conception of a tragedy of ultimate values drastically understates the transformability of society through politics', and implies 'an arbitrary limit upon collective experiments in the forms of common life'.[21]

Both respect for nature and the imperative to satisfy basic human needs are based on the injunction not to dominate or degrade life. The attitude of respect for human and cultural diversity nurtures and is nurtured by respect for environmental and ecological diversity. Our ethical injunctions and our psychological attitudes can and should cohere. One crucial and often neglected link between conservation and development are human beings cognizant of the important facts, informed by right values, and moved by appropriate attitudes.

Most fundamentally, we need to avoid the nature/human dichotomy just as we need to circumvent the market/state disjunction. We can do this by recognizing that people live in mixed, natural-social systems. The Bribri Indians of Talamanca, who live in harmonious interaction with their natural surroundings, successfully model such a system. Respect for the stability, diversity, integrity, and beauty of their tropical forest home requires, and is required by, respect for the cultural identity and attractiveness of the Bribris themselves. Part of what we learn from them is precisely their love for, and restrained use of, their environment.[22] Like so many of our dichotomies, the nature/human dichotomy, when absolutized, does more harm than good. Our ethical choices are usually between different sorts of 'mixed' natural-social community, and we should look for the best ways to practise a 'mixed management' that combines both human and environmental concerns.

With the 'respect for nature' principle added to our earlier two principles, we can identify steps to get from the present Costa Rican environment-development impasse to a future of authentic sustainable development. Among these means would be development projects such as the New Alchemy Group in Talamanca, Teproca-Cot on the side of Irazú Volcano, and Santa Rosa National Park in Guanacaste. In all three projects we find communities practising democratic self-management, environmental respect, cultural restoration, and generating income that contributes to basic-needs satisfaction. The first project emphasizes tropical nurseries (*viveros*). The second practices organic farming and commercial weaving with local materials. The third, which has had a significant impact on Costa Rica's commitment to sustainable development, generates local income through the restoration and conservation of a dry tropical forest.

In addition to formulating and evaluating micro projects and national policy, our principles help systematize and articulate an alternative ecodevelopment vision. One function of development ethics is to provide an inspiring long-term focus for our often frustrating short-term and middle-term labours.

The real opportunity for personal development

If the basic-needs principle provides a foundation for individual self-realization or growth, our fourth principle, personal development, provides the scaffolding. A developed society guarantees the basic-needs satisfaction of all its members. A developed society also provides all its members — regardless of race, religion, gender, wealth, or age — with real opportunities to actualize the best that is within them. It provides enabling conditions and not just legal permissibility. A developed society, however, does not and cannot *guarantee* that all its members will reach maximal human achievement. But a developed society *can* provide the means and the non-coercive encouragement for its members to develop as far and as fast as they can. A developing society, such as Costa Rica, has the responsibility to allocate some human and material resources to this development goal as well as to the previous three. Costa Rica's generally excellent educational system which, however, increasingly excludes the poorest of the poor, could be a major vehicle for human growth.

What is the content of this ideal of human development? It can be summed up by the ancient Greek ideal of *praxis*, partially translated as 'free, productive activity'.[23] Praxis can occur in one's work, although unfortunately much modern work is coercive antipraxis. It can also occur in artistic, athletic, and scientific activity — be it professional or leisure. Praxis can occur at home, in loving and child-rearing, as well as in the public space of communal and political activity. Costa Rican liberals are right in emphasizing human activity and work. They misunderstand both due to liberalism's atomism and its notion of freedom as simply absence of constraint.

Praxis occurs if and only if we engage in activity that realizes our highest capacities. Among these capacities are intentionality, self-determination, creativity, solidarity, and rationality.

We act intentionally when we act on purpose and for a purpose instead of being the pawns of accident, necessity, or blind habit. Freedom as self-determination occurs when we choose from an array of genuine alternatives with respect to our action or our character. We are creative when we act in ways that are both original and aesthetically pleasing. We realize our capacity for solidarity when we deliberate together, promote the general interest, and act in concert for common goals. Praxis is rational in the sense that it is informed by traditional wisdom as well as scientific understanding, selects feasible ends given existing means, chooses the best means for given ends, and justifies certain goals as best. Crucial to rational action is critical thinking in the context of ongoing communal dialogue.

A truly developed society does not just permit people to live lives of *praxis*. It provides them with the necessary means, especially education, to pursue this good life. It does so because *praxis* is good in itself, and because the person who engages in praxis will strive to realize our other three ethical principles: basic-needs satisfaction, the precondition for praxis; democratic self-determination, one social manifestation of praxis; and respect for nature, the rational recognition of our role in the natural-social community. A society that is conducive to the realization of praxis, then, will also tend to be a society of just, participative ecodevelopment.

While he does not use the term 'praxis', H.C.F. Mansilla articulates a Latin American development vision that combines a personal ideal similar to praxis with the social ideals of 'just, participatory ecodevelopment':

Explicitly contraposed to the majority of contemporary theories of development, the critical theory of modernization . . . [embraces] the values and dimensions that belong to the sphere of goals, properly designated, and of a rationality that transcends instrumentalism: effective political participation, critical conciousness with respect to public problems, individual power-free happiness, culture without ideology, communal life without bureaucracy, well-being free of luxury and obsession with grandeur, conservation of nature, sustainable equilibrium of various ecosystems of our biosphere, and the progress of liberty in the framework of individual autonomy.[24]

Much needs to be done to define just, participatory ecodevelopment. We need to show in detail how its principles emerge from criticism of the assumptions of other Costa Rican development options. We also need to reflect more on which principles should take precedence in situations where all cannot be satisfied. Moreover, it is important to generate from this abstract, philosophical vision a concrete model for Costa Rican development. Such a model will include both macro- and micro-development policies and institutions, such as tax structure, agricultural policy, external indebtedness, balance of payments, dependence on external aid, and regional relations, including regional peace. Authentic development in Costa Rica will require a certain kind of regional, hemispheric, and even global development. Finally, we need to show how this model is feasible in the long run and explore more fully the transformative practice relevant for its implementation. Philosophical clarification, criticism, and invention is both one task of development ethics and a necessary condition for Costa Rica to find a development path that is just and good as well as new.

It is appropriate to close with some remarks by Manuel Formosa, a Costa Rican thinker whose ideals of personal and social development have influenced this vision:

The only alternative that it is possible to set forth, even though it concerns the long run, has to be that of radical change that enables us to establish the basis for our life together not in competition but in mutual aid, not in the profit motive but in solidarity, in living not in order to have something but in order to be something. Never before has humanity been so close to the power to do it, given the productivity that work has achieved. For this reason, we cannot abandon now the ideals that enable us to live in full democracy with social justice, equality with liberty. It is clear that the revolution will not be made simply by thinking about it. Yet undoubtedly we must begin by restating the things that are important. For unless we do so, we will never reach them.[25]

Notes

1 Oscar Arias Sánchez, 'Mensaje presidencial', *La Nación* (May 1987): 7A.
2 Manual Rojas Bolaños, 'Ocho tesis sobre la realidad nacional', in Edelberto Torres Rivas *et al.*, *Costa Rica: Crisis y Desafíos* eds, (San José, Costa Rica: DEI, 1987), 27.
3 Luis Camacho, 'Ciencia, tecnología y desarrollo desde el punto de vista de los derechos humanos' in E. Roy Ramíriz, ed., *Ciencia, Responsabilidad y Valores* (Cartage: Editorial Tecnología de Costa Rica, 1985), 25–38; Manuel Formoso, 'La alternativa: repensar la revolución', *Seminario Universidad* (October 1987): 5; and E. Roy Ramírez, 'Desarrollo y ética', *Revista Comunicación* 2, 2 (1986): 22–5.
4 Helio Fallas Venegas, 'Crisis económica y transformación social en Costa Rica' in Jorge Rovira Mas, ed., *Costa Rica hoy: la crisis y sus perspectivas* (San José: Editorial Universidad Estatal a Distancia, 1984), 57–81; Helio Fallas Vanegas, *Crisis económica en Costa Rica* (San José: Editorial Nueva Decada, 1981); Leonardo Garnier, 'Crisis, desarrollo y democracia en Costa Rica' in Edelberto Tores Rivas *et al.*, eds, *Costa Rica: Crisis y Desafíos* (San José: DEI, 1987); José Luís Vega Carballo, *Hacia una Interpretación del Desarrollo Costarricense: Ensayo Sociológico*, 5th edn (San José: Editorial Provenir, 1986), 381–433; Gerardo Budowski, 'Conservation and the Future Environment of Mankind' in *Ökologie und Lebensschutz in internationaler Sicht* (Freiburg: Rombach, 1975), 439–51; William McLarney, 'An Interview with Alvaro Umaña', *Amicus Journal* 10 (1988): 39–41; Francisco Morales Hernández, 'Hacia un sector de economía laboral en Costa Rica

— S.E. L.', paper presented to the ICASIS-CRIES conference: 'Crisis y opciones en Centroamérica', San José, 12–15 May 1986; Manuel Rojas Bolaños, 'Ocho tesis'; and the bimonthly journal of CEPAS, *Costa Rica: Balance de la Situación.*

5 Jerome Segal, *What is Development?*, Center for Philosophy and Public Policy: Working Paper DN-1 (October 1986): 10–27. For the interpretation of Costa Rica, see Jorge Rovira Mas, *Estado y política económica en Costa Rica 1948–1970* 2nd. ed. (San José, Costa Rica: 1983) and *Costa Rica en los años 80* (San José, Costa Rica: Editorial Porvenir, 1987).

6 Rojas Bolaños, 'Ocho tesis', 25.

7 Garnier, 'Crisis, desarrollo y democracia', 37.

8 Germán Serrano Pinto, 'La dimensión social del trabajo y la redistribución de la riqueza en el modelo social cristiano', *Fragua del pensamiento Social Cristiano* 3 (November 1986): 5–7; Ennio Rodrígrez Céspedes, '¿Ocaso del intervencionismo en Costa Rica?', *Revista de Ciencias Sociales* 24 (October 1982): 7–18.

9 Garnier, 'Crisis, desarrollo y democracia', 37.

10 Roberto Mangabeira Unger, *Social Theory: Its Situation and Task* (Cambridge: Cambridge University Press, 1987), 15.

11 CEPAS, *Costa Rica: Balance de la Situación* 22 (August–October, 1987): 10.

12 Ibid., 20.

13 David Crocker, *Praxis and Democratic Socialism: The Critical Social Theory of Marković and Stojanović* (Atlantic Highlands, New Jersey: Humanistic Press, 1983), 256–73.

14 Mitchell Seligson, 'Development and Participation in Costa Rica: The Impact of Context' in John A. Booth and Mitchell Soligson, eds, *Political Participation in Latin America, Citizen and State* I (New York: Holmes and Meier Publishers, 1978), 144–5.

15 Branko Horvat, ed., *Self-Managing Socialism* (New York: International Arts and Sciences Press, 1975).

16 Tessie Whelan, 'A Tree Falls in Central America', *The Amicus Journal* 10 (Fall, 1988): 30.

17 H.C.F. Mansilla, 'Esbozo de una teoría crítica de la modernización: La marcha victoriosa de la racionalidad instrumentalista en América Latina', *Folio Humanística* 24 (April 1986): 275.

18 J. Baird Callicott, 'The Search for an Environmental Ethic', in Tom Regan, ed., *Matters of Life and Death: New Introductory Essays in Moral Philosophy* 2nd edn (New York: Random House, 1986), 381–424.

19 Unger, *Social Theory*, 36.

20 Jorge A. Mora, *Costa Rica: Agricultura de cambio y producción campesina* (Heredia: Universidad Nacional, 1988); Joanne Omang, 'The Hands-on Level of Deforestation', *Smithsonian* 17 (1987): 56–67; and Anabelle Porras and Beatriz Villarreal, *Deforestación en Costa Rica (Implicaciones sociales, económicas y legales)* (San José: Editorial Costa Rica, 1986).

21 Unger, *Social Theory*, 37.

22 Gloria Mayorga, Paula Palmer and Juanita Sanches, *Cuidando los regalos de dios: Testimonios de la reserva indígena Cocles/Kéköldi* (San José: Universidad de Costa Rica, 1988).

23 Mihailo Marković, *From Affluence to Praxis: Philosophy and Social Criticism* (Ann Arbor: University of Michigan Press, 1973).

24 Mansilla, 'Esbozo', 272.

25 Formoso, 'La alternativa', 5.

Africa and the
Middle East

13 Traditional African land ethics
C. K. Omari

Land and natural resources differ considerably between traditional African and other societies. The differences are rooted in cultural and socio-economic relationships and in organizational development. They concern the value that is attached to land, the distribution of and access to land, and the right to use land for individual and community welfare. Such differences influence the human-to-land relation and the ethical issues that stem from it.

Most of the materials presented in this chapter were collected by the author, beginning with initial field work in the late 1960s and early 1970s among the societies of Tanzania.

Ownership rights versus possession rights

Wherever in the world the capitalist mode of production is predominant, ownership of land and access to its natural resources is based on individual rights. These rights are usually stipulated in legal documents which may have resulted from a democratic process or may have been legislated by an elite who happened to control and influence community decisions. Land and its natural resources belong to someone and are commodities. Profit and exploitation of water, forests, minerals, and animals for the benefit of the individual are explicit motives for land ownership. Once one has the right of occupancy, one usually has also the right of access to all the resources therein, although in some states and countries special permission must be obtained in order to exploit natural resources. Real estate and marketing systems are organized, and management skills are developed to enhance this system of economic development.

In Africa today, many states are governed by this mode of land use and management. This is one result of the impact of a money economy on African societies, which has altered considerably the traditional concepts of land use and attitudes towards natural resources. The ethical implications of this change are considerable.

In traditional African societies, there was a difference between 'ownership rights' and 'possession rights'. These two concepts constituted both a legal and social framework for individuals as well as social groups. One aspect could not exist without the other, since both concepts were interwoven in the fabric of the society.

With respect to ownership rights, it was the social group that was considered the owner of the land. This could be a clan, a kinship group, or a family. Every member of the social group had the right to ownership and had an obligation to see that this right was maintained and observed. To have the right of ownership meant a great responsibility for both the individual and the community, because the ultimate owner of the land was God, who is above all human beings. Thus, among the Kikuyu of Kenya, the land, *Githaka*, was owned by *mbari*, a social unit equivalent to a clan. The land was given to them by God.[1] Among the Chagga of northeastern Tanzania, the *kihamba*, a geographical area, was owned by the whole clan. The same was true of the Pare people of northeastern Tanzania with regard to the clan land, or *kithaka*.[2]

The important thing which united all African societies with regard to ownership of land was that land was considered a communal property belonging to both the living and the dead. Those ancestors who had lived on the land belonged to the same social unit which owned and controlled the land, and each individual who used the land felt a communal obligation for its care and administration before passing it to the next generation.

It was the duty of the head of the clan to oversee all matters related to land and its proper use and management. He was to assure that each member of the clan had access to the land. New members were assigned new areas of land where they could settle, build their houses, and raise the crops necessary for their subsistence. It was the responsibility of the new member to look after the farm plot since he had a 'possession right', but ultimate ownership rested with the social group or clan.

In some societies, individuals were allowed temporarily to transfer their piece of land to someone else who was in need. Such transfer was not in the manner of today's transfer of land and properties. No monetary transaction occurred between the owner and the new occupier. The individual was merely exercising his 'possession rights', while the 'ownership right', a community thing, continued to be preserved. Even within this practice, a consultation between the members of the family or clan had to take place before the piece of land was released to someone within or outside it. This was done in part to assure that every member of the group had enough land to cultivate. The obligation to see that each married male had access to the means of production, and that each individual had the right to exercise his freedom within the general structure of approved communal rights and obligations, were ethical considerations in land distribution and ownership.

In most cases a distinction prevailed between the family or clan and the larger community with respect to natural resources. Among the Pare of northeastern Tanzania, the individual family was allowed to exercise a limited authority in relation to ownership and control of farming land, but forests and water sources were controlled communally. Among semi-pastoral and pastoral people like the Maasai, grazing land and water for animals were also controlled communally. Everyone had access to these resources, but the ultimate control and ownership rested with the community. That is why transhumance and nomadism have been common phenomena among pastoralists. For them, grazing land is communal since it was given to the social group by God, who continued to exercise control through his ever-watching eye.[3] When sources of water were owned by the larger society, the village headman, or head of the clan, was in charge of the distribution process. This ensured that each family had access to water for irrigation, which was very important in a subsistence economy.

In the case of forests related to places of worship and initiation rite centres, control was left to the individual clan rather than the whole community. For example, among the Pare of northeastern Tanzania, each clan had its own forest in which its youth were trained and initiated into adulthood. Also, each clan, and sometimes even each lineage, had its own worshipping place which was considered sacred. No other person was allowed to worship in these places except the owners, since they were family- rather than community-based. People were united by their worship at these places, and individuals felt a sense of belonging and identity when they met. They also felt that they were using these places as trustees of a larger transgenerational family.[4] Later, religious centres of this nature became strong political institutions among certain clans, especially after the creation of a centrally-orientated authority among the Pare people.

These forests and shrubs were respected by the whole community. No one was supposed to cut the trees from these areas; it was considered morally wrong to do so. Firewood and building materials were fetched from places other than these sacred places.

Reverence for natural resources

The reverence of Africans towards nature and natural places was a religious attitude and practice which, while it developed around the religious thought and history of a particular social group, indirectly served other social functions in the whole community. In the case of shrines and initiation rite centres, taboos developed around the destruction of trees, shrubs, and the sacred places themselves. The forests, certain kinds of trees, animals, and sources of water were preserved in the name of religion.

Perhaps people did not plan to practise such attitudes in the way a modern person would conserve the forests, but out of their religious beliefs and values and their reverence for sacred public places, an ecological and environmental concern was developed. As a result, in traditional African societies there was a balanced ecosystem; people and nature interacted in such a way that the harmony between them was maintained. These attitudes were stronger when they were attached to the ownership of land through myth. These may have been myths of the origin of the clan, of the place where the ancestors were given power, or of something with special historical meaning to the whole social group. In this way, belief in sacred places served as a common history which united all generations of the same social unit.[5]

In many instances, when people went to worship in sacred places, they were carrying out religious acts for the purpose of preserving harmony and tranquility in the community. They were fulfilling their obligation towards their God by an act of appeasing the ancestors or evil spirits, by praising and giving thanks to God, or by praying for peace and harmony in the community. For this reason, it is difficult for Africans to differentiate between religious and social action. There was always an interaction between the so-called 'religious' and 'secular' worlds, and both were interwoven in the same entity — the community.

The Africans anticipated no change in the future of their communities. The forests and shrubs of their worshipping places were preserved for both present and future generations. It was believed that if one destroyed the holy places, the ancestors would be angry, and as a result some misfortune might befall the community. It was also believed that future generations would face terrible misfortunes if God, who had entrusted these resources to them, was displeased by their misuse or destruction.

To dismiss these religious attitudes and values because they were suited to an underdeveloped, pre-modern world is not to appreciate the community function they served with respect to ecology and natural conservation.

For example, among the Luguru and Zaramo people of eastern Tanzania, there is a myth about Kolelo, a mythical hero believed to possess the power to bring rain. People from these areas worshipped near or in the direction of Morogoro where the Uluguru mountains are and where Kolelo was thought to live. As a result of this belief, the forests around this area and mountain were preserved. This made the area green and beautiful all the time. Streams of water constantly ran down from the mountains. Such reverence, besides being a symbol of unity among the ethnic groups concerned, had an important function among them. Uluguru country is hilly. It enabled the peasants of the hilly Uluguru countryside to grow various types of vegetables and beans in sufficient quantities to feed not only the adjacent Morogoro town but even the city of Dar es Salaam about 125 miles away. Without this forest cover, their fields would have been washed away by soil erosion. Current lumbering practices are a threat to this and other areas.

In traditional African societies, religious taboos and restrictions took the place of aforestation campaigns which are now being waged by governments like that of Tanzania. People knew their responsibilities towards natural resources without being reminded through special campaigns. Positive values towards the use of natural resources were inculcated from generation to generation through songs, proverbs, and stories. Sometimes religious ceremonies or rituals, for example rituals for rain-making, strengthened natural resource values.

Each ethnic group developed its own taboos and restrictions towards animals according to its religious belief system and the values related to its historical development. Certain animals and birds, like the tortoise and python among the Pare people, were considered totems. It was believed that if these animals were killed, children would be caught up by rushes and wounded. Other species were killed only for special purposes. These may have been kinship or lineage totems, or may have been preserved for special purposes. Among the Pare, a kind of forest monkey with white spots (*mbega*) was not supposed to be killed. It was looked upon as a symbol of beauty and religious significance. Its skin was specifically used for the ceremonial caps worn by the chief at public ceremonies, or by the medicine man when performing rituals for the public interest. Since these monkeys were rare in the area, such religious restrictions kept them from being exterminated. Animals like leopards, whose skins were used by the traditional healers, were also protected. Only when such a skin was needed was anyone authorized to hunt and kill a leopard. The killing of certain animals, such as the owl, was believed to be a bad omen. Thus, animal species were preserved for generations as a result of the system of religious values and beliefs.

The impact of a money economy and development

African societies are now undergoing great changes due to the impact of Western value systems, especially as they are embodied in Western economic systems.

A money economy has not only altered social relations among people, but it has also affected people's attitudes towards nature and natural resources. Because of the new values inculcated through Western education and religions like Christianity and Islam, people now see natural resources as objects for exploitation and profit-making. Resources are used for individual private gain and satisfaction. Furthermore, the Western concept of individual achievement through power relationships has undermined the communal decision-making processes which helped communities maintain a balance between available resources and their use by individuals. Instead, decisions about resource use are now based on a bureaucratic and legal system.

Many of the economic activities which seem to threaten the African ecology are done in the name of development. In many cases a foreign multinational company conducts the activities alone; sometimes, it collaborates with the local government or agents. Whether these local governments or agents are aware of the long-term environmental effects on their countries is not always clear. One thing is clear, however: they are lured by the profit they get out of such business, and on the basis of a bureaucratic decision procedure, they allow it. As a result, 'development' has acquired a negative meaning.

The mismanagement of the environment and the imbalance in the ecological system brought about by modern economic and value systems have led to 'environmental bankruptcy' in Africa.[6]

In the name of development — and with foreign investment — about 130,000 square kilometers of Africa's tropical rainforests are lost every year. In Tanzania precious ebony trees (*mpingo*) have been cut wildly and mercilessly, without any consideration for their future use and benefit to the society at large. In Kenya and Tanzania there is a scarcity of charcoal due to the lack of proper trees for making it. Mali, in West Africa, one of the countries worst hit by drought in the 1970s and early 1980s, is facing a critical shortage of fish due to low water levels in the Niger River. The Niger River used to produce 100,000 tons of fish for export annually. Now, major fish processing plants along the river banks have either suspended operations or closed down. The country has been left barren because of commercial deforestation. Climatologists have warned us that due to the environmental disturbance, especially to forests and water sources, rainfall in Africa will remain uncertain for the next ten to twenty years.

Yet, viewed in an ethical context, it is the human who has changed rather than the environment. Value systems which used to help keep balance between humans and the environment are no longer in place; instead, we have value systems controlled and motivated by the greedy accumulation of capital on an individual basis. As a result, even ethical decisions regarding the management of land and natural resources are guided by a production principle and the social principles that emerge from it.

Drought has been with the African people for a long time. What we have witnessed in the 1970s and 1980s is nothing new. In the past however, people knew how to deal with nature and the environment. They knew how to use dams and furrows for irrigation; they knew how to protect forests and water sources through belief systems and value systems attached to places. They acted as custodians of these resources for future generations within the kinship social group.

The introduction of a money economy with its capitalist mode of production, the introduction of religions like Christianity and Islam, and the introduction of state control of natural resources have destroyed the indigenous belief systems to the extent of altering production relations. This affects ethical decisions. The emphasis is no longer on how the community will benefit from the restoration or preservation of the forests and other natural resources, but on what the 'state class' or individual will get through the exploitation of these resources. People have been led to believe in 'modern' civilization and its destructive operations; they have been led to worship money, big business, or state institutions which have profit as their priority. People's loyalties and concern are for these institutions rather than for the community where ecological and environmental issues are of primary concern. Decisions are made at high levels of the state bureaucracy without prior consultation with the local people whose so-called development is at stake.

Thus, because of these new attitudes towards natural resources and their management, people have been persuaded to cut down trees for export to earn foreign exchange which is badly needed by many governments. But this has been done at the expense of the local environment and ecology. Furthermore, what is earned from the sale of these products rarely benefits the local people. An example from Tanzania illustrates this process.

In an effort to modernize agriculture and meet world market demands, the government of Tanzania, with the assistance of the World Bank, started tobacco production in the 1970s among the Nyamwezi people of western Tanzania. The project involved clearing bush areas for cultivation of the crop, which was a crucial feature in Tanzania's capital development and export programme. Since tobacco processing requires firewood, a great number of trees were harvested. This programme of tobacco production among the Nyamwezi was termed 'a success' by some scholars.[7] One wonders, a success on what terms? People from this area were forced to buy food crops as a result of this production system, a phenomenon which had not been observed among the Nyamwezi in the past. Moreover, due to extensive deforestation, the firewood shortage has been a problem in this area ever since.

The impact of religious and political changes

Perhaps we cannot return to the old religious belief systems. Few people in Tanzania profess to be followers of the traditional religious system which shaped their lives and values in the past. It is estimated, for example, that of 22 million people in Tanzania, 44 per cent are Christians, 32.5 per cent are Muslim, and 22.8 per cent are traditionalists. All of these religions influence individuals as well as communities. Moreover, state intervention through the policy of *ujamaa* development has also altered production relations among the people.

The impact of Christianity and Islam has been to shift considerably the attitudes among people of certain African communities away from traditional communal ownership of land and means of production. In Tanzania, in those communities where Islam has been predominant, as in Zanzibar, Pemba, the coast, and the central corridor of the mainland, a feudal mode of production has been admired and practised. The growth and expansion of a plantation economy in Zanzibar and Pemba could not have survived in the nineteenth and early twentieth centuries had it not been for slavery. To this day, on these islands, a successful person is one who has people who work for him or her. Such a person is called a *mwinyi*, a person who has properties and controls others. Along the coast, a successful person is one who has several hundred coconut trees and employs others to work on the coconut farm.

In Tanzania, where the Christian religion has dominated, capitalist tendencies are noticed. In areas like Kilimanjaro, Arusha, Pare, West Lake, and the southern Highlands, individual as well as small family-unit production farms have been emphasized, especially in coffee producing areas. Individual achievement and success, competition and profit making are stressed. People in these areas were buying and selling land before the state intervened in the 1960s.

Then came the state and its policy mechanism, especially the *Arusha Declaration* of 1967.[8] In this policy document, land and the major means of production were nationalized, and thus became the property of the state. No one was supposed to own a large tract of land or exploit laborers. It was also during this time that rural communities called *ujamaa* villages were organized to facilitate social development in the countryside. In 1975, the establishment of the Ujamaa and Village Act 1975 gave these rural social units the power to own and control land and all other natural resources within the village, except if such resources were under the ministry of the central government.

In both the 1967 Arusha Declaration and the 1975 Village Act, the aim was to reemphasize communal ownership of the means of production. Each village was to establish a governing council consisting of twenty-five members elected from among the villagers of the same unit, and from these members five different committees were to be established. One of these committees was to be responsible for the production and distribution of resources. In this way it was ensured that, besides the communal land and ownership of the means of production, every villager had personal access to land and its utilization. Other resources like water, forests, and some minerals were controlled communally. Minerals with foreign export value, like gold, diamonds, coal, and precious stones were controlled by the state.

I have cited Tanzania for examples of land and resource use, and thereby I have illustrated a trend throughout Africa. In the case of Tanzania, reorganization did not satisfactorily return communal control to the villagers. Control by the state *did* bring bureaucracy to the village level. Although the villagers have a measure of control over land and resources, the penetration of state machinery to the village level is obvious. Also, due to reorganization problems and food shortages, in 1983 the Tanzanian government reintroduced the large-scale farming which had been eliminated in 1967. This new direction in ownership and control of land has resulted in the following types of land tenure:

• large forests, national parks, and other designated areas belonging to the state;

- village communal areas — controlled by the villagers as communal social units;
- large-scale farms — individually owned and state-owned away from the village farms;
- individually owned farms — these may be family farms within the village communal land or outside.

In all these, however, the values that operate in relation to land use are more capitalist than communal. Interaction and the exchange of goods centre around profit and market value.

In Tanzania, as in many African countries, the development of land and resources has been guided by the principles of market demand at the village, national, or international level. Villagers no longer cultivate their land for subsistence. Through extension workers, marketing boards and other established economic institutions, the state directs the peasants in what to grow and what not to grow. Land must be used to the maximum so that it produces an export surplus which will bring in profits to help run the state apparatus. Thus, the peasants' traditional values of communal interest are undermined. This is true even at the village level where democratic procedures are supposedly in place. It is the state which decides what to plant and where to sell the products.

The hope of communal solidarity

Sustainable development contradicts the present value system and practices. To take sustainable development seriously would involve programmes which enabled villagers to utilize land and land resources for their and the land's mutual benefit. It would involve local planning and decision-making processes, including decisions regarding what to plant and where to sell the produce. Furthermore, it would mean projects which boosted a community's self-reliance and self-esteem through the better utilization of land and resources for present and future generations.

It is on this level that I think governments and private non-governmental organizations should cooperate to initiate programmes on better land management which are supported by all the people at the village level. Communal solidarity, which is a part of the traditional African value system, should be utilized fully not only for the present generation, but for the future as well.

Traditional religions and Christian and Islamic belief systems ideally teach stewardship and responsibility towards land. Traditional religions and the Christian and Islamic religions include teachings which condemn greedy and selfish attitudes towards land use and management of resources. The concern for others, the concern that all of us are stewards for someone else, should guide us in this issue. For Africans, land belongs to all, living and dead. We will live in this land where our foreparents lived and where our great-great-grandchildren will live. To make sure that all benefit from this wealth, we have to take care of it properly now. This value system cuts across all ethnic groups in Africa.

Wherever we are, the land, its resources, and the environment contribute to our survival. If we destroy them, through bad policies or by sheer greed, we are responsible, and the present and future generations will suffer. We are responsible for what has happened in our society through 'development' and other forms of exploitation of land and resources in the name of the state or the market. We cannot go on without asking ethical questions about our relations to the land. We cannot remain silent without raising the question of who is responsible and what we can do to stop the present destruction.

Notes

1 Jomo Kenyatta, *Facing Mount Kenya* (New York: Vintage Books, 1962).
2 C.K. Omari, *God and Worship among the Pare* (Dar es Salaam: University of East Africa, 1970).
3 Ibid.
4 I.N. Kimambo and C.K. Omari, 'The Development of Religious Thought and Centres among the Pare' in T.O. Ranger and I.N. Kimambo, eds, *Historical Study of African Religion* (London: Heinemann, 1972), 111–35.
5 B.C. Ray, *African Religions: Symbol, Ritual, and Community* (Englewood Cliffs, New Jersey: Prentice Hall, 1976).
6 C.K. Omari, 'The Churches and the Food Question in Africa', Keynote speech, Lutheran World Federation World Service Meeting, Bulawayo, Zimbabwe, 11–16 May, 1986.
7 J. Boesen and A.J. Mohale, *The 'Success Story' of Peasant Production in Tanzania* (Uppsala: Scandinavian Institute of African Studies, 1979).
8 Julius K. Nyerere, *Ujamaa: Essays on Socialism* (Dar es Salaam and Nairobi: Oxford University Press, 1968).

14 Communalism: The moral factor in African development
Jimoh Omo-Fadaka

It is generally agreed that conservation is necessary. So the question 'Why conservation?' is not at issue. Rather, the issue is 'How conservation?' Conservation may be defined as the management of human use of the biosphere so that it may yield the greatest *sustainable* benefit to present generations while maintaining its potential to meet the needs and aspirations of future generations. Conservation and development are mutually dependent activities in the process of improving life for human beings.

Yet, how does one develop a conservation ethic in today's climate of increasing interest in material goods and decreasing interest in spiritual and ethical matters? The answer requires a new problem-solving approach by everyone involved — scientists, governments, and local people.

But how is this change to be brought about within the established political machinery of society? Pundits may agree on a theoretical course of action for legislative and social reform, but their deliberations are meaningless without the support of those affected. And while democracy implies decision-making by the people, it is within the ranks of the establishment that cooperation has to be initiated. That is political reality.

But it is not only politicians, scientists, technicians, ecologists, environmentalists, voluntary agencies, or individuals of good will who will solve this problem, but also poets, priests, philosophers, and artists. For the conservation of nature is above all an ethical matter. Poets, writers, musicians, artists, and religious communities in Africa can contribute to creating a culture that retrieves the communal ethics of African culture. They can help to sharpen the inherent feelings humans have about their place in nature. Only by the development of a conservation ethic or conscience can the political will to solve conservation problems be developed.

The key phrase in developing a conservation ethic is *sustainable development*. No long-term gain accrues to the nation or the people who are victims of a 'trial and error' approach to resource development. Inventory assessment and land capability for sustained use are keys to conservation, as well as keys to rational development. The list of development projects which failed because this kind of assessment was not carried out is a long one. People have suffered tremendous dislocation when these projects faltered.

An appropriate conservation ethic must first be reflected in government development policies. If only a few upper- and middle-class people are reaping most of the benefits of development, it will be difficult to convince the people to have a conservation ethic. If, on the other hand, government policies aim at equitable development and distribution of resources, particularly for the poor majority, then a conservation ethic is possible.

By and large, non-industrial countries possess a conservation ethic within their own cultural setting. Most farmers have positive feelings towards the land; many forest-dwelling people feel themselves to be part of the living forest, each part of which has its own spirit. And most religions contain within them the raw materials of a conservation ethic. These values are usually lost when either a Western free enterprise or a Soviet communist industrial model of development is adopted. They are temporarily thrown out of balance by the temptations of increased consumption of manufactured luxury goods, the so-called 'consumer goods'. Hence, the need for the reactivation and redevelopment of traditional ethics wherever and whenever possible.

For this reason, religious motivations should be brought to bear upon conservation problems. This is vitally important in development, since religions teach us how to sacrifice materially and be rewarded spiritually. While people must not be brainwashed or hoodwinked by religious *hocus-pocus*, the answers to the basic questions lie as much in morality as they do in technology.

Capitalist and Marxist development patterns

The lessons of the First United Nations Development Decade (1961–70) and the Second United Nations Development Decade (1971–80) have shown quite clearly that the adoption of alien patterns of development is not the way to tackle problems as complex and deep-rooted as those faced by many non-industrial countries. The problems confronting non-industrial countries cannot be solved by imitating the capital-intensive technological pattern of free enterprise. Many present-day problems resulting from this type of development took root in the colonial past. This development pattern has failed to solve poverty. In fact, poverty is growing worse.

The Soviet pattern of development is also unlikely to solve the problems of non-industrial nations. Soviet achievements have obvious appeal because of the speed with which the Soviet economy was modernized. During the initial stages of development, Soviet planners faced the same problem of how to modernize a backward peasant economy that African countries face. But there are certain negative aspects of the Soviet experiment.

First, the implementation of Soviet planning has been on authoritarian lines. The forced march towards an industrialized and socialistic society has been characterized by an enforced austerity, a deliberate lowering of living standards while the resources necessary for creating modern industry were being accumulated, and a systemic exploitation of the peasant masses. Second, the rate of growth in the agricultural sector of the Soviet economy has been slow. Soviet agriculture is still poorly managed and its yield rates, after more than fifty years of revolutionary government, compare unfavourably with those of the pre-revolutionary era. Third, in the technologically developing socialist societies, workers have become increasingly preoccupied with material possessions, and as a result, new privileged classes have emerged, based on the ownership of possessions and the monopoly of power.

Classical Western economics and the ideology of *laissez-faire*, as well as Marxist socialism, are products of the nineteenth century English Industrial Revolution. They bear no relevance to conditions in African countries. The Soviet model is no more capable of solving our problems than the Western model. The economies of non-industrial countries are markedly different from those of the Soviet Union, the United States, or Japan.

As President Nyerere of Tanzania has rightly pointed out, European socialism and Soviet communism are meant for large-scale industrial economies with highly centralized and bureaucratic planning. He concludes that although there is some truth in the notion of African communism, African societies are, by and large, commun*al* rather than commun*ist*. Their economic arrangements express a communitarian ethos of democratic socialism rather than the Soviet kind of socialism.

African communalism

Communalism, then, is the basis of the traditions of African countries. This has fundamental ethical and philosophical implications. The communal organization in Africa is not just a matter of individuals clinging together to eke out an existence; nor is it comparable, except superficially, to the organization of rural communities in Europe; nor does it trace its evolution from an urban cultural centre. It is a form of communal organization which has evolved its own philosophical system and its own way of interpreting and projecting reality. In brief, it is a communal structure which has affirmed its particularity through forms of religion and thought arising directly out of its own organization.

African countries need to develop on their own, to invest their traditional concepts with new meanings and not slavishly to accept the standards of the industrialized countries — capitalist or communist — as gospels of development. They should pioneer their own way of development which avoids the pitfalls of both capitalism and communism. They may draw on the experiences of other countries as long as they modify the models to suit their unique conditions. Emphasis should be placed on developing economic systems and patterns of development which are best suited to indigenous requirements and realities. African countries should look at the past as well as the present, and their future course of action should be guided dialectically and related to concrete experience.

Indeed, African countries should try to avoid becoming battlegrounds for competing foreign ideologies, for it is only when Africans assume an identity rooted in their culture that they have anything to share with the outside world. The whole point of being international and cosmopolitan is to be able to receive a visitor and say: 'This is my culture, my place, and I share it with you; what is *your* culture about?' If Africans deny and relinquish their cultural identity, the benefits of expanded human identity will be lost, and every African will become a displaced person.

Bioregional development

Perhaps the best way to describe what non-industrial countries should be is to describe what they should *not* be. They should *not* turn into urbanized industrial societies where cities swell up like infected glands, attracting to themselves manpower which cannot conceivably be employed in any productive capacity. Instead, they should try by every means to avoid the horrors of rampant urbanization and avoid as well the pollution and environmental problems that go hand in hand with urbanization.

The cause of poverty in many countries is not backwardness or lack of resources, but decay of the rural structure. Most development plans bypass the rural areas where between 80 and 90 per cent of the populations of these countries live and work. Non-industrial countries must recognize the importance of their agricultural base, since, for the foreseeable future, the great mass of their population will be farmers. They must first bring their agricultural productivity to the level at which a sustained policy of industrialization is possible. Therefore, the base of development should be rural, not urban; a *bottom-up*, or bioregional, pattern of development which takes account of indigenous conditions, not a top-down one which disregards these realities.

Hence, development should emphasize a country's traditional rural culture. This can be achieved by deurbanization and decentralization and by locating a large number of a country's industries in rural areas.

Literature describing ecologically based, low-impact technology is needed to support small-scale village communities. Such literature should contain information on low-cost building materials; low-cost dams; low-cost energy, such as wind, water, solar, and biogas; low-cost medicine; low-cost transportation; labour-intensive methods; workshop technology; and all those things which the village needs to be self-sufficient, self-reliant, and largely self-governing.

This does not mean that local, small-scale village activities should always prevail. Certain services may need to be provided at national, state, provincial, district, or county levels. Transportation networks need national coordination. Copper mines, smelters, and petroleum refineries require a massive input of energy and labour that cannot be supplied by a few wind generators.

Equally, however, one does not need a gigawatt power plant to meet the energy needs of farms and villages. In fact, supplying energy needs in such a way inevitably results in feelings of alienation, dependency, and helplessness which accompany the lack of understanding or control over the means of survival. This tendency to make everything huge and heavy should be avoided as much as possible. Urban and rural development should be organized specifically to suit the differing conditions of cities, towns, villages, and rural communities.

Authority to solve local problems should be held at the local level. Development should be localized, human-scale, and intended to solve human problems. Nothing should be done by a national government, state, province, district, or county that can be done better by the village. Nothing should be referred to the national government that can be solved by a state, province, district, county, or village. Those most likely to live with the consequences of development decisions should have the most active role in reaching those decisions.

We might do well to reflect that 'poverty' as it is known today was almost unknown in pre-colonial Africa. Although the pre-colonial era in Africa was not a Golden Age, for African countries had many problems before colonialists came, there was no 'overpopulation' in the sense of a rate of population increase greater than the rate of increase of food production. The system of land tenure provided each family with the land required to feed its members. Each family considered it a sacred duty to look after those members who were incapable of looking after themselves.

There was no unemployment, underemployment, or malnutrition. Colonial rule gave grist to the mill of poverty and overpopulation. The people who suffered most from specific nutritional deficiencies were those brought most fully into the colonial economy — the urban workers. Those who managed in spite of colonial rule to maintain their traditional pattern of nutrition remained generally healthy.

The radical changes in structure and institutions which are the only way African countries can rescue themselves from poverty need a popular base and popular support. The people as a whole should be allowed to see their cultural experience develop by its own logic. This is vital. In African countries, as elsewhere, political change will remain of little long-term value unless it is cultural change as well. But cultural change becomes possible only when the people fight their own mental battles; others cannot do it for them.

Development, in other words, cannot be grafted onto a country like a foreign body. It must grow within the country at a grassroots level, utilizing readily available resources. The real implementers of development are the people who either see their own needs and problems or are made aware of them. Development should proceed at a population's own pace and standards; the techniques of development should be simple, practical, and economical — ones which the people can afford, understand, and benefit from.

When communities discover their own potential power to initiate development, the spirit engendered becomes their most valuable asset, one that can set them firmly on the road to self-reliance.

Basis for change

The problem, then, for African leaders and peoples during the Third United Nations Development Decade (1981–90) and beyond is to discover the means whereby African traditional, social, economic, and cultural institutions can regain the high road of their own history. They need to do this before the whole continent is further darkened by the spectre of increasing poverty — a horror that will have no meaning or direction, if only because it will spring from a repudiation of the only forces in African life that might have prevented it.

One way to start repairing the casualties of development which have been brought about by the imitation of Northern development patterns is to outline some strengths in the African traditional way of life on which programmes of modernization could be based:

- The pattern of communal land rights and collective responsibility could form the basis of cooperative work, whether in business ventures or community development projects.
- Decision-making by consensus could be examined by political leaders with a view to adapting its value for modern parliamentary procedures.
- The philosophy of shared responsibility for the young, the sick, and the elderly could be embraced in modern social welfare programmes.
- Classless and non-elitist social forms could be brought into newly planned educational structures.

Finally, no unidimensional explanation or solution to the environment and development problems we face today is possible. It is important to stress *interlinkages* among multiple dimensions — the interlinkage between environment, on the one hand, and patterns of development, lifestyle, poverty, overconsumption, resources, population, cultural survival, energy, food, technology, genetic resources, pesticides, chemical fertilizers, biotechnology, land use, soil conservation, development assistance, conservation, and environmental protection, on the other hand. All these will need to be considered in all their ramifications. Then we should determine prescriptive solutions and effective actions to alter whatever damages the quality of life.

In so doing, we should avoid a linear approach to causation. This means greater stress on understanding the process and less on isolating causes. Ours should be a normative approach, not a purely analytical one. There must be a fit between ideas and the societal forces that are working for desirable change, peace, and transformation.

Grassroots movements

Grassroots movements are forces working for moral alternatives. We need to identify those engaged in desirable change. These include movements for environmental protection; for tribal and cultural survival; against deforestation; for ecology; and for alternative development, technology, and energy. In Africa, non-governmental organizations such as Action for Development in Mauritius, Agri-Service in Ethiopia, the Tanzania Environment Society, Wildlife Clubs of Uganda, the Association of Women's Clubs of Zimbabwe, and the Evangelical Fellowship of Kenya are engaged in this transformation.

Grassroots movements are a new form of organization on the scene. So far, their potential seems to be to act as catalysts to transform the climate of public opinion. Most movements, however, have small constituencies. Many also lend themselves to being co-opted by the state. If they become successful, they invite the wrath of the state. Yet, it seems that a new social class is in the making which consists of sensitive, educated, and erstwhile members of the middle and lower classes who constitute a public-regarding 'moral vanguard'. While this countertrend is arising, the masses are taking to consumerism. This raises a serious dilemma: since the grassroots movements have the masses as their constituency, how are they to bring about a transition to the concept of sustainable development, conservation, and environmental protection?

The solution that appears most obvious is that grassroots movements all over Africa should form a coalition. Together they can mount the pressure to protect the African environment and improve the quality of life. Yet, it is easier to say this than to say how it can be done. So we end, as we began, with the all-important question of 'how'. How do we make the modern state an instrument of moral transformation, first by demilitarizing it and then by liberating it from the global tentacles of domination, monopoly, and ecological and cultural exploitation?

15 'The range of the mountains is his pasture' — environmental ethics in Israel
Bill Clark

Equus hemionus hemippus — a subspecies of Asian wild ass — was the smallest of the modern equids. It stood barely one metre at the shoulder. Yet, this mammal was an important element in the ecological dynamics of its Asian habitat, and an important factor in the cultural heritage of the region, one of the cradles of human civilization. At one time, *Equus hemionus hemippus* ranged along the arid and semi-arid fringe of southwest Asia's fertile crescent, from Mesopotamia westward to the Land of Israel. In Xenophon's classic *Anabasis* it was known as '*emionos*, from which we derive the modern scientific name for the entire species. In the ancient biblical texts of Job, Jeremiah, and the Psalms, the wild ass, known in Hebrew as *pere'*, serves as the incarnate symbol of wildness and freedom.

Like so many other creatures wild and free, *Equus hemionus hemippus* was subjected through the millennia to both intensive and extensive efforts at domestication. These efforts began at least as early as the ancient Sumerians. All failed. The final effort to domesticate *hemippus* was made in Vienna's Schönbrunn Zoo early in the twentieth century. There, Professor Otto Antonius could not even get this equid to accept a small halter. Humanity tried to subjugate this wild animal right to the very end. And it resisted right to the very end. *Equus hemionus hemippus* passed into extinction in 1927, untamed.

Since the creation of the state of Israel in 1948, wildlife protection laws have been enacted and rangers employed to enforce them. In the 1960s, Israel initiated its Hai-Bar programme to reintroduce locally extinct species. Hai-Bar means 'wild life'. The presupposition of the programme is that a great variety of animal species once lived in the Land of Israel. This is attested throughout the pages of the Bible. Since ancient times they have been exterminated or driven to very low population levels. The intention of Hai-Bar is to seek out surviving individuals of locally extinct species, return them to the Land of Israel, and reintroduce them into the ecological dynamics of appropriate habitats. In effect, this is the creation of a second Noah's ark. For many Israelis, it means renewing their ancient covenant with God and the Land. To date, the Hai-Bar programme has returned more than a dozen species of biblical desert animals to Israel, including the ostrich, the white oryx antelope (the prototype of the mythical unicorn), and the Nubian ibex.

One of the reintroduced species is *Equus hemionus*. Since the *hemippus* type is extinct, Israeli conservationists selected the *onager* subspecies as the most suitable substitute. On 17 February 1968, three pairs of *Equus hemionus onager* were brought to Israel from a European zoo. After quarantine, the equids were released into eight square kilometres of fenced natural habitat at the Hai-Bar wildlife restoration facility in the Negev Desert. The following year, another three pairs of *onager* were acquired directly from Iran. The work at Hai-Bar involved two objectives. First, the equids had to be bred in numbers sufficient to initiate a reintroduction programme. Second, they had to be professionally guided to the point where they regained natural behavioural patterns and herd dynamics. The effort involved a major investment of funds, land, talent, manpower, and concern.

Finally, in the spring of 1982, five bachelor males were released beside the desert spring of Ein Saharonim. They were closely monitored and, within a few months, Israeli conservationists were convinced that the animals were tough enough to withstand the rigours of the desert. The following year, eight *onagers* — one stallion, five mares, and two juvenile males — which had lived as a socially cohesive unit at Hai-Bar were released in midsummer, the most difficult season for wildlife in the desert.

In all, the project has been responsible for five releases totaling twenty-eight animals. Sixteen births have been recorded in the wild, including the 1988 births of foals born to mares who were themselves born in the wild — thus attaining a second filial generation, an important milestone for a reintroduction effort. Follow-up studies indicate that the animals are integrated well into their habitat. They have become part of the ecological dynamics of the desert. And this is as it should be.

The biblical conservation heritage

More than two millennia ago, the faithful Job asked:

Who has given freedom to the wild ass? Who has unfettered this animal? I have made the wilderness his home, and the barren Land his dwelling place. He scorns the multitude of the city, and he rejects the commands of a driver. The range of the mountains is his pasture (Job 39:5–8).

The Hebrew Bible is a tremendous treasure to modern Israel. It carries moral messages of great antiquity which are nevertheless valid to this day. It even suggests that non-human species do not exist simply for the pleasure or use of man. Indeed, this heresy is central to the reintroduction of the wild ass in the Negev Desert.

Even the most secular of Israelis will agree that the Bible is vital to the ethical fibre of the society. And many will also lament the misinterpretations of the scriptures across the ages. Consider, for example, the oft-quoted passage of Genesis 1:26:

And God said: Let us make man in our image, after our likeness; and let him have dominion over the fish of the sea, and over the fowl of the air, and over the cattle, and over the earth, and over every creeping thing that creepeth upon the earth.

How many ecological atrocities have been committed because unscrupulous plunderers have held this passage to be a divine licence for blind exploitation? What rapacity has been committed because the key word in this passage, 'dominion', has so often been equated with 'domination'?

There are nearly a dozen different Hebrew words which have been translated into English as 'dominion' or 'rule'. In biblical Hebrew, however, each of these words has a meaning much more precise than merely the exercise of authority. Some words are used to characterize the rule of tyrants, while others refer to responsible stewardship, and yet other words denote the power of intellectual persuasion. What sort of 'dominion' is envisioned by Genesis 1:26? A strong argument can be made that the basic intent of the passage is to impose upon humanity a very considerable responsibility for the well-being of 'every creeping thing that creepeth upon the earth'. That this is the most correct meaning of this passage may be inferred from the many religious ceremonies and laws which assured the conservation of nature in ancient Israel.

For example, there is a whole body of traditional Jewish law which concerns itself with animal welfare. This is known as *ṣa'ar ba'ălê ḥayyîm*, or literally, 'sympathy for life'. Most of this body of law consists of rabbinical interpretations of biblical law. There are biblical laws which require assistance to lost, injured, or overburdened animals. Exodus 23:4 and 5 stipulate, respectively, that upon coming across a strayed animal, one must return it to its owner, even if the owner is one's enemy; and that an animal in distress must be helped. 'If thou seest the ass . . . lying under his burden . . . thou shalt surely unload . . . him.' Protecting animals is also a part of proverbial Judaism: 'A righteous man careth for the life of his beast; but the mercies of the wicked are cruelty' (Proverbs 12:10). In Exodus 23:12 the Bible requires Jewish farmers not only themselves to rest after working for six days, but also extends the day of rest to the farmer's domestic animals — 'that thy ox and thy ass may repose'. In Deuteronomy 25:4, the Bible forbids teasing an animal with the sight of food: 'Thou shalt not muzzle the ox when he thresheth out the corn.' Orthodox Jewish tradition calls for the offering of a prayer while donning new clothes for the first time. But it prohibits such a prayer if the new clothes are made of fur or leather, because such garments are made at the cost of life.

The ancient concept of 'sabbatical' comes from the biblical concept of 'sabbath' — taking every seventh day as a day of rest and rejuvenation. In the case of farmers, however, it is every seventh year. Under Jewish law (both traditional and modern) the sabbatical is a *requirement*. In it we may find perhaps one of the very first human laws aimed at sustainable development. Sabbatical law requires a farmer to leave all fields fallow every seventh year. He is not allowed to prune, cultivate, spread fertilizer, or pull weeds — and he is not allowed to harvest a single grain. This permits the fields a periodic rest so that they may be used on a sustainable basis. But the biblical requirement does not stop at sustainable utilization. It goes on to say that the fallow fields are to be open to wildlife (or 'beasts of the field').

In contemporary terms, every time one opens a bottle of kosher wine, one is promoting 'sustainable use' and also helping wildlife. Rabbinical councils will not classify wine as kosher unless they inspect the vineyards and are certain (among other things) that those vineyards were left unharvested every seventh year since the day they were planted. Furthermore, those unharvested fields must have been made available to wildlife. This, of course, is delightful for the birds, which find unprotected, ripe wine grapes a very enjoyable repast. But many mammals also thrive on grapes. Wolves, for one, have an incredible sweet tooth. Foxes also love grapes. In Proverbs the Israeli fox got his grapes and 'spoiled the vine' in the process. Vine leaves are edible for many species of herbivores.

But kosher law has yet another requirement. During years of production, kosher fields must be left 10 per cent *unharvested* — 'one-tenth portion of which shall be given unto the Lord so the beasts of the field may eat'. Slice into some kosher bread, and it's an act of shameless conservation! For bread to get the rabbi's seal, it must be made of grain which came from fields that are left fallow one year in seven; and during the six years that those fields are harvested, one-tenth of the crop must be left to stand in the field for wildlife.

Today many people in Israel continue to keep the spirit of the biblical conservation heritage. Each year 400,000 Israelis — one tenth the entire population — participate in some activity of the Society for the Protection of Nature in Israel (SPNI). Hundreds of thousands of others visit nature reserves and national parks. Millions have planted trees on denuded and neglected land.

The creation of 240 nature reserves (20 per cent of Israel's total land area), national forests (another 12 per cent), national parks, conservation zones, and 'protected' military zones has resulted in approximately 50 per cent of Israel's total land area being set aside for conservation.

Many of the nature reserves were set aside in order to assure the use of various resources on a sustainable basis. There are many reserves in the Upper Galilee, for example, and the main function of these is to protect the headwaters of the Jordan River, which is the country's most important source of fresh water.

Other reserves were declared to protect the wild progenitors of important domestic plants. Wild wheat, wild barley, and even wild cabbages may be found in Israeli nature reserves. Here, a genetic resource is being conserved. It is important to understand, for example, that more than 90 per cent of the world's wheat is of one type — semi-dwarf. This means the world's most basic food crop is based on an extremely narrow genetic base. If semi-dwarf ever ran into genetic problems, there could be mass starvation around the world. But preservation of the wild type of wheat preserves genetic material which can be used to protect and enhance domestic food crops.

Some years ago, a type of fungus or 'rust' was affecting barley production around the world. Botanical geneticists went to nature reserves in Israel and started working with wild barley. They eventually uncovered the gene which made wild barley resistant to 'rust' and this gene was 'spliced' into domestic types. Most of the rust-free barley growing in the world today is propagated from genetic stock obtained in an Israeli nature reserve.

The only possible 'use' of many other nature reserves, such as those employed in the Hai-Bar programme, is the simple inspiration they give to people who view — or perhaps I should say 'behold' — wild animals running freely in the desert. This is a thrilling sight which quickens anyone's pulse. Here tremendous resources are poured into conservation work simply because there is an *ethical imperative* to restore the vacated ecological niches in the desert habitats.

Conservation in Israel is a bold statement which proclaims to the world: we respect the land, and we shall act responsibly toward it.

Toward a world conservation ethic for animals

It is vital to re-emphasize that *Equus hemionus onager* was reintroduced in Israel for the sake of nature itself, and not necessarily for the benefit or 'use' of the human population. In keeping with this kind of effort, there is now before the world community a proposed International Convention for the Protection of Animals.

The proposed Convention is an effort to create a multilateral treaty which will introduce explicit ethical concerns for nature in general, and the animal kingdom in particular, by way of international law. Fundamental principles of the proposed Convention acknowledge that humans and animals coexist within interdependent ecosystems and that they share a common evolutionary heritage. It confirms that humans, as moral beings, have an obligation to act as responsible stewards, that life itself has intrinsic value, and that no animal should be killed unnecessarily or be subjected to cruel acts or to unnecessary suffering. Such principles are the expression of moral concerns shared by many people around the world.

The proposed Convention's operative passages are analogous to The Hague and Geneva Conventions, and this may be demonstrated by way of example. Where The Hague Convention prohibits the use of specific weapons in war such as glass shrapnel, mustard gas, and dum-dum or hollow point bullets, because they are understood to cause unnecessary human suffering, so the proposed Convention for the Protection of Animals would ban steel-jaw traps and practices such as killing nursing mother primates in order to capture their infants.

And where the Geneva Convention establishes basic standards of care for captive prisoners of war, so the proposed Convention would establish basic standards of housing, nutrition, socialization, veterinary attention, and other welfare requirements for captive animals.

Today, millions of people accept spurious distinctions between humanity and the rest of the animal kingdom. Acceptance is encouraged by those people and institutions who stand to lose by any acknowledgement of kinship in all life. For if all organisms share a common biological origin, there arise many questions concerning rights and values.

It is absolutely imperative that any conservationist who claims concern with ethics must be concerned with cruelty. Ethics, in its most fundamental definition, involves a system of moral principles. Morality, in its most fundamental definition, involves the distinction between right and wrong. The imposition of unnecessary cruelty on defenseless animals is one of the most conspicuous moral issues of conservation. If conservation is to concern itself at all with ethics, it must confront this issue.

Some initial work is readily available. For example, there is the statement in the United Nations' World Charter for Nature: 'Every life form is unique, warranting respect regardless of its worth to man. To accord other organisms such recognition, man must be guided by a moral code of action.'[1] Much support for this ethic already exists within the various societies and cultures of the world. It is important to emphasize at this point the merits of the Judao-Christian heritage. There is a certain vogue among many conservationists to seek new inspiration by exploring the obscure tenets of alien cultures. Frequently, this inclination is a reflection of dissatisfaction with the conservationist's own Western cultural heritage. Indeed, there is a pronounced tendency to reject the great spiritual treasures which can be found at the source of Western civilization. Too often, these seminal works are either ignored, distorted, or suppressed.

But kinship of life is a key to ethical conservation. And it is a very old key indeed:

That which happens to men happens also to animals; as one dies, so dies the other; yes, they all share one breath; so man has no pre-eminence above an animal; for all is vanity. All go to one place; all are made of dust and all return to dust again. Who knows for certain that a human spirit ascends upward, while an animal's spirit descends into the earth? Therefore, I understand that there is nothing better than for a man to rejoice in his own work; for who shall bring him to see what shall be after him? (Ecclesiastes 3: 19–22)

Notes

1 Wolfgang E. Burherme and Will A. Irwin, *The World Charter for Nature: A Background Paper* (Berlin: Erich Schmidt Verlag GmbH, 1983).

16 Islamic environmental ethics, law, and society
Mawil Y. Izzi Deen (Samarrai)

Islamic environmental ethics, like all other forms of ethics in Islam, is based on clear-cut legal foundations which Muslims hold to be formulated by God. Thus, in Islam, an acceptance of what is legal and what is ethical has not involved the same processes as in cultures which base their laws on humanistic philosophies.

Muslim scholars have found it difficult to accept the term 'Islamic Law', since 'law' implies a rigidity and dryness alien to Islam. They prefer the Arabic word *Sharī'ah* (Shariah) which literally means the 'source of water'. The Shariah is the source of life in that it contains both legal rules and ethical principles. This is indicated by the division of the Shariah relevant to human action into the categories of: obligatory actions (*wājib*), — those which a Muslim is required to perform; devotional and ethical virtues (*mandūb*), — those actions a Muslim is encouraged to perform, the non-observance of which, however, incurs no liability; permissible actions (*mubāḥ*), — those in which a Muslim is given complete freedom of choice; abominable actions (*makrūh*), — those which are morally but not legally wrong; and prohibited actions (*ḥaram*), — all those practices forbidden by Islam.

A complete separation into the two elements, law and ethics, is thus unnecessary in Islam. For a Muslim is obliged to obey whatever God has ordered, his philosophical questions having been answered before he became a follower of the faith.

The foundation of environmental protection

In Islam, the conservation of the environment is based on the principle that all the individual components of the environment were created by God, and that all living things were created with different functions, functions carefully measured and meticulously balanced by the Almighty Creator. Although the various components of the natural environment serve humanity as one of their functions, this does not imply that human use is the sole reason for their creation. The comments of the medieval Muslim scholar, Ibn Taymīyah, on those verses of the Holy Qur'ān which state that God created the various parts of the environment to serve humanity, are relevant here:

In considering all these verses it must be remembered that Allah in His wisdom created these creatures for reasons other than serving man, for in these verses He only explains the benefits of these creatures [to man].[1]

The legal and ethical reasons for protecting the environment can be summarized as follows:[2] First, the environment is God's creation and to protect it is to preserve its values as a sign of the Creator. To assume that the environment's benefits to human beings are the sole reason for its protection may lead to environmental misuse or destruction.

Second, the component parts of nature are entities in continuous praise of their Creator. Humans may not be able to understand the form or nature of this praise, but the fact that the Qur'ān describes it is an additional reason for environmental preservation:

The seven heavens and the earth and all that is therein praise Him, and there is not such a thing but hymneth his praise; but ye understand not their praise. Lo! He is ever Clement, Forgiving (Sūrah 17: 44).[3]

Third, all the laws of nature are laws made by the Creator and based on the concept of the absolute continuity of existence. Although God may sometimes wish otherwise, what happens, happens according to the natural law of God (sunnah), and human beings must accept this as the will of the Creator. Attempts to break the law of God must be prevented. As the Qur'ān states:

Hast thou not seen that unto Allah payeth adoration whosoever is in the heavens and whosoever is in the earth, and the sun, and the moon, and the stars, and the hills, and the trees, and the beasts, and many of mankind (Sūrah 22: 18).

Fourth, the Qur'ān's acknowledgment that humankind is not the only community to live in this world — 'There is not an animal in the earth, nor a flying creature flying on two wings, but they are peoples like unto you' (Sūrah 6: 38) — means that while humans may currently have the upper hand over other 'peoples', these other creatures are beings and, like us, are worthy of respect and protection. The Prophet Muḥammad (peace be upon him) considered all living creatures worthy of protection (hurmah) and kind treatment. He was once asked whether there will be a reward from God for charity shown to animals. His reply was very explicit: 'For [charity shown to] each creature which has a wet heart there is a reward.'[4] Ibn Ḥajar comments further upon this tradition, explaining that wetness is an indication of life (and so charity extends to all creatures), although human beings are more worthy of the charity if a choice must be made.[5]

Fifth, Islamic environmental ethics is based on the concept that all human relationships are established on justice ('adl) and equity (iḥsān): 'Lo! Allah enjoineth justice and kindness' (Sūrah 16: 90). The prophetic tradition limits benefits derived at the cost of animal suffering. The Prophet Muḥammad instructed: 'Verily Allah has prescribed equity (iḥsān) in all things. Thus if you kill, kill well, and if you slaughter, slaughter well. Let each of you sharpen his blade and let him spare suffering to the animal he slaughters.'

Sixth, the balance of the universe created by God must also be preserved. For 'Everything with Him is measured' (Sūrah 13: 8). Also, 'There is not a thing but with Us are the stores thereof. And We send it not down save in appointed measure' (Sūrah 15: 21).

Seventh, the environment is not in the service of the present generation alone. Rather, it is the gift of God to all ages, past, present and future. This can be understood from the general meaning of Sūrah 2:29: 'He it is Who created for you all that is in the earth' The word 'you' as used here refers to all persons with no limit as to time or place.

Finally, no other creature is able to perform the task of protecting the environment. God entrusted humans with the duty of viceregency, a duty so onerous and burdensome that no other creature would accept it: 'Lo! We offered the trust unto the heavens and the earth and the hills, but they shrank from bearing it and were afraid of it. And man assumed it' (Sūrah 33:72).

The comprehensive nature of Islamic ethics

Islamic ethics is founded on two principles — human nature, and religious and legal grounds. The first principle, natural instinct (*fitrah*), was imprinted in the human soul by God at the time of creation (Sūrah 91: 7–8). Having natural instinct, the ordinary individual can, at least to some extent, distinguish not only between good and bad, but also between these and that which is neutral, neither good nor bad.[6] However, an ethical conscience is not a sufficient personal guide. Due to the complexities of life an ethical conscience alone cannot define the correct attitude to every problem. Moreover, a person does not live in a vacuum, but is affected by outside influences which may corrupt the ability to choose between good and evil. Outside influences include customs, personal interests, and prevailing concepts concerning one's surroundings.[7]

The religious and legal grounds upon which Islamic ethics is founded were presented by the messengers of God. These messengers were possessed of a special nature, and since they were inspired by God, they were able to avoid the outside influences which may affect other individuals.

Legal instructions in Islam are not negative in the sense of forcing the conscience to obey. On the contrary, legal instructions have been revealed in such a way that the conscience approves and acknowledges them to be correct. Thus the law itself becomes a part of human conscience, thereby guaranteeing its application and its success.

An imported, alien law cannot work because, while it may be possible to make it legally binding, it cannot be made morally binding upon Muslims. Muslims willingly pay the poor-tax (*zakāh*) because they know that if they fail to do so they will be both legally and ethically responsible. Managing to avoid the legal consequences of failure to pay what is due will not help them to avoid the ethical consequences, and they are aware of this. Although a Muslim poacher may be able to shoot elephants and avoid park game wardens, if a framework based on Islamic principles for the protection of the environment has been published, he knows that he will not be able to avoid the ever-watchful divine Warden. The Muslim knows that Islamic values are all based on what God loves and wants: 'And when he turns away [from thee] his effort in the land is to make mischief therein and to destroy the crops and the cattle; and Allah loveth not mischief' (Sūrah 2: 205).

When the Prophet Solomon and his army were about to destroy a nest of ants, one ant warned the rest of the colony of the coming destruction. When Solomon heard this he begged God for the wisdom to do the good thing which God wanted him to do. Solomon was obviously facing an environmental problem and needed an ethical decision; he begged God for guidance:

Till, when they reached the Valley of the Ants, an ant exclaimed: O, ants! Enter your dwellings lest Solomon and his armies crush you, unperceiving.
    And [Solomon] smiled, laughing at her speech, and said: My Lord, arouse me to be thankful for Thy favor wherewith Thou hast favored me and my parents, and to do good that shall be pleasing unto Thee, and include me among [the number of] Thy righteous slaves (Sūrah 27: 18–19).

Ethics in Islam is not based on a variety of separate scattered virtues, with each virtue, such as honesty or truth, standing isolated from others. Rather virtue in Islam is a part of a total, comprehensive way of life which serves to guide and control all human activity.[8] Truthfulness is an ethical value, as are protecting life, conserving the environment, and sustaining its development within the confines of what God has ordered. When 'Āisha, the wife of the Prophet Muḥammad, was asked about his ethics she replied: 'His ethics are the whole Qur'ān.' The Qur'ān does not contain separate scattered ethical values. Rather it contains the instructions for a complete way of life. There are political, social and economic principles side by side with instructions for the construction and preservation of the earth.

Islamic ethical values are based not on human reasoning, as Aristotle claimed values to be, nor on what society imposes on the individual, as Durkheim thought, nor on the interests of a certain class, as Marxists maintain. In each of these claims values are affected by circumstances. In Islam, ethical values are held to be based on an accurate scale which is unalterable as to time and place.[9] Islam's values are those without which neither persons nor the natural environment can be sustained.

The human–environment relationship

As we have seen, within the Islamic faith, an individual's relationship with the environment is governed by certain moral precepts. These originate with God's creation of humans and the role they were given upon the Earth. Our universe, with all its diverse component elements was created by God and the human being is an essential part of His Measured and Balanced Creation. The role of humans, however, is not only to enjoy, use and benefit from their surroundings. They are expected to preserve, protect and promote their fellow creatures. The Prophet Muḥammad (peace be upon him) said: 'All creatures are God's dependents and the best among them is the one who is most useful to God's dependents.[10] The Prophet of Islam looked upon himself as responsible for the trees and the animals and all natural elements. He also said: 'The only reasons that God does not cause his punishment to pour over you are the elderly, the suckling babes, and the animals which graze upon your land'[11] Muḥammad prayed for rain when he was reminded that water was short, the trees suffering from drought, and animals dying. He begged for God's mercy to fall upon his creatures.[12]

The relationship between human beings and their environment includes many features in addition to subjugation and utilization. Construction and development are primary but our relationship to nature also includes meditation, contemplation and enjoyment of its beauties. The most perfect Muslim was the Prophet Muḥammad who was reported by Ibn 'Abbās to have enjoyed gazing at greenery and running water.[13]

When reading verses about the Earth in the Holy Qur'ān, we find strong indications that the Earth was originally a place of peace and rest for humans:

Is not He [best] Who made the earth a fixed abode, and placed rivers in the folds thereof, and placed firm hills therein, and hath set a barrier between the two seas? Is there any God beside Allah? Nay, but most of them know not! (Sūrah 27: 61)

The Earth is important to the concept of interrelation. Human beings are made from two components of the Earth — dust and water.

And Allah hath caused you to grow as a growth from the earth, And afterward He maketh you return thereto, and He will bring you forth again, a [new] forthbringing. And Allah hath made the earth a wide expanse for you That ye may thread the valleyways thereof (Sūrah 71: 17–20).

The word 'earth' (arḍ) is mentioned twice in this short quotation and in the Qur'ān the word occurs a total of 485 times, a simple measure of its importance.

The Earth is described as being subservient to humans: 'He it is Who hath made the earth subservient unto you, so walk in the paths thereof and eat of His providence' (Sūrah 67: 15). The Earth is also described as a receptacle: 'Have we not made the earth a receptacle both for the living and the dead' (Sūrah 77: 25–26).[14] Even more importantly, the Earth is considered by Islam to be a source of purity and a place for the worship of God. The Prophet Muḥammad said: 'The earth is made for me [and Muslims] as a prayer place (masjid) and as a purifier.' This means that the Earth is to be used to cleanse oneself before prayer if water is unobtainable.[15] Ibn 'Umar reported that the Prophet of Islam said: 'God is beautiful and loved everything beautiful. He is generous and loves generosity and is clean and loves cleanliness'.[16]

Thus it is not surprising that the Islamic position with regard to the environment is that humans must intervene in order to protect the Earth. They may not stand back while it is destroyed. 'He brought you forth from the earth and hath made you husband it' (Sūrah 11: 61). For, finally, the Earth is a source of blessedness. And the Prophet Muḥammad said: 'Some trees are as blessed as the Muslim himself, especially palm.'[17]

The sustainable care of nature

Islam permits the utilization of the natural environment but this utilization should not involve unnecessary destruction. Squandering is rejected by God: 'O Children of Adam! Look to your adornment at every place of worship, and eat and drink, but be not prodigal. Lo! He loveth not the prodigals' (Sūrah 7: 31). In this

Qur'ānic passage, eating and drinking refer to the utilization of the sources of life. Such utilization is not without controls. The component elements of life have to be protected so that their utilization may continue in a sustainable way. Yet even this preservation must be undertaken in an altruistic fashion, and not merely for its benefit to human beings. The Prophet Muḥammad said: 'Act in your life as though you are living forever and act for the Hereafter as if you are dying tomorrow.'[18]

These actions must not be restricted to those which will derive direct benefits. Even if doomsday were expected imminently, humans would be expected to continue their good behaviour, for Muḥammad said: 'When doomsday comes if someone has a palm shoot in his hand he should plant it.[19] This ḥadīth encapsulates the principles of Islamic environmental ethics. Even when all hope is lost, planting should continue for planting is good in itself. The planting of the palm shoot continues the process of development and will sustain life even if one does not anticipate any benefit from it. In this, the Muslim is like the soldier who fights to the last bullet.

A theory of the sustainable utilization of the ecosystem may be deduced from Islam's assertion that life is maintained with due balance in everything: 'Allah knoweth that which every female beareth and that which the wombs absorb and that which they grow. And everything with Him is measured' (Sūrah 13:8). Also: 'He unto Whom belongeth the sovereignty of the heavens and the earth, He hath chosen no son nor hath He any partner in the sovereignty. He hath created everything and hath meted out for it a measure' (Sūrah 25:2).

Humans are not the owners, but the maintainers of the due balance and measure which God provided for them and for the animals that live with them.

And after that He spread the earth,
And produced therefrom water thereof and the pasture thereof,
And He made fast the hills,
A provision for you and for your cattle (Sūrah 79:30–33).

The Qu'rān goes on to say:

But when the great disaster cometh,
The day when man will call to mind his [whole] endeavor (Sūrah 79:34–35).

Humans will have a different home (ma'wā) or place of abode, different from the Earth and what it contains. The word ma'wā is the same word used in modern Arabic for 'environment'. One cannot help but wonder if these verses are an elaboration on the concept of sustainable development, a task that humans will undertake until their home is changed.

Sayyid Quṭb, commenting on these verses, observes that the Qur'ān, in referring to the origin of ultimate truth, used many correspondences (muwāfaqāt) — such as building the heavens, darkening the night, bringing forth human beings, spreading the earth, producing water and plants, and making the mountains fast. All these were provided for human beings and their animals as providence, and are direct signs which constitute proof as to the reality of God's measurement and calculation. Finally, Sayyid Quṭb observes that every part of God's creation was carefully made to fit into the general system, a system that testifies to the Creator's existence and the existence of a day of reward and punishment.

At this point, one must ask whether it is not a person's duty to preserve the proof of the Creator's existence while developing it. Wouldn't the wholesale destruction of the environment be the destruction of much which testifies to the greatness of God?

The concept of the sustained care of all aspects of the environment also fits into Islam's concept of charity, for charity is not only for the present generation but also for those in the future. A story is told of 'Umar ibn al-Khaṭṭāb, the famous companion of the Prophet. He once saw that an old man, Khuzaymah ibn Thābit, had neglected his land. 'Umar asked what was preventing him from cultivating it. Khuzaymah explained that he was old and could be expected to die soon. Whereupon, Umar insisted that he should plant it. Khuzaymah's son, who narrated the story, added that his father and 'Umar planted the uncultivated land together.[20]

This incident demonstrates how strongly Islam encourages the sustained cultivation of the land. Land should not be used and then abandoned just because the cultivator expects no personal benefit.

In Islam, law and ethics constitute the two interconnected elements of a unified world view. When considering the environment and its protection, this Islamic attitude may constitute a useful foundation for the formulation of a strategy throughout, at least, the Muslim world. Muslims who inhabit so much of the developing world may vary in local habits and customs but they are remarkably united in faith and in their attitude to life.

Islam is a religion of submission to God, master of all worlds. The Earth and all its inhabitants were created and are dominated by God. All Muslims begin their prayers five times a day with the same words from the Holy Qur'ān: 'Praise be to Allah, Lord of the Worlds' (Sūrah 1:1). These opening words of the Qur'ān have become not only the most repeated but also the most loved and respected words for Muslims everywhere. Ibn Kathīr, like many other Qur'ānic commentators, considers that the word 'worlds' (ʿālamīn) means the different kinds of creatures that inhabit the sky, the land, and the sea. Muslims submit themselves to the Creator who made them and who made all other worlds. The same author mentions that Muslims also submit themselves to the signs of the existence of the Creator and His unity. This secondary meaning exists because 'worlds' comes from the same root as signs; thus the worlds are signs of the Creator.[21]

A Muslim, therefore, has a very special relationship with those worlds which in modern times have come to be known as the environment. Indeed, that these worlds exist and that they were made by the same Creator means that they are united and interdependent, each a part of the perfect system of creation. No conflict should exist between them; they should exist in harmony as different parts of the whole. Their coexistence could be likened to an architectural masterpiece in which every detail has been added to complete and complement the structure. Thus the details of creation serve to testify to the wisdom and perfection of the Creator.

The practice of Islamic environmental ethics

Islam has always had a great influence on the formation of individual Muslim communities and the policy making of Muslim states. Environmental policy has been influenced by Islam and this influence has remained the same throughout the history of the Islamic faith.

The concept of *ḥimā* (protection of certain zones) has existed since the time of the Prophet Muḥammad. *Ḥimā* involved the ruler or government's protection of specific unused areas. No one may build on them or develop them in any way. The Mālikī school of Islamic law described the requirements of *ḥimā* to be the following.[22] First, the need of the Muslim public for the maintenance of land in an unused state. Protection is not granted to satisfy an influential individual unless there is a public need. Second, the protected area should be limited in order to avoid inconvenience to the public. Third, the protected area should not be built on or cultivated. And fourth, the aim of protection (Zuhaylī 5:574) is the welfare of the people, for example, the protected area may be used for some restricted grazing by the animals of the poor.

The concept of *ḥimā* can still be seen in many Muslim countries, such as Saudi Arabia, where it is practised by the government to protect wildlife. In a less formal way it is still practised by some bedouin tribes as a custom or tradition inherited from their ancestors.

The *ḥarīm* is another ancient institution which can be traced back to the time of the Prophet Muḥammad. It is an inviolable zone which may not be used or developed, save with the specific permission of the state. The *ḥarīm* is usually found in association with wells, natural springs, underground water channels, rivers and trees planted on barren land or *mawāt*.[23] There is careful administration of the *ḥarīm* zones based on the practice of the Prophet Muḥammad and the precedent of his companions as recorded in the sources of Islamic law.

At present the role of Islam in environmental protection can be seen in the formation of different Islamic organizations and the emphasis given to Islam as a motive for the protection of the environment.

Saudi Arabia has keenly sought to implement a number of projects aimed at the protection of various aspects of the environment, for example, the late King Khalid's patronage of efforts to save the Arabian oryx from extinction.

The Meteorology and Environmental Protection Administration (MEPA) of Saudi Arabia actively promotes the principles of Islamic environmental protection. In 1983 MEPA and the International Union for the Conservation of Nature and Natural Resources commissioned a basic paper on the Islamic principles for the conservation of natural environment.[24]

The Islamic faith has great impact on environmental issues throughout the Arab and Muslim world. The first Arab Ministerial Conference took as its theme 'The Environmental Aspects of Development' and one of the topics considered was the Islamic faith and its values.[25] The Amir of Kuwait emphasized the fundamental importance of Islam when he addressed the General Assembly of the United Nations in 1988. He explained that Islam was the basis for justice, mercy, and cooperation between all humankind; and he called for an increase in scientific and technological assistance from the North to help conserve natural and human resources, combat pollution and support sustainable development projects.

Finally, it is imperative to acknowledge that the new morality required to conserve the environment which the World Conservation Strategy (Section 13.1) emphasizes, needs to be based on a more solid foundation. It is not only necessary to involve the public in conservation policy but also to improve its morals and alter its attitudes. In Muslim countries such changes should be brought about by identifying environmental policies with Islamic teachings. To do this, the public education system will have to supplement the scientific approach to environmental education with serious attention to Islamic belief and environmental awareness.

Notes

1 Aḥmad Ibn Taymīyah, *Majamūʿ Fatawā* (Rabati Saudi Educational Attaché, n.d.), 11:96–97.
2 Mawil Y. Izzi Deen (Samarrai), 'Environmental Protection and Islam', *Journal of the Faculty of Arts and Humanities, King Abdulaziz University* 5 (1985).
3 All references to the Holy Qur'ān are from *The Meaning of the Glorious Koran*, trans. Mohammed M. Pickthall, (New York: Mentor, n.d.).
4 Ibn Ḥajar al-ʿAsqalānī, *Fatḥ al-Bārī bi-Sharḥ Ṣaḥīḥ al-Bukhārī*, edited by M. F. ʿAbd al-Bāqī, M. al-Khāṭib, and A. B. Bāz 1959; 1970 (Beirut: Dār al-Maʿrifah, 195; 197), 5: 40.
5 Ibid., 5: 42.
6 Muḥammad ʿAbd Allah Draz, *La Morale du Koran*, trans. into Arabic by A. Shahin and S. M. Badāwī (Kuwait: Dār al-Risālah, 1973), 28.
7 Ibid.
8 Sayyid Quṭb, *Muqāwamāt al-Tasawwur al-Islāmī* (Cairo: Dār al-Shurūq, 1985), 289.
9 Ibid., 290.
10 Ismāʿil Ibn Muḥammad al-ʿAjlūnī, *Kashf al-Khafāʾ wa Muzīl al-Ilbās*, edited by A. al-Qallash (Syria Damascus: Muʾassasat al-Risālah, 1983), 1: 458.
11 Ibid., 1:213.
12 Ibn Ḥajar, *Fatḥ al Bārī*, 2: 512.
13 ʿAjlūnī, *Kashf al-Khafāʾ*, 1: 387.
14 N.J. Dawood, trans. *The Koran* (New York: Penguin, 1974): 54.
15 Muḥammad Ibn Ismāʿīl al-Bukhāri, *Ṣaḥīḥ al-Bukhāri* (Istanbul: Dār al-Ṭibaʿah al-Amīrah, 1897), 1: 86.
16 Ajlūnī, *Kashf al-Khafāʾ*, 1: 260.
17 Bukhāri, *Ṣaḥīḥ al-Bukhāri*, 1: 22, 6: 211.
18 Aḥmad Ibn al-Husayn al-Bayhāqī, *Sunan al-Bayhaqī al-Kubrā* (Hyderabad, India: n.d.), 3: 19.
19 Ibid., 3: 184.
20 Soūti, *al-Jāmiʿ al-Kabīr*, manuscript (Cairo: Egyptian General Committee for Publication, n.d.).
21 M. A. al-Sabunī, *Mukhtaṣar Tafsīr Ibn Kathīr* (Beirut: Dār al-Qurʾān al-Karīm, 1981), 1: 21.
22 Wahbah Muṣṭafa Zuḥayli, *al-Fiqh al-Islāmī wa ʿAdilatuhu* (Damascus: Muʾassasat al-Risālah 1985).
23 Ibid., 5: 574.

24 A.H. Bakader, A.T. al-Sabbagh, M.A. al-Gelinid, and M.Y. Izzi Deen (Samarrai), *Islamic Principles for the Conservation of the Natural Environment* (Gland, Switzerland: International Union for the Conservation of Nature and MEPA, 1983).
25 *Habitat and the Environment* (Tunis: Economic Affairs Department of the Directorate of the Arab League, 1986).

Asia

17 *Satyagraha* for conservation: Awakening the spirit of Hinduism
O. P. Dwivedi

The World Commission on Environment and Development acknowledged that to reconcile human affairs with natural laws 'our cultural and spiritual heritages can reinforce our economic interests and survival imperatives'.[1] But until very recently, the role of our cultural and spiritual heritages in environmental protection and sustainable development was ignored by international bodies, national governments, policy planners, and even environmentalists. Many fear that bringing religion into the environmental movement will threaten objectivity, scientific investigation, professionalism, or democratic values. But none of these need be displaced in order to include the spiritual dimension in environmental protection. That dimension, if introduced in the process of environmental policy planning, administration, education, and law, could help create a self-consciously moral society which would put conservation and respect for God's creation first, and relegate individualism, materialism, and our modern desire to dominate nature in a subordinate place. Thus my plea for a definite role of religion in conservation and environmental protection.

From the perspective of many world religions, the abuse and exploitation of nature for immediate gain is unjust, immoral, and unethical. For example, in the ancient past, Hindus and Buddhists were careful to observe moral teachings regarding the treatment of nature. In their cultures, not only the common person but also rulers and kings followed those ethical guidelines and tried to create an example for others. But now in the twentieth century, the materialistic orientation of the West has equally affected the cultures of the East. India, Sri Lanka, Thailand, and Japan have witnessed wanton exploitation of the environment by their own peoples, despite the strictures and injunctions inherent in their religions and cultures. Thus, no culture has remained immune from human irreverence towards nature. How can we change the attitude of human beings towards nature? Are religions the answer?

I believe that religion can evoke a kind of awareness in persons that is different from scientific or technological reasoning. Religion helps make human beings aware that there are limits to their control over the animate and inanimate world and that their arrogance and manipulative power over nature can backfire.

Religion instils the recognition that human life cannot be measured by material possessions and that the ends of life go beyond conspicuous consumption.

As a matter of fact, religion can provide at least three fundamental mainstays to help human beings cope in a technological society. First, it defends the individual's existence against the depersonalizing effects of the technoindustrial process. Second, it forces the individual to recognize human fallibility and to combine realism with idealism. Third, while technology gives the individual the physical power to create or to destroy the world, religion gives the moral strength to grow in virtue by nurturing restraint, humility, and liberation from self-centredness.[2] Directly and indirectly, religion can be a powerful source for environmental conservation and protection. Thus, we need a strategy for conservation that does not ignore the powerful influence of religions, but instead draws from all religious foundations and cultures.

World religions, each in their own way, offer a unique set of moral values and rules to guide human beings in their relationship with the environment. Religions also provide sanctions and offer stiffer penalties, such as fear of hell, for those who do not treat God's creation with respect. Although it is true that, in the recent past, religions have not been in the forefront of protecting the environment from human greed and exploitation, many are now willing to take up the challenge and help protect and conserve the environment. But their offer of help will remain purely rhetorical unless secular institutions, national governments, and international organizations are willing to acknowledge the role of religion in environmental study and education. And I believe that environmental education will remain incomplete until it includes cultural values and religious imperatives. For this, we require an ecumenical approach. While there are metaphysical, ethical, anthropological and social disagreements among world religions, a synthesis of the key concepts and precepts from each of them pertaining to conservation could become a foundation for a global environmental ethic. The world needs such an ethic.

The religion and environment debate

In 1967, the historian, Lynn White, Jr, wrote an article in *Science* on the historical roots of the ecological crisis.[3] According to White, what people do to their environment depends upon how they see themselves in relation to nature. White asserted that the exploitative view that has generated much of the environmental crisis, particularly in Europe and North America, is a result of the teachings of late medieval Latin Christianity, which conceived of humankind as superior to the rest of God's creation and everything else as created for human use and enjoyment. He suggested that the only way to address the ecological crisis was to reject the view that nature has no reason to exist except to serve humanity. White's proposition impelled scientists, theologians, and environmentalists to debate the bases of his argument that religion could be blamed for the ecological crisis.

In the course of this debate, examples from other cultures were cited to support the view that, even in countries where there is religious respect for nature, exploitation of the environment has been ruthless. Countries where Hinduism,

Buddhism, Taoism and Shintoism have been practised were cited to support the criticism of Thomas Derr, among others, that 'We are simply being gullible when we take at face value the advertisement for the ecological harmony of nonwestern cultures'. Derr goes on to say:

even if Christian doctrine had produced technological culture and its environmental troubles, one would be at a loss to understand the absence of the same result in equally Christian Eastern Europe. And conversely, if ecological disaster is a particularly Christian habit, how can one explain the disasters non-Christian cultures have visited upon their environments? Primitive cultures, Oriental cultures, classical cultures — all show examples of human dominance over nature which has led to ecological catastrophe. Overgrazing, deforestation and similar errors of sufficient magnitude to destroy civilizations have been committed by Egyptians, Assyrians, Romans, North Africans, Persians, Indians, Aztecs, and even Buddhists, who are foolishly supposed by some Western admirers to be immune from this sort of thing.[4]

This chapter challenges Derr's assertion with respect to the role of the Hindu religion in the ecological crisis. We need to understand how a Hindu's attitude to nature has been shaped by his religion's view of the cosmos and creation. Such an exposition is necessary to explain the traditional values and beliefs of Hindus and hence what role Hindu religion once played with respect to human treatment of the environment. At the same time, we need to know how it is that this religion, which taught harmony with and respect for nature, and which influenced other religions such as Jainism and Buddhism, has been in recent times unable to sustain a caring attitude towards nature. What are the features of the Hindu religion which strengthen human respect for God's creation, and how were these features repressed by the modern view of the natural environment and its resources?[5]

The sanctity of life in Hinduism

The principle of the sanctity of life is clearly ingrained in the Hindu religion. Only God has absolute sovereignty over all creatures; thus, human beings have no dominion over their own lives or non-human life. Consequently, humanity cannot act as a viceroy of God over the planet, nor assign degrees of relative worth to other species. The idea of the Divine Being as the one underlying power of unity is beautifully expressed in the Yajurveda:

The loving sage beholds that Being, hidden in mystery,
wherein the universe comes to have one home;
Therein unites and therefrom emanates the whole;
The Omnipresent One pervades souls and matter like warp and woof in created beings (Yajurveda 32.8).[6]

The sacredness of God's creation means no damage may be inflicted on other species without adequate justification. Therefore, all lives, human and non-human, are of equal value and all have the same right to existence. According to the Atharvaveda, the Earth is not for human beings alone, but for other creatures as well:

Born of Thee, on Thee move mortal creatures;
Thou bearest them — the biped and the quadruped;
Thine, O Earth, are the five races of men, for whom
Surya (Sun), as he rises spreads with his rays
the light that is immortal (Atharvaveda 12.1–15).[7]

Srsti: God's creation

Hindus contemplate divinity as the one in many and the many in one. This conceptualization resembles both monotheism and polytheism. Monotheism is the belief in a single divine Person. In monotheistic creeds that Person is God. Polytheism, on the other hand, believes in the many; and the concept of God is not monarchical. The Hindu concept of God resembles monotheism in that it portrays the divinity as one, and polytheism in that it contemplates the divinity as one in many. Although there are many gods, each one is the Supreme Being. This attitude we may call non-dualistic theism.

The earliest Sanskrit texts, the Veda and Upanishads, teach the non-dualism of the supreme power that existed before the creation. God as the efficient cause, and nature, *Prakrti*, as the material cause of the universe, are unconditionally accepted, as is their harmonious relationship. However, while these texts agree on the concept of non-dualistic theism, they differ in their theories regarding the creation of the universe. Why have different theories been elaborated in the Veda and the Upanishads? This is one of the most important and intriguing questions we can ask. A suitable reply is given in the Rigveda:

He is one, but the wise call him by different names; such as Indra, Mitra, Varuna, Agni, Divya — one who pervaded all the luminous bodies, the source of light; Suparna — the protector and preserver of the universe; whose works are perfect; Matriswa — powerful like wind; Garutman — mighty by nature (Rigveda 1.164.46).[8]

The Hindu concept of creation can be presented in four categories. First is the Vedic theory, which is followed by further elaboration in Vedanta and Sankhya philosophies; the second is Upanishadic theory; the third is known as Puranic theory; and the fourth is enunciated in the great Hindu epics *Ramayana* and *Mahabharata*. Although the Puranic theory differs from the other three, a single thought flows between them. This unifying theory is well stated in the Rigveda:

The Vedas and the universal laws of nature which control the universe and govern the cycles of creation and dissolution were made manifest by the All-knowing One. By His great power were produced the clouds and the vapors. After the production of the vapors, there intervened a period of darkness after which the Great Lord and Controller of the universe arranged the motions which produce days, nights, and other durations of time. The Great One then produced the sun, the moon, the earth, and all other regions as He did in previous cycles of creation (Rigveda 10:190.1–3).

All the Hindu scriptures attest to the belief that the creation, maintenance, and annihilation of the cosmos is completely dependent on the Supreme will. In the *Gita*, Lord Krishna says to Arjuna: 'Of all that is material and all that is spiritual in this world, know for certain that I am both its origin and dissolution.' (*Gita*

7.6).[9] And the Lord says: again 'The whole cosmic order is under me. By my will it is manifested again and again and by my will, it is annihilated at the end' (Gita 9.8). Thus, for ancient Hindus, both God and Prakriti (nature) was to be one and the same. While the Prajapati (as mentioned in Regveda) is the creator of sky, the earth, oceans, and all other species, he is also their protector and eventual destroyer. He is the only Lord of creation. Human beings have no special privilege or authority over other creatures; on the other hand, they have more obligations and duties.

Duties to animals and birds

The most important aspect of Hindu theology pertaining to treatment of animal life is the belief that the Supreme Being was himself incarnated in the form of various species. The Lord says: 'This form is the source and indestructible seed of multifarious incarnations within the universe, and from the particle and portion of this form, different living entities, like demi-gods, animals, human beings and others, are created' (Srimad-Bhagavata Book I, Discourse III: 5).[10] Among the various incarnations of God (numbering from ten to twenty-four depending upon the source of the text), He first incarnated Himself in the form of a fish, then a tortoise, a boar, and a dwarf. His fifth incarnation was as a man-lion. As Rama he was closely associated with monkeys, and as Krishna he was always surrounded by the cows. Thus, other species are accorded reverence.

Further, the Hindu belief in the cycle of birth and rebirth where a person may come back as an animal or a bird gives these species not only respect, but also reverence. This provides a solid foundation for the doctrine of ahimsa — non-violence against animals and human beings alike. Hindus have a deep faith in the doctrine of non-violence. Almost all the Hindu scriptures place strong emphasis on the notion that God's grace can be received by not killing his creatures or harming his creation: 'God, Kesava, is pleased with a person who does not harm or destroy other non-speaking creatures or animals' (Visnupurana 3.8.15). To not eat meat in Hinduism is considered both an appropriate conduct and a duty. Yajnavalkya Smriti warns of hell-fire (Ghora Naraka) to those who are the killers of domesticated and protected animals: 'The wicked person who kills animals which are protected has to live in hell-fire for the days equal to the number of hairs on the body of that animal' (Yajnavalkyasmriti, Acaradhyayah, v. 180). By the end of the Vedic and Upanishadic period, Buddhism and Jainism came into existence, and the protection of animals, birds and vegetation was further strengthened by the various kings practicing these religions. These religions, which arose in part as a protest against the orthodoxy and rituals of Hindu religion, continued its precepts for environmental protection. The Buddhist emperor, Ashoka (273–236 BCE), promoted through public proclamations the planting and preservation of flora and fauna. Pillar Edicts, erected at various public places, expressed his concerns about the welfare of creatures, plants and trees and prescribed various punishments for the killing of animals, including ants, squirrels, and rats.

Flora in Hindu religion

As early as in the time of Regveda, tree worship was quite popular and universal.

The tree symbolized the various attributes of God to the Regvedic seers. Regveda regarded plants as having divine powers, with one entire hymn devoted to their praise, chiefly with reference to their healing properties. (Regveda 10.97) During the period of the great epics and Puranas, the Hindu respect for flora expanded further. Trees were considered as being animate and feeling happiness and sorrow. It is still popularly believed that every tree has a *Vriksa-devata*, or 'tree deity', who is worshipped with prayers and offerings of water, flowers, sweets, and encircled by sacred threads. Also, for Hindus, the planting of a tree is still a religious duty. Fifteen hundred years ago, the Matsya Purana described the proper ceremony for tree planting:

Clean the soil first and water it. Decorate trees with garlands, burn the guggula perfume in front of them, and place one pitcher filled with water by the side of each tree. Offer prayer and oblation and then sprinkle holy water on trees. Recite hymns from the Regveda, Yajur and Sama and kindle fire. After such worship the actual plantation should be celebrated. He who plants even one tree, goes directly to Heaven and obtains Moksha (Matsya Purana 59.159).

The cutting of trees and destruction of flora were considered a sinful act. *Kautilya's Arthasastra* prescribed various punishments for destroying trees and plants:

For cutting off the tender sprouts of fruit trees or shady trees in the parks near a city, a fine of six panas shall be imposed; for cutting of the minor branches of the same trees, twelve panas, and for cutting off the big branches, twenty four panas shall be levied. Cutting off the trunks of the same, shall be punished with the first amercement; and felling shall be punished with the middlemost amercement (*Kautilya's Arthasastra* III 19: 197).[11]

The Hindu worship of trees and plants has been based partly on utility, but mostly on religious duty and mythology. Hindu ancestors considered it their duty to save trees; and in order to do that they attached to every tree a religious sanctity.

Pradushana: Pollution and its prevention in Hindu scriptures

Hindu scriptures revealed a clear conception of the ecosystem. On this basis a discipline of environmental ethics developed which formulated codes of conduct (*dharma*) and defined humanity's relationship to nature. An important part of that conduct is maintaining proper sanitation. In the past, this was considered to be the duty of everyone and any default was a punishable offence. Hindu society did not even consider it proper to throw dirt on a public path. Kautilya wrote:

The punishment of one-eighth of a pana should be awarded to those who throw dirt on the roads. For muddy water one-fourth Pana, if both are thrown the punishment should be double. If latrine is thrown or caused near a temple, well, or pond, sacred place, or government building, then the punishment should increase gradually by one pana in each case. For urine the punishment should be only half (*Kautilya's Arthasastra* II 36: 145).[12]

Hindus considered cremation of dead bodies and maintaining the sanitation of the human habitat as essential acts. When, in about 200 BCE, Caraka wrote about *Vikrti* (pollution) and diseases, he mentioned air pollution specifically as a cause of many diseases.

The polluted air is mixed with bad elements. The air is uncharacteristic of the season, full of moisture, stormy, hard to breathe, icy cool, hot and dry, harmful, roaring, coming at the same time from all directions, badsmelling, oily, full of dirt, sand, steam, creating diseases in the body and is considered polluted (*Caraka Samhita, Vimanastanam* III 6:1).[13]

Similarly, about water pollution, Caraka Samhita says:

Water is considered polluted when it is excessively smelly, unnatural in color, taste and touch, slimy, not frequented by aquatic birds, aquatic life is reduced, and the appearance is unpleasing (*Caraka Samhita, Vimanastanam* III 6:2).[14]

Water is considered by Hindus as a powerful media of purification and also as a source of energy. Sometimes, just by the sprinkling of pure water in religious ceremonies, it is believed purity is achieved. That is why, in Regveda, prayer is offered to the deity of water: 'The waters in the sky, the waters of rivers, and water in the well whose source is the ocean, may all these sacred waters protect me (Regveda 7.49.2). The healing property and medicinal value of water has been universally accepted, provided it is pure and free from all pollution. When polluted water and pure water were the point of discussion among ancient Indian thinkers, they were aware of the reasons for the polluted water. Therefore Manu advised: 'One should not cause urine, stool, cough in the water. Anything which is mixed with these unpious objects, blood and poison, should not be thrown into water (*Manusmrti* IV: 56).[15]

Still today, many rivers are considered sacred. Among these, the river Ganges is considered by Hindus as the most sacred and respectable. Disposal of human waste or other pollutants has been prohibited since time immemorial:

One should not perform these 14 acts near the holy waters of the river Ganga: i.e., remove excrement, brushing and gargling, removing cerumen from body, throwing hairs, dry garlands, playing in water, taking donations, performing sex, attachment with other sacred places, praising other holy places, washing clothes, throwing dirty clothes, thumping water and swimming (*Pravascitta Tatva* 1.535).

Persons doing such unsocial activities and engaging in acts polluting the environment were cursed: 'A person, who is engaged in killing creatures, polluting wells, and ponds, and tanks and destroying gardens, certainly goes to hell (*Padmapurana, Bhoomikhanda* 96: 7–8).

Effectiveness of Hinduism in conservation

The effectiveness of any religion in protecting the environment depends upon how much faith its believers have in its precepts and injunctions. It also depends upon how those precepts are transmitted and adapted in everyday social interactions. In the case of the Hindu religion, which is practised as *dharma* — way of life — many of its precepts became ingrained in the daily life and social institutions of the people. Three specific examples are given below to illustrate this point.

The caste system and sustainable development

The Hindu religion is known for its elaborate caste system which divides individuals among four main castes and several hundred sub-castes. Over the centuries, the system degenerated into a very rigid, hereditarily determined, hierarchical, and oppressive social structure, particularly for the untouchables and lower castes. But the amazing phenomenon is that it lasted for so many millennia even with centuries of domination by Islamic and Christian cultures.

One explanation by the ecologist, Madhav Gadgil, and the anthropologist, Kailash Malhotra, is that the caste system, as continued until the early decades of the twentieth century, was actually based on an ancient concept of sustainable development which disciplined the society by partitioning the use of natural resources according to specific occupations (or castes); and 'created' the right social milieu in which sustainable patterns of resource use were encouraged to emerge'.[16] The caste system regulated the occupations that individuals could undertake. Thus, an 'ecological space' was created in ancient Hindu society which helped to reduce competition among various people for limited natural resources. A system of 'resource partitioning' emerged whereby the primary users of natural resources did not worry about encroachment from other castes. At the same time, these users also knew that if they depleted the natural resources in their own space, they would not survive economically or physically because no one would allow them to move on to other occupations. Religious injunctions also created the psychological environment whereby each caste or sub-caste respected the occupational boundaries of the others. In a sense, the Hindu caste system can be seen as a progenitor of the concept of sustainable development.

But the system started malfunctioning during the British Raj when demands for raw materials for their fast-growing industrial economy had to be met by commercial exploitation of India's natural resources. As traditional relationships between various castes started disappearing, competition and tension grew. The trend kept on accelerating in independent India, as each caste (or sub-caste) tried to discard its traditional role and seize eagerly any opportunity to land a job. When this happened, the ancient religious injunction for doing one's prescribed duty within a caste system could no longer be maintained; this caused the disappearance of the concept of 'ecological space' among Hindus. There is no doubt that the caste system also degenerated within and became a source of oppression; nevertheless, from an ecological spacing view point, the caste system played a key role in preserving India's natural riches for centuries.

Bishnois: Defenders of the environment

The Bishnois are a small community in Rajasthan, India, who practise a religion of environmental conservation. They believe that cutting a tree or killing an animal or bird is blasphemy. Their religion, an offshoot of Hinduism, was founded by Guru Maharaj Jambaji, who was born in 1451 CE in the Marwar area. When he was young he witnessed how, during a severe drought, people cut down trees to feed animals but when the drought continued, nothing was left to feed the animals, so they died. Jambaji thought that if trees are protected, animal life would be sustained, and his community would survive. He gave 29 injunctions and principal among them being a ban on the cutting of any green tree and killing of any animal or bird. About 300 years later, when the King of Jodhpur wanted to build a new palace, he sent his soldiers to the Bishnois area where trees were in abundance. Villagers protested, and when soldiers would not pay any attention to the protest, the Bishnois, led by a woman, hugged the trees to protect them with their bodies. As soldiers kept on killing villagers, more and more of the Bishnois came forward to honour the religious injunction of their Guru Maharaj Jambaji. The massacre continued until 363 persons were killed defending trees. When the king heard about this human sacrifice, he stopped the operation, and gave the Bishnois state protection for their belief.[17]

Today, the Bishnois community continues to protect trees and animals with the same fervour. Their community is the best example of a true Hindu-based ritual defence of the environment in India, and their sacrifices became the inspiration for the Chipko movement of 1973.

The Chipko movement

In March 1973, in the town of Gopeshwar in Chamoli district (Uttar Pradesh, India), villagers formed a human chain and hugged the earmarked trees to keep them from being felled for a nearby factory producing sports equipment. The same situation later occurred in another village when forest contractors wanted to cut trees under licence from the Government Department of Forests. Again, in 1974, women from the village of Reni, near Joshimath in the Himalayas, confronted the loggers by hugging trees and forced contractors to leave. Since then, the *Chipko Andolan* (the movement to hug trees) has grown as a grassroots ecodevelopment movement.[18]

The genesis of the Chipko movement is not only in the ecological or economic background, but in religious belief. Villagers have noted how industrial and commercial demands have denuded their forests, how they cannot sustain their livelihood in a deforested area, and how floods continually play havoc with their small agricultural communities. The religious basis of the movement is evident in the fact that it is inspired and guided by women. Women have not only seen how their men would not mind destroying nature in order to get money while they had to walk miles in search of firewood, fodder and other grazing materials, but, being more religious, they also are more sensitive to injunctions such as *ahimsa*. In a sense, the Chipko movement is a kind of feminist movement to protect nature from the greed of men. In the Himalayan areas, the pivot of the family is the woman. It is the woman who worries most about nature and its conservation in order that its resources are available for her family's sustenance. On the other hand, men go away to distant places in search of jobs, leaving women and old people behind. These women also believe that each tree has a *Vriksadevata* (tree god) and that the deity *Van Devi* (the Goddess of forests) will protect their family welfare. They also believe that each green tree is an abode of the Almighty God *Hari*.

The Chipko movement has caught the attention of others in India. For example, in Karnataka state, the Appiko movement began in September 1983, when 163 men, women, and children hugged the trees and forced the lumberjacks to leave. That movement swiftly spread to the adjoining districts. These people are against the kind of commercial felling of trees which clears the vegetation in its entirety. They do recognize the firewood needs of urban people (mostly poor) and therefore do not want a total ban on felling. However, they are against indiscriminate clearing and would like to see a consultative process established so that local people are able to participate in timber management.

These three examples are illustrative of the practical impact of Hinduism on conservation and sustainable development. While the effectiveness of the caste system to act as a resource partitioning system is no longer viable, the examples of Bishnois and Chipko/Appiko are illustrative of the fact that when appeal to secular norms fails, one can draw on the cultural and religious sources for 'forest *satyagraha*'. ('Satyagraha' means 'insistance or persistence in search of truth'. In this context, the term 'forest satyagraha' means 'persistence in search of truth pertaining to the rights of trees'.)

Loss of respect for nature

If such has been the tradition, philosophy, and ideology of Hindu religion, what then are the reasons behind the present state of environmental crisis? As we have seen, our ethical beliefs and religious values influence our behaviour towards others, including our relationship with all creatures and plant life. If, for some reason, these noble values become displaced by other beliefs which are either thrust upon the society or transplanted from another culture through invasion, then the faith of the masses in the earlier cultural tradition is shaken. As the foreign culture, language and system of administration slowly takes root and penetrates all levels of society, and as appropriate answers and leadership are not forthcoming from the religious leaders and Brahmans, it is only natural for the masses to become more inward-looking and self-centered. Under such circumstances, religious values which acted as sanctions against environmental destruction do not retain a high priority because people have to worry about their very survival and freedom; hence, respect for nature gets displaced by economic factors.

That, it seems, is what happened in India during the 700 years of foreign cultural domination. The ancient educational system which taught respect for nature and reasons for its preservation was no longer available. On the other hand, the imported culture was unable to replace the ancient Hindu religion; consequently, a conflict continued between the two value systems. The situation became more complex when, in addition to the Muslim culture, the British introduced Christianity and Western secular institutions and values. While it is too easy to blame these external forces for the change in attitudes of Hindus towards nature, nevertheless it is a fact that they greatly inhibited the religion from continuing to transmit ancient values which encourage respect and due regard for God's creation.

The Hindu religion teaches a renunciation of worldly goods, and preaches against materialism and consumerism. Such teachings could act as a great source of strength for Hindu societies in their struggle to achieve sustainable development. I detect in countries like India and Nepal a revival of respect for ancient cultural values. Such a revival need not turn into fundamentalism; instead it could be based on the lessons learned from environmental destruction in the West, and on the relevant precepts enshrined in the Hindu scriptures. That should not cause any damage to the secularism now practised in India. As a matter of fact, this could develop into a movement whereby spiritual guidance is made available to the secular system of governance and socioeconomic interaction.

Hope for our common future

Mahatma Gandhi warned that 'nature had enough for everybody's need but not for everybody's greed'. Gandhi was a great believer in drawing upon the rich variety of spiritual and cultural heritages of India. His *satyagraha* movements were the perfect example of how one could confront an unjust and uncaring though extremely superior power. Similarly, the Bishnois, Chipko, and Appiko people are engaged in a kind of 'forest *satyagraha*' today. Their movements could easily be turned into a common front — 'stayagraha for the environment', — to be used against the forces of big government and big business. This could include such other movements as *Mitti Bachao Abhiyan* (save the soil movement), *Van Mahotsava* (tree planting ceremony), *Chetna March* (public awareness march), *Kalpavriksha* (voluntary organization in Delhi for environmental conservation), and many others. The Hindu people are accustomed to suffering a great level of personal and physical hardships if such suffering is directed against unjust and uncaring forces. The minds of the Hindu people are slowly being awakened through the Chipko, Appiko, Bishnois, Chetna March, and other movements. *Satyagraha* for conservation could very well be a rallying point for the awakened spirit of Hinduism.

Hindu culture, in ancient and medieval times, provided a system of moral guidelines towards environmental preservation and conservation. Environmental ethics, as propounded by ancient Hindu scriptures and seers, was practised not only by common persons, but even by rulers and kings. They observed these fundamentals sometimes as religious duties, often as rules of administration or obligation for law and order, but either way these principles were properly knitted with the Hindu way of life. In Hindu culture, a human being is authorized to use natural resources, but has no divine power of control and dominion over nature and its elements. Hence, from the perspective of Hindu culture, abuse and exploitation of nature for selfish gain is unjust and sacreligious. Against the continuation of such exploitation, the only viable strategy appears to be *satyagraha* for conservation.

Notes

1 World Commission on Environment and Development, *Our Common Future* (New York: Oxford University Press, 1987), 1.
2 O.P. Dwivedi, 'Man and Nature: A Holistic Approach to a Theory of Ecology', *The Environmental Professional* 10 (1987): 8–15.
3 Lynn White, Jr, 'The Historical Roots of Our Ecologic Crisis', *Science* 155 (March 1967): 1203–7.
4 Thomas S. Derr, 'Religion's Responsibility for the Ecological Crisis: An Argument Run Amok', *World View* 18 (1975): 43.
5 These questions have been examined in detail in O.P. Dwivedi and B.N. Tiwari, *Environmental Crisis and Hindu Religion* (New Delhi: Gitanjali Publishing, 1987).
6 *The Yajurveda*, trans. Devi Chand, (New Delhi: Munsiram Manoharlal Publishers, 1982).
7 *The Atharvaveda*, trans. Devi Chand, (New Delhi: Munsiram Manoharlal Publishers, 1982).
8 *Rigveda*, comp. Mahrishi Dayanand Saraswati, (New Delhi: Sarvadeshik Arya Pratinidhi Sabha, 1974), 12 vols.
9 *The Bhagavad Gita*, commentator Swami Chidbhavananda, (Tirruchirapalli: Sri Ramakrishna Tapovanam, 1974).
10 *Srimad Bhagavata Mahapurana*, trans. C. L. Goswami and M. A. Sastri, (Gorakhpur: Gita Press, 1982), 2 vols.
11 R. Shamasastry, ed., *Kautilya's Arthasastra* (Mysore: Mysore Publishers, 1967), 224.
12 Ibid., 166.
13 *Caraka-Samhita*, trans. Priyavrat Sharma, (Varanasi: Chaukhambha Orientalia, 1983) I, 315.
14 Ibid.
15 *Manusmriti* (*The Laws of Manu*), trans. G. Buhler, (Delhi: Motilal Banarsidass, 1975), 137.
16 Centre for Science and Environment, *The State of India's Environment 1984–85*, the Second Citizens' Report (New Delhi: CSE, 1985), 162.
17 Ibid., 164.
18 Chandi Prasad Bhatt, 'The Chipko Andolan: Forest Conservation Based on People's Power' in eds. Anil Agrawal, Darryl D'Monte, and Ujwala Samarth *The Fight for Survival*, (New Delhi: Centre for Science and Environment, 1987), 51.

18 A Buddhist perception of a desirable society

S. Sivaraksa

Those who have not made a profound study of Buddhism tend to think of it as merely a way of personal salvation for escapists in search of spiritual enlightenment. Unlike disciples of the world's other great religions, Buddhists have no recognized international leaders to hand down pronouncements on social justice or environmental concern for the faithful. Nor do Buddhists have an international organization like the World Council of Churches or the World Muslim League, whose resolutions on such matters as racial discrimination often have an impact on local religious communities. Although the present Dalai Lama is greatly revered, he is the spiritual head of the Tibetan tradition only.

Although the World Fellowship of Buddhists exists with headquarters in Bangkok, as a social organization it lacks a significant perception of desirable models of society. Indeed, it has never been known to make any statement against social injustice anywhere, nor has it ever demanded government intervention for Buddhist victims in countries like Bangladesh. It has never been known to send a peace delegation to reconcile differences among Buddhists, or between Buddhists and other religious groups, as in Sri Lanka. Nor has it ever pursued policies on world disarmament, unemployment, overpopulation, or ecological imbalances.

Many Western universities have philosophy departments or divinity schools that challenge people to think more deeply about their role in modern society. Some progressive theological seminaries prepare their seminarians for post-industrial society. Medical ethics and the problems of life and death are often studied by leading theologians and physicians. Meanwhile, some leading Muslims in the Middle East want to pursue their own model of a desirable society. Unfortunately, many scholars in Buddhist Asia follow the secular West so blindly that Buddhism has no social application whatsoever. It would seem that leading Buddhist scholars, especially in Japan, cannot see the wood for the trees. Actually, people need to know how to apply Buddhist teachings if they are to inspire people in the creation of a desirable society in the near future.

It has been said that the Buddhist Middle Path is in fact a slippery path that accommodates anything whatsoever. Most established Buddhist leaders tend to sit on the fence, avoiding comment either on the right-wing reactionary perspective or on the revolutionary left. Many of the same Buddhists claim spiritual happiness despite the fact that, in many so-called Buddhist countries, the majority of people face enormous suffering. At best, only scattered pockets of calm exist, and even these places may disguise a great deal of suffering and the presence of undesirable elements. Anyone who assiduously studies the internal structures of many Buddhist temples may accumulate certain alarming facts not usually available to the casual observer.

Compromise on the path to social justice

The preceding discourse should not discourage those who wish to understand Buddhism thoroughly. Buddhism has its contradictions, as do all religions. The message of the Buddha is in fact so radical that most so-called leaders and scholars find it difficult to follow. Therefore, they compromise, carrying out their own pursuits by ignoring social injustice or by not bothering with the development of a 'desirable society'. Often they quote certain scriptural passages to support their particular way of life.

Yet Buddhism is not a religion of sacred books; Buddhists are discouraged from paying respect to the Buddha's words uncritically. While there are many interpretations, many schools of thought, and different religious traditions, it is generally agreed that if Buddhists are serious about the Buddha's teachings, they will concur on certain fundamental principles. For example, one of the key elements in Buddhism is found in the following passage:

Whatever are the states of which you, Gotami, may know; these states lead to passion, not to passionlessness; they lead to bondage, not to absence of bondage; they lead to piling up [of rebirths], not to the absence of piling; they lead to wanting much, not to wanting little, not to solitude; they lead to indolence, not to putting forth of energy; they lead to difficulty in supporting oneself, not to ease in supporting oneself; of such states you should know with certainty, Gotami: this is not Dhamma, this is not Discipline, this is not the Teacher's instruction (Vinaya II.259; Abhidhamma IV.280).[1]

To follow that passage precisely, one needs to be radicalized in a way that most lay Buddhists, even many monks and nuns, are not.

The Buddha's teachings allow compromise even in the *sangha*; this is at once the strength and weakness of Buddhism. Indeed, throughout Buddhist history, only the most enlightened disciples and radically committed Buddhists have relied entirely on the teaching of the Buddha, which is seen as supremely righteous, understanding, rational, meaningful, spiritual, and self-reliant. The teachings are also full of compassion and selflessness, which in social terms implies democracy, tolerance, and egalitarianism.

The majority of people combine the Buddha's teachings with other religious traditions and local customs, relying on more contemporary political and economic models, as well as on the sciences and new technologies. The Buddha spoke very little on economics and politics. In fact, it is believed that the Buddha even discouraged the faithful from pursuing these disciplines seriously. Yet, he never condemned them outright.

If Buddhist leaders have 'skilful means' — that is, if they are aware of and practise the essence of Buddhism — they should know how to use it for their own happiness and the happiness of others and, bearing in mind the principles cited above, for less greed, less hatred, and less ignorance. In other words, righteousness and ethics are key words in adjusting human behaviour for the benefit of the world. This will in turn affect natural phenomena, as is said in a discourse of the Buddha:

When kings are righteous, the ministers of kings are righteous. When ministers are righteous, brahmans and householders are also righteous. The townsfolk and villagers are righteous. This being so, moon and sun go right in their course. This being so, constellations and stars do likewise; days and nights, months and fortnights, seasons and years go on their courses regularly; winds blow regularly and in due season . . . Rains fall seasonably, the crops ripen in due season . . . when crops ripen in due season, men who live on these crops are long-lived, well-favoured, strong and free from sickness.[2]

Indeed, the Buddha even spoke about an ideal society thus: 'If people are righteous, mindful, using enlightenment as a guideline for their way of life, they can achieve the desirable society.' He also said:

O Bhikkhus, in the city of Benares there would be a kingdom named Ketumati, which would be prosperous, wealthy and highly populated, with an abundance of food.
    O Bhikkhus, in this land of India, there would be eighty-four thousand cities which would take Ketumai as their model and guide.
    A righteous King Chakrawarti would be born in this kingdom.
They would then live in peace and justice throughout this earth that has the great seas as its boundary (Dhammapada III.75).

Most Buddhists presume that such an ideal state will only be possible during the time of the future Buddha, Maitreya. Some post-canonical texts state that the teachings of the present Buddha, Gautama, will last only 5000 years. Since the decline was supposed to begin 2500 years after the Buddha's death and 2532 years have already passed, there would seem to be no hope for any 'desirable' society in the near future. Even the destruction of the entire Earth in a nuclear holocaust would be understandable, since greed, hatred, and delusion seem to be in control of world affairs. Small groups scattered around the world who share the Buddhist interpretation of the 'right view' based on self-reliance, non-exploitation of others, and mindfulness of self and society are preparing themselves for enlightenment or hope for rebirth in the time of the future Buddha.

Buddhism, like any other world religion, supports the status quo if a society is on the whole righteous. Should a society lose that legitimacy, Buddhism will draw upon its prophetic element and support social upheaval — hence the millennial movements in Buddhist history. The very existence of independent states around the thirteenth century in mainland Southeast Asia was in part due to Theravadin Buddhist influences. These small states rebelled against the Srivijaya and Khmer empires, which mixed Mahayana Buddhism with Hinduism for the benefit of the ruling elites, and at the expense of various peoples and vassal states. Once they became independent, those states used the *sangha* as a model for righteous democracy, freedom, and egalitarianism.

In Buddhist terminology *sangha* refers both to the holy brotherhood of Bhikkhu who leave home for the homeless life in order to strive for enlightenment, and to any disciple who has reached the state of sainthood or has become 'awake'. At its best, the Buddhist *sangha* has the special characteristics of: constant cultivation of mindfulness concerning human existence; and complete accessibility to the people. Both are important if the ethical and spiritual values of Buddhism are to be transmitted to the surrounding society. The independent states combined the *sangha* with elements of local beliefs, technologies, and some forms of feudalism. Much later in the 1850s, King Mongkut of Siam declared that a sovereign retained his right to the throne only so long as his people wanted him. Since then, every Siamese king's first announcement on the day of his coronation is: 'We shall reign righteously.' Without righteousness, society cannot exist.

The limits of the ability of religion to influence society

A contradiction in the Buddha's teaching is contained in the following quotes:

So long as the brethren shall establish nothing that has not been already prescribed, and abrogate nothing that has been already established, and act in accordance with the rules of the order as now laid down, the Sangha [Holy Order] will last forever (Dhammapada II.77; Abhidhamma IV.20).

At the same time he also said: 'When I am gone, Ananda, let the Order, if it should so wish, abolish all the lesser and minor precepts.'

Even with such guidelines, only three months after the Master's passing away, the committee of 500 monks, all of whom had reached the status of Enlightened One, *Arahat*, could not decide what were the major and what were the minor rules. Out of respect for Buddha, they decided unanimously not to alter any rule at all.

This decision led to the first schism about one hundred years later. The Southern School, which is now known as Theravada, claims to follow the dictum of the Elders who held the First Council almost immediately after the cremation of the body of the Buddha, while the Northern School, which is now known as Mahayana, claims to follow the general advice of the Buddha, instead of adhering strictly to rules and regulations which may be out of date.

Despite the two main schools of thought, Buddhists agree that the teaching can be divided into two main categories: *ādibramacariya*, the Essence of the Noble Life; and *abhisamācāra*, rules of conduct appropriate for local customs of certain times and places.

Although Theravadins claim to adhere strictly to the rules laid down over 2500 years ago, they have in fact changed their lifestyle. Today, most monks' lodgings have chairs, desks, clocks, radios, and electric fans; some even have telephones, televisions, refrigerators, air conditioners, and automobiles. At the same time, there are those who vow to practice austerity and refuse motorized transportation, electricity, and other modern conveniences. Some refuse money altogether. Others would not mind having an account in the bank, while the majority feel that in this day and age one might as well keep some money for practical purposes.

Since the time of Emperor Ashoka in the third century BCE, there existed a

Dhammaraja theory: if the king were righteous, he had the right to rule; at the same time he had the duty to support the *sangha* which in turn legitimatized kingship. The *sangha* acted as middlemen between the rulers and the ruled by applying simple Buddhist ethics on behalf of a fairly flexible society which was not too exploitative. Although some kings were quite oppressive, they lacked the mechanisms or technologies to implement their wishes entirely. Besides, on rare occasions, the people's support for the *sangha* could build into an opposition party which encouraged the people to depose wicked kings. Theravada Buddhism had no theory regarding just war, nor could monks be directly involved in political affairs.

However, when Theravadin countries were colonized by Western governments, some political leaders became champions of the struggle for independence and looked to the good old times of the Dhammaraja period, despite the fact that the kings in the past may not have been very righteous.

Once modern independence was established, some political leaders in Buddhist countries saw themselves as Dhammarajas. Unfortunately, some politicians, whether they be Buddhist, Muslim, or Christian, work only for their own political ends. They use certain passages of the scriptures to support their position, rather than seeking the essence of the noble life.

Although Siam was never colonized by the West, the absolute monarchy came to an end in 1932. After that, each government used the monarchy to legitimize itself, as if carrying on the Dhammaraja concept. But Buddhist countries are no different from secular or so-called religious nations in the Third World; those with power become even more powerful, while the common people are really powerless. The situation has deteriorated greatly since the Dhammaraja period, because now modern transportation and technology, as well as centralized bureaucracies, are in collaboration with multinational corporations to exploit the people more effectively than ever before. Their concept of a desirable society is to imitate the First World and ignore its negative elements entirely.

Thailand today has more prostitutes (half a million) than monks (250,000); child labour and malnutrition are also widespread. Almost no guarantee exists for basic human rights. It is feared that Thailand is not alone in this unfortunate state of affairs. Since Sri Lanka expressed the wish to join ASEAN, she has become more and more like Thailand. Burma, Laos, and Kampuchea may have fewer prostitutes, but citizens of those countries hardly enjoy political freedom. The same could be said of Vietnam and China, which were once Buddhist countries.

In China, Buddhism has been mixed with Taoism and Confucianism for so many centuries that they have become the Three Ways. Most of the past contributions of Buddhism to Chinese culture have been lost.

As for Japan, when a Buddhist priest was asked how traditional Japanese religion had responded to the tremendous winds of change in that country, he smiled and gave a small shrug. Shintoism and Buddhism, he said, have simply not quarrelled with technology, development, or militarism. They have been very flexible; Japan has shown a unique tendency to avoid any great strain between the pull of religion and the push of the modern age. Asked whether religion had lost its influence in Japan, the same Buddhist priest demurred cheerfully: 'Being Japanese is itself a kind of religion.'

When Indian Buddhism blended with Hinduism, it lost its essence. Hence, it disappeared from the subcontinent, although Buddhist historians claimed that the disappearance of Buddhism was due to the Muslim invasion. Indeed, when Dr Ambedkar led multitudes of untouchables to embrace Buddhism on the eve of Indian independence, there was a good chance of a Buddhist revival in the land of its birth. But after the untimely death of Ambedkar, the Buddhists had no spiritual leader, especially not for the poorest of the poor. Hence, the Buddhists in India are still at the margin of that country's resources, finding it hard even to exist from day to day, let alone to look for a desirable society in the future.

Hopeful signs

Buddhists have been taught to look at things as they really are. When they see things negatively, they are encouraged to look at the positive side as well. For instance, when the Tibetans were driven out of their country, they established themselves in India and many Western countries. Their sufferings helped them to understand the modern world in a way which most other Buddhist leaders, having been co-opted by the status quo, have been unable to reach. Hence, the Tibetan presence in India contributed greatly to the revival of Indian Buddhism and its propagation in the West.

Buddhism first attracted Western interest with the British conquest of Ceylon, and later with the formation of the Pali Text Society in London in 1881, and the Buddhist Society of Great Britain and Northern Ireland in 1907. Until recently, the scope of these societies has been limited to scholarly pursuit or individual practice. But the Buddhist Peace Fellowships in many Western cities have put Buddhist study into practice by aiming to improve their societies collectively. Rather than sit on the fence, they have taken a firm Buddhist stand for justice through loving kindness and non-violence.

Recently, positive action has become characteristic of some Japanese Buddhist monks, who have protested against armaments and nuclear war; walked around the island of Sri Lanka for reconciliation between the Sinhalese Buddhists and Tamil Hindus; and stood firm with native Americans who refused to be driven out of their lands despite the fact that the American National Guard threatened to shoot them. In Japan itself, the lay Buddhist organization (Rissho Kosei-kai) has established the Niwano Peace Prize and Niwano Foundation to encourage studies toward a peaceful world. With other leading institutions, the foundation helps support the World Conference on Religion and Peace, which could be very positive indeed.

In China, Buddhist leaders suffered for their faith during the Cultural Revolution but have managed to secure the right to their religious practices. The Buddhist Association is active in restoring the religion in China, and the Institute for the Study of World Religions has a strong Buddhist chapter that collaborates with scholars abroad.

Vietnamese Buddhists have suffered fates similar to their Tibetan counterparts. As a result, they have helped the West to understand suffering and how to find its cause as well as its cure through the Noble Eightfold Path. Although the Van Hanh Buddhist University in Vietnam was nationalized as a secular place of learning, the government allowed the Buddhist Institute to exist in order to continue serious research work. This unique institute sprang from both the Theravada and Mahayana traditions, retaining scholars versed in Pali, Sanskrit, and German languages. Appropriate contacts at the United Nations University could establish widespread benefits for all concerned.

Hong Kong may not look very Buddhist, but many Buddhist nuns in the colony have achieved a level of scholarship more profound than any that I have come across in Southeast Asia. In Sri Lanka, too, research has been conducted by leading Buddhist women regarding their own role. They remind us that, in encountering contradictions *vis-à-vis* the position of women in Buddhism, we should neither gloss over them nor become defensive. At the same time, we need to study the position of feminists who condemn Buddhism for exploiting women in Asia.

Like their contemporaries in many other Buddhist countries, young Thai intellectuals have returned to critical study of the sacred teaching. Naturally, they are striving for their own Buddhist politics, economics, and social sciences — away from Western domination. Buddhist monks like Buddhadasa Bhikkhu and Phra Depavedi (Payutto) are not only leading lights within the kingdom, but are also known abroad to those interested in the social aspects of Buddhism.

There are, of course, numerous other positive signs that could be linked together to form a platform for appropriate studies on desirable future societies.

Proposals

I wish to incorporate the traditional *sila*, or basic rules for Buddhist morality, as a framework for building desirable societies. They are:

● to abstain from killing;
● to abstain from stealing;
● to abstain from sexual misconduct;
● to abstain from false speech;
● to abstain from intoxicants that cause heedlessness.

From the Buddhist point of view, *sila* is one of three practices necessary in order to develop oneself. The other two are *samādhi* (meditation) and *paññā* (wisdom). These three should be developed simultaneously. In Buddhism, when you practice *paññā* (wisdom) you will see that you are connected to other human beings socially and connected to nature ecologically. You are not a separate entity living life apart from other human beings or nature.

When one becomes a Buddhist, one declares reverence to the 'triple gems' which are Buddha, *dharma*, and *sangha*. In essence, this is a vow that one will develop onself to become a Buddha or an Enlightened One; that one will understand nature and the law of nature which is *dharma*; and that one will seek and help to build a Buddhist ideal society called *sangha*. It can be said, in modern language, that one has a commitment to develop oneself, society, and nature in order to live in harmony with oneself, society, and nature.

Now, with the three practices (basic rules, meditation, and wisdom) and the

three domains of concern (person, society, nature) in mind, let us proceed to build
desirable societies from basic rules.

To abstain from killing

Killing is not restricted to human beings killing each other or to war. When we
deprive people of the means to live properly, we are also engaged in a kind of
killing. From a Buddhist perspective, a person's happiness is interdependent with
the happiness of societies, and a human's harmony is interdependent with
nature's harmony. For example, it can be said that modern farming, which was
propagated in the name of the Green Revolution, has done damage to natural
harmony. Modern farming treats soil as inorganic matter. The use of chemical
fertilizers and insecticides deprives soil of its fertility. In this process, agriculture
becomes the mining of topsoil. Now we know very well that human beings cannot
live on this planet without topsoil. By mining our topsoil we are killing ourselves.

We cannot reduce forests to a kind of resource, either. By naming forests
'resources' we have destroyed them. The loss of species through ecological
damage is also an act of killing performed by ignorance, and there is no need to
mention nuclear waste, nuclear dumping, and nuclear war which are acts of
suicide by *homo sapiens*, our own species.

To abstain from stealing

There is much that needs to be determined concerning the right means of
livelihood and generosity versus traditional theft. People should be encouraged to
study and comment on the New Economic Order from the Buddhist perspective.
They should especially, comment on appropriate and inappropriate
development models; right and wrong consumption; unequal and just marketing;
the degradation of natural resources; and the way to cure economic problems.

Where do Buddhists stand when it comes to a new economic ethic on a national
and international scale? Many Christian groups have done studies on
multinational corporations and international banking. We ought to learn from
them and use their findings for our own Buddhist position.

To abstain from sexual misconduct

On issues of sex, people should be encouraged to study the role of the so-called
'weaker' sex that has been exploited by its male counterpart throughout their
mutual history.

Studies should also be concentrated on the rights of all human beings. The
Universal Declaration of Human Rights, good and useful though it is, was
created from a limited Western perspective. Not even the United Nations Charter
had Buddhist input.

Sex issues should also involve population problems and the Buddhist concept
of birth control. To address the issue of abortion, we need to return to the first

precept of respect for life and death. How far should we allow Western science and technology to interfere with birth and death, and where does the Buddhist concept of health and medicine fit in?

To abstain from false speech

In the area of concern for truth and falsehood, we need to take mass media and education seriously. The Buddhists are far behind their Muslim and Christian brothers and sisters in this respect. The Muslim Pesantran educational institutions in Indonesia should be examined by Buddhists to see how they retain Islamic and traditional principles in the light of modern society while also projecting a vision for the future. We need a workable Buddhist education that is not limited to the classroom. We need to expand the Right View through the mass media so that truth will triumph over falsehood. The dignity of human beings should take precedence over a consumer culture where people have more than they really need.

Using truthfulness as the guideline, research should be conducted at the university level toward curbing political propaganda and commercial advertisements. Unless we have alternatives to what is available, we shall not be able to overcome the vast falsehood and indoctrination that is perpetrated in the name of national security and the cultural well-being of humankind.

To abstain from intoxicants that cause heedlessness

The fifth precept should encourage us not only to study drug problems and find solutions, but also to overcome the problems of intoxication on a large scale. The usual religious preaching against intoxicants does not get us anywhere. We must examine the beer, wine, spirit, and drug industries to identify their power base.

At the same time, one should use this precept to study the practice of mindfulness in order to develop and share our spiritual critical awareness (*yonisomanasikāra*). This sense of self-criticism, which will help us to be humble without false pretense, brings with it a sense of being natural in one's dealing with other beings, be they human or otherwise.

Notes

1 F. Max Müller, ed., *Sacred Books of the East* (Oxford: Clarendon Press, 1882).
2 *The Book of Gradual Sayings* II, trans. F. L. Woodward, (London: Pali Text Society, 1951–5), 85.

19 Ancient wisdom and sustainable development from a Chinese perspective

Simon Sui-cheong Chau and Fung Kam-Kong

At the end of the twentieth century, the rivers and lakes of our planet are dying, the seas are poisoned, and the continents are becoming garbage dumps. The supposedly most intelligent animal which ever walked the Earth is killing every fellow coinhabitant. This is the world our generation is handing over to posterity. As more and more of us wake up to this painful reality, the air of helplessness thickens. We may lose our battle for survival. This chapter is an attempt to show that the scenario could be different. A little ancient sanity could help.

It is not difficult to explain what went wrong from an ecological point of view. One single word can do the job — 'development', as it is commonly understood today.

The so-called First World (primarily the West and Japan) is upsetting the ecological balance of our delicate biosphere with its wasteful way of life. With one-quarter of the total world population, it is using three-quarters of the world's resources, shamelessly, to the jealousy and anger of the rest. And 'the rest' is losing little time catching up. In the 1980s, the Second World — Russia, Eastern Europe and China, among others — shook off its ideological burdens and took decisive steps to imitate the West. While its degree of success remains to be seen, the outcome, whatever it may be, gives little comfort. If these giants should succeed in 'modernization' (which amounts to little more than trying to adopt a Western style of life, as symbolized by Coca Cola and jeans), they will add a fatal pollution burden to the Earth (imagine 1 billion Chinese each throwing away a packet of tissues a day). Then there are the Third World countries' prospects for development. Can they, with 60 per cent of the world population, industrialize without aggravating the Earth's pollution and resource depletion problems? There are few hopeful signs. Their eventual failure to industrialize is no more heartening. As inequality in the distribution of wealth increases and hardship and discontent grow among the 'have-nots', it needs little imagination to see the outcome — given the general availability of deadly weapons we have so smartly created.

It is animal instinct to ask, in the face of imminent calamity, what we should do.

The way of ethics

This question, what we should do, is one which concerns action and behaviour. It can be interpreted on two levels: social policy, and individual action. The first is formulated by the government and other organizations within the establishment; the second is a result of personal choices. Thus, there are two questions: what our governments should do, and what each of us should do. Take the example of the present ozone layer crisis. We can demand action on two levels: governments should cooperate to stop the production and use of chlorofluorocarbons; each of us should be informed of the danger of the use of chlorofluorocarbons and stop using them.

Many of us rely heavily on government action to solve public problems without realizing its limits. Governments are basically guided by the principle of utility. They have to be convinced that to act is more beneficial than not to act. It is utterly unrealistic and unreasonable to expect our governments to play the roles of prophets or saviours. Usually the most governments can do is avoid further deterioration of the situation. Rarely can a government attack a problem at its roots.

Furthermore, expecting the government to do a lot is not only unrealistic but also dangerous. Direct intervention in too many aspects of our lives often leads to authoritarianism. It is wise and necessary to demand that our governments take more pollution control measures and allocate more resources to the civil sector to promote ecological wisdom. But government intervention is not sufficient to solve public environmental problems.

We also have to be serious about individual action. When we ask what we (as individuals) should do, we may get four kinds of answer: we should do X because we *like* to do so; we should do X because the law *requires* us to do so; we should do X because everybody *does* so; and we should do X because upon reflection we reach the conclusion that we *ought* to do so. These answers represent the four systems which generally govern human behaviour: emotion, law, custom, and ethics. Emotion is someone's subjective condition. It certainly has great influence on one's behaviour, as Freud and other psychologists emphasized. Law and custom are external systems one is obliged to obey. Their defiance carries a price in the form of punishment. Ethics is an internal value system which one chooses to adopt *after reflection*. It requires the exercise of free will and reason. These systems are often mixed up in people's minds. It is important to differentiate among them. It is also important to understand their implications.

Subjective value systems are often dangerous, especially when they are universalized ('Everyone must do this because I like it'). Neither are law or custom satisfactory; if I do X just because the law or custom says I must, then I will stop doing X or choose to do Y whenever the police and other people are not looking. Actually, one of the greatest problems facing us today is that whenever either law or custom fails to stop people from doing antisocial things, people act according to their impulse or personal interest. Helpful as they are in guiding our behaviour, law and custom are not reliable. Moreover, even when the things law and custom oblige me to do are right, it is possible that I obey without understanding the rationale for the actions. Thus, I give up my freedom and dignity as an independent being, and become the slave of external forces.

Because of considerations such as these, many sages have emphasized the building up of ethics, that is, the cultivation of one's heart and mind. Although they understood the role external systems play in the formation of human character, they insisted that only by cultivating one's heart and mind are things really changed.

But there are two basic conceptions of ethics. According to the first, there are certain objective principles of behaviour which everyone should understand after rational reflection, and which should be universally followed. We may call this a system of obligatory ethics. There is another system of ethics which is not objective, but *unique*. This may be called a system of contextual ethics.

What does 'contextual ethics' mean? It means that one chooses to do something purely on the basis of one's condition and values, without implying that the particular actions chosen ought to be adopted universally. Such moral choice is neither subjective or objective. Rather, it comes from rational reflection and is adopted according to one's personal situation and choice of orientation. When a person does A, it is because he or she thinks that A suits him or her well. He or she knows that this choice does not necessarily suit everybody. A second person can justifiably choose to do B, while a third can very well choose to do C, all without contradiction. In other words, we can each do different things and be equally justified, without necessarily implying that others are less 'right'.

It is in this spirit that we present the following observations which we believe may be of help to others who care about the fate of our civilization.

The way of Chinese Taoism

Twenty-three centuries ago, the Chinese Taoist philosopher Chuang Tzu (369–286 BCE) told this story in his essay 'The Secret of Caring for Life':

Your life has a limit but knowledge has none. If you use what is limited to pursue what has no limit, you will be in danger. If you understand this and still strive for knowledge, you will be in danger for certain! . . .

Cook Ting was cutting up an ox for Lord Wen-hui. At every touch of his hand, every heave of his shoulder, every move of his feet, every thrust of his knee — zip! zoop! He slithered the knife along with a zing, and all was in perfect rhythm, as though he were performing the dance of the Mulberry Grove or keeping time to the Ching-shou music.

'Ah, this is marvelous!' said Lord Wen-hui. 'Imagine skill reaching such heights!'

Cook Ting laid down his knife and replied, 'What I care about is the Way, which goes beyond skill. When I first began cutting up oxen, all I could see was the ox itself. After three years I no longer saw the whole ox. And now, now I go at it by spirit and don't look with my eyes. Perception and understanding have come to a stop and spirit moves where it wants. I go along with the natural makeup, strike in the big hollows, guide the knife through the big openings, and follow things as they are. So I never touch the smallest ligament or tendon, much less a main joint.

'A good cook changes his knife once a year — because he cuts. A mediocre cook changes his knife once a month — because he hacks. I've had this knife of mine for nineteen years and I've cut up thousands of oxen with it, and yet the blade is as good as though it had just come from the grindstone.'

'Excellent!' said Lord Wen-hui. 'I have heard the words of Cook Ting and learned how to care for life!'[1]

There are several interesting points in this story. Chuang Tzu compares worldly affairs with the ox, and the self with the knife. As long as one follows the natural composition or 'make up' of the ox, one can work beautifully without effort. But whenever coercion is involved, not only will the ox be damaged but the knife will suffer even more.

This, in essence, is what our generation is doing with the Earth. We use every means to exploit and upset the natural order. Furthermore, our destruction of the planet is but a reflection of our destruction of ourselves. Instead of accepting things as they come, the modern person tries to conquer, to possess, and to dominate. We think we know better. This is self-defeating because, as Chuang Tzu says, we 'use what is limited to pursue what has no limit'. Turning to material possessions for gratification is cutting and hacking clumsily with the proverbial knife. In the end, it is we ourselves who suffer.

In another story, Chuang Tzu spoke through the mouth of the greatest saint of Chinese history. He cooked up a fictional dialogue between Confucius and his most beloved disciple, Yen Hui. The latter, in his youthful enthusiasm, wanted to go to the neighbouring state and save it from the stupid leadership of its immature ruler. He was sure that his virtue and wisdom would enable him to do a good job, thereby sparing the people there of untold hardship. But when he bid farewell to Confucius, the master warned him sternly:

'Ah,' said Confucius, 'you will probably go and get yourself executed, that's all. The Way doesn't want things mixed in with it. When it becomes a mixture, it becomes many ways; with many ways, there is a lot of bustle; and where there is a lot of bustle, there is trouble — trouble that has no remedy! The Perfect Man of ancient times made sure that he had it in himself before he tried to give it to others. When you're not even sure what you've got in yourself, how do you have time to bother about what some tyrant is doing?

'Do you know what it is that destroys virtue, and where wisdom comes from? Virtue is destroyed by fame, and wisdom comes out of wrangling. Fame is something to beat people down with, and wisdom is a device for wrangling. Both are evil weapons — not the sort of thing to bring you success. Though your virtue may be great and your good faith unassailable, if you do not understand men's spirit, though your fame may be wide and you do not strive with others, if you do not understand men's minds, but instead appear before a tyrant and force him to listen to sermons on benevolence and righteousness, measures and standards — this is simply using other men's bad points to parade your own excellence. You will be called a plaguer of others. He who plagues others will be plagued in turn. You will probably be plagued by this man.'[2]

To many of us, the argument that virtue and wisdom are 'evil weapons' cannot but sound bizarre. But Chuang Tzu was in fact making two points. First, obligatory ethics can be dangerous. It is good to be virtuous and wise. Yet the moment you try to make others strive in the same direction, you are imposing your system of behaviour and value on the world. This, according to Chuang Tzu, is dangerous. Second, you cannot truly win an argument. Even if you manage to win in words and logic, you will not win your opponent's heart. When you enter into a debate, you are often forced to behave foolishly. Confrontation must be avoided as much as possible. To sum up, trying to convince others to do good things is not advisable. What, then should/can one do?

Chuang Tzu provides us with an answer. Again, it is through Confucius' mouth in a fictional dialogue with Yen Hui, who, in desperation, asks 'Please tell me what to do.'

'You must fast!' said Confucius. 'I will tell you what that means. Do you think it is easy to do anything while you have [a mind]? If you do, Bright Heaven will not sanction you.'

Yen Hui said, 'My family is poor. I haven't drunk wine or eaten any strong foods for several months. So can I be considered as having fasted?'

'That is the fasting one does before a sacrifice, not the fasting of the mind.'

'May I ask what the fasting of the mind is?'

Confucius said, 'Make your will one! Don't listen with your ears, listen with your mind. No, don't listen with your mind, but listen with your spirit. Listening stops with the ears, the mind stops with recognition, but spirit is empty and waits on all things. The Way gathers in emptiness alone. Emptiness is the fasting of the mind.'

Yen Hui said, 'Before I heard this, I was certain that I was Hui. But now that I have heard it, there is no more Hui. Can this be called emptiness?'

'That's all there is to it,' said Confucius. 'Now I will tell you. You may go and play in his bird cage, but never be moved by fame. If he listens, then sing; if not, keep still. Have no gate, no opening, but make oneness your house and live with what cannot be avoided. Then you will be close to success.'

'It is easy to keep from walking; the hard thing is to walk without touching the ground. It is easy to cheat when you work for men, but hard to cheat when you work for Heaven. You have heard of flying with wings, but you have never heard of flying without wings. You have heard of the knowledge that knows, but you have never heard of the knowledge that does not know. Look into that closed room, the empty chamber where brightness is born! Fortune and blessing gather where there is stillness.'[3]

The most inspiring part of this story is the instructions ascribed to the Master: 'Make your will one! Don't listen with your ears, listen with your mind. No, don't listen with your mind, but listen with your spirit.' Chuang Tzu proposed a method to cultivate the heart and mind. To begin with, one learns to concentrate totally ('make your will one'). Then, one abandons the use of sense organs and uses one's heart and mind instead. Finally, even the heart and mind are abandoned and one comprehends and feels the *Chi* (literally, 'breath', but translated above as 'spirit'). The method can be explained as follows:

Begin with total concentration. By closing the sense organs, one minimizes the influences of external objects that lead to attachment to the outside world. For example, one will not feel happy on being praised, or feel sad on being criticized. Neither will one cling to a rich person in order to benefit from such a relationship, or despise a poor person because one cannot take advantage of him.

When the heart and mind manage to rid themselves of the influences of external objects, one can then train them to liberate themselves from the influences of internal ones. These are the various kinds of images and memories we harbour inside us. For example, daydreaming diverts our attention from the work before us so that we can no longer concentrate.

When one manages to liberate oneself from the bondage of external and internal objects, one's *Chi* is empty and the Way naturally comes in. This is the 'fasting of the mind', an attitude of 'letting go', as opposed to that of 'taking'. In the passage quoted above, Chuang Tzu makes use of the image of the birdcage to illustrate this point. The key to success lies in emptying one's mind. The moment you have achieved this, the Way is with you. When Yen Hui realizes that there is no more Hui, he has attained the ideal mode of existence. If all this sounds incomprehensible, some Chinese Buddhist teachings may help.

The way of Chinese Buddhism

Among the innumerable Chinese Buddhist texts, a well-known piece is from the Zen master Shen Xiu (606–706 CE) in the form of a Zen poem:

The body is like a bodhi tree,
The mind is like a framed mirror.
One ought to wipe it frequently
To make sure that no dust is collected.

This is the kind of inspiration Zen Buddhism has to offer to us mortals who choose to live an earthly life and still remain pure in heart. Shen Xiu's point is that, like a mirror which attracts dust, it is all too easy for our mind to be tied down by any kind of desire. One of the most irresistible desires is that of possession, both material (wealth, objects) and non-material (love, power, fame). As long as we treasure them, these things inevitably enslave us. In seeking to possess them, we are in fact possessed by them. This is the main cause of human suffering. The Zen poem reminds us that the moment our mind is aroused by such desire, we must eliminate it at once. In other words, we should 'let go' instead of allowing ourselves to 'take'.

Shen Xiu's choice of the mirror to symbolize our mind and heart is revealing. A mirror never strives for an image which has yet to arrive, nor does it retain one that is gone. This is certainly not the case with our mind and heart. While working in the office, we are frequently occupied by thoughts concerning the party that weekend, and cannot drive away from our mind and heart the scene of unpleasant confrontation with the boss earlier in the day. In such a manner, our mind and heart are rather like a videotape playing fast forward or rewinding back all the time. Such images never bother the mirror, which always truthfully reflects the sight of just that particular moment, without adding or subtracting irrelevant elements. We are advised to live every moment as it comes, and let go of all other matters which disturb our heart and mind. By doing so, we can gain peace of mind.

It is interesting to note that Chuang Tzu used the very same image — the mirror: 'The Perfect Man uses his mind like a mirror — going after nothing, welcoming nothing, responding but not storing. Therefore he can win over things and not hurt himself.'[4] The ideal of 'going after nothing, welcoming nothing' was explained above. 'Responding but not storing' refers to the peculiar nature of the mirror which forms an image after the arrival of an object, but not before, and never intends to take possession of it. Applying this principle to everyday life, we should not attempt to add to, or subtract from, the things we encounter; in other words, we must not take and own them, nor should we reject or escape from them. The best attitude is to let them be, let them come and go, and so never allow our heart and mind to be disturbed.

Another Zen story illustrates this point very well. There was once a Zen master who, on being asked how he practised the Way, answered: 'When I'm hungry I eat, and when I'm sleepy I go to bed.' The caller was puzzled by his answer and asked him: 'Then in what way are your practices different from the practices of ordinary people?' And the master explained: 'The ordinary people not only want to eat when they're hungry, they also want to eat well. When they fail to find good food, they're not satisfied, and so cannot eat happily. Then when they do have good food, they want to have it again and again, or they want even better food next time. In this way, they cannot concentrate on their present meal. When they are sleepy they want a comfortable bed, and yet when they have it their minds are occupied by thoughts concerning yesterday and tomorrow.'

It is logical for the reader to assume that Shen Xiu must have been influenced by Chuang Tzu. However, these ideas are common in Buddhist scriptures. For example, in the Heart Sutra, one of the most well-known Chinese Buddhist scriptures, is this saying: 'All things are but appearances having no substance: they neither arise nor become extinct, neither become defiled, nor become pure, neither increase nor decrease by themselves.'[5] Since things have no substance, there is no reason for our hearts and minds to be affected by them. By thinking that things 'neither arise nor become extinct', we realize that there is no point in chasing after them. This is the same idea as Chuang Tzu's *Chi* which just 'waits on all things', while 'neither increase nor decrease by themselves' corresponds to Chuang Tzu's 'going after nothing, welcoming nothing'.

The perennial philosophy

This teaching is also found in another wonderful culture. It is referred to as *Karma Yoga* in ancient Indian wisdom. (*Karma* is a Sanskrit term meaning 'action-influence'.) In the holy song of the *Bhagavad Gita* such ideas are frequent:

He who restrains his organs of action but continues in his mind to brood over the objects of sense . . . is said to be a hypocrite [a man of false conduct].
But he who controls the senses by the mind, O Arjuna, and without attachment engages the organs of action in the path of work, he is superior.
Do thou thy allotted work, for action is better than inaction; even the maintenance of thy physical life cannot be effected without action.
Therefore, without attachment, perform always the work that has to be done, for man attains to the highest by doing work without attachment.[6]

It is clear from these passages that the ancient sages held very similar views concerning these matters. We witness a merging of the great philosophical and religious traditions.

It is important to note that neither the *Bhagavad Gita* nor Chuang Tzu advises people to abandon the world and escape into the mountains to become hermits. Chuang Tzu made the point clear in his story. The cook never gives up his work.

He occupies himself working with his knife day after day, but in a natural way, following the order of 'heaven'. So we, too, should work and get things done. As long as we follow the natural Way, there is 'plenty of room' for us to 'play about'. Liberty lies in detachment from inappropriate human intervention.

Buddhism, regarded by many as a religion or philosophy which denies and abandons this world, in fact holds very much the same view. Hui Neng (638–713 CE), another Zen master, explained his philosophy of life in this poem:

The Buddhist Way is in this world,
It is never separated from our daily-life consciousness.
To look for wisdom outside this world
Is like looking for horns on a rabbit.

This idea was echoed by Jesus who taught that heaven is never very far; it is among people and within our hearts. The ideal way to live, therefore, is to submerge oneself in earthly affairs like everybody else, accept things as they come and go, and try not to be tied down by them.

As explained earlier, *Karma Yoga* is the fulfilment of one's duties without regard for eventual success or failure. In Christian terms, the real meaning of sacrifice is very much the same: one gives without attempting to take anything back. This idea is repeatedly explained in the *Diamond Sutra*, one of the most important Chinese Buddhist classics: 'The Compassionate Lord should not attach to any objects. The Compassionate Lord, in the true manner should practice charity without attaching to any appearance.'[7] In other words, one does good deeds without premeditation, without deliberately thinking about it, and without remembering it afterwards. This is the ideal frame of mind.

There is a consensus of opinion among these sages that, to live freely, one should try to be like floating clouds and running waters, accepting the fact that one comes and goes. Everything in life, including life itself, follows a natural pattern of coming and going. You cannot force life to come when it is not ready; neither can you keep it, for it will leave without a trace. In a word, you should never attempt to 'take' anything; otherwise, you suffer. If we can manage to let go of the desire to treasure (to 'take'), and treat *everything* in life as 'let-go-able', we will be liberated from our slavery. For example, we fear death primarily because we cannot imagine ourselves ceasing to exist. We regard ourselves (the 'I-ness') as very important. The more we can ignore this 'I-ness' in our consciousness, the less pain and apprehension we will feel in our rendezvous with death.

The same idea appears in Christian teachings: Jesus, for example, told us not to worry about tomorrow, as the sparrows do not sow or harvest and they are well taken care of by God.

The perennial philosophy centres around a style of living, or attitude towards life. The idea is that by letting go the desire to possess and dominate we will not make unnecessary demands on life, thereby attaining a state of real peace of mind. If we can do that, our lives and the world will both be very different.

A note of caution is useful here. The attitude of detachment being proposed is very different from one of irresponsible indulgence. The latter is no more than an immediate gratification of sensual or psychological needs, without regard to the consequences of one's action. Such irrational behaviour is one of the plagues destroying our civilization and threatening the survival of our species. The ancient wisdom is just the opposite — one's mind and heart have no desire to take, to possess, or to dominate. Because of this, one is able to appreciate the way of the world rationally and coolly, and to behave naturally, like the mirror with dust that reflects everything at the moment with absolute clarity. Achieving this, one will be able to work like Cook Ting, operating according to the law of nature without inappropriate human intervention.

This is, incidentally, what green movements all over the world are striving to achieve.

The way before us

In a recent talk on 'Where is the Green Movement Going?', a colleague of ours, a leader of the local Buddhist modernization movement, relates the green ideal to ancient wisdom in this way:

Now we know that, although there are external causes for environmental pollution, basically it is a problem of the mind: it is our greed, our desire to possess, our inflation of the self. So, in addition to introducing legal regulations, we must also establish a philosophy of non-greediness to sublimate men's desires. By exhorting the virtue of thriftiness, resources will no longer be wasted. We must not think that such a value system is a backward one which belongs to an agricultural society. Rather, it is an excellent way to counterbalance men's selfishness, and it has stood the test of philosophizing and practice down through the ages. We cannot allow the selfish elements within human nature to triumph; the same applies to agricultural as well as industrial societies. Therefore, the path ahead for the green movement should, on the one hand, make good use of the present legal system, and on the other, learn humbly from ancient civilizations. We have to learn from history, digging up ideas that are eternal, so as to reconstruct the world of values for the modern man.[8]

What is going to happen if more people eventually adopt this ancient philosophy? On a personal level, more of us should be leading happier lives, as we understand that the source of happiness lies not in possessing external objects, but in peace of mind. A considerable amount of our psychological and physical illness will disappear. On the social level, when more people adopt this philosophy, there will be more sacrifice — giving up our possessions in order to help those in need, so that basic needs will be met universally. On a national level, the prevalent consumerist way of life will fade away, taking away with it our apparently insolvable pollution and resource depletion problems. This will also lead to the reduction of all kinds of international conflict and struggle.

Yet, before this utopia is created, we must demand that our governments take every kind of necessary measure so as to make sure that our ecology will not deteriorate to the point that we all perish before more people have the chance to think about choosing this philosophy of life. To state it briefly, we absolutely need to demand that our governments and international bodies halt the trend of environmental deterioration. But whether things will permanently change for the better is a matter of choice for each of us.

The West, with its unending enthusiasm for discovery and innovation, has done the human community a great service by providing modern societies with various tools and material comforts. Now, just as the rest of the world is imitating the West, it is alarming to note that things are going disastrously wrong, and the cause somehow lies in the basic philosophy of life of many Westerners. As described by Eric Fromm, this philosophy is wanting 'to have' rather than 'to be'. It is our belief that the ancient art of living based on 'letting go' may provide one of the alternatives for those who ask, in the face of mounting threats to the Earth, what we should do.

Notes

1 *Chuang Tzu: Basic Writings*, Burton Watson, ed. and trans. (New York: Columbia University Press, 1964), 46–47.
2 Ibid., 50–51.
3 Ibid., 53–55.
4 Ibid., 95.
5 Authors' translation.
6 *The Bhagavad Gita*, trans. S. Radhakrishnan. (Bombay: Blackie & Son, 1977).
7 Translated by Lan Yuk Yim.
8 Fok Tou-hui, 'Where is the Green Movement Going?', *The Light of Dharma* 81 (February 1989): 1. Authors' translation.

The Experience of Women

20 The daughters of Earth: Women's culture as a basis for sustainable development
Hilkka Pietilä

It is not by chance that we speak so often of world crisis these days. Although each of us may view it somewhat differently, those familiar with the global situation and with ongoing trends in world economics agree there is an economic crisis, a human crisis, and an environmental crisis.

Development of a major part of the world has not only stagnated, but in great regions, like Africa, declined. During the 1980s, the quality of people's lives has deteriorated rather than improved. Environmental deterioration — drought, desertification, and erosion — has also continued and become widespread. The countries of the South have fallen into endless debt, their choices of action and policy curtailed.

Our mother, Gaia, seems to be at the edge of an unforeseen dilemma, of having either to totally shake us off her surface or else to force us to adjust to the ancient rules of her household. Difficult as it is for us to believe, we could be one of those extinct species fairly soon — in Gaian time.

In this situation, we are still speaking about the economic adjustment of developing countries and controlled structural change in industrialized societies. What does economic adjustment mean? The management of existing loans leading to additional debt? The adjustment of the poor to declining services and the closing of their schools and health centres? The adjustment of whole nations to the depletion of their natural resources and the pollution of air and water?

And what does 'controlled structural change' mean where expansion and internationalization of corporations have transformed political leaders into mere puppets of economic power; where national economies are no longer self-reliant, but vulnerable and dependent in every way; and where economic sovereignty was surrendered long ago for the cheap price of conspicuous consumption?

The paramount thrust of the report of the World Commission on Environment and Development, *Our Common Future*, is the concept of 'sustainable development'.[1] The report stresses that unless we make development in all countries ecologically sustainable, there will not be a future. This commission was led by a woman; two others of its twenty-one members were women, one woman for every six men. In spite of having had women's participation in its formation, the report omits any discussion of the potential within women's culture to provide practical and philosophical guidelines for sustainable development. By so doing, it omits the energy, creativity, and traditions of half of humanity at a time when we need to mobilize all available human resources to pave a new way toward a sustainable common future.

This is one more indication of how women's culture is invisible to the eyes of decision-makers, whether they are men or women. Or is it perhaps the failure of a small minority in the commission to make itself heard by the dominating majority? Whichever, it becomes all the more important to have a place in this book to highlight the possible alternative philosophies hidden in the midst of us, to hear an account from the women's perspective of the historical path which has led us here, and to explore the values of women's culture — an untapped source of fresh ideas for the future.

Woman in mythology

The mythology of humankind is full of parables and expressions combining woman and nature, mother and Earth, the fertility of women and nature. The goddesses of fertility are always women. There are many names for the goddesses of Earth, Nature, and Fertility — the Universal Mother — Gaia, Astarte, Isis, Ceres, Diana, Venus, Ilmatar, Lilith, and Maria.

In 1979, Wiona LaDuke, a native American woman, brought a message to the people of Europe concerning the hazards of uranium mining. This message of the International Traditional Elders ended like this:

They tell us to farm the land — how dare you ask us to cut our mother's hair,
They tell us to mine the land — how dare you ask us to level our mother's breast,
They tell us to plough the land — how dare you ask us to cut our mother's side.[2]

What is the experience of women themselves? How would they define their relationship with nature? Do women associate themselves with these ancient myths? References to the relationship of women with nature can be found in the folklore of many nations. It is said that women invented agriculture at the dawn of history when their men were out hunting; that they founded animal husbandry by taming the cubs of wild animals by breastfeeding them; that they discovered the healing arts by collecting berries and flowers, herbs and plants for use as medicine and dyes. In these folktales we see a relationship between women and nature which is cooperative, which easily develops into notions of caring and nurturing, mutually giving and receiving.

The experience women have of their own bodies also provides an excellent and everpresent bridge to nature. The menstrual cycle follows the stages of the moon; even fertility follows the rhythm of the seasons to some degree. Women feel themselves as a part of the eternal cycle of birth, growth, maturation, and death which flows through them, not outside them. In this way, women experience nature as a process uniting all living things.

A dualistic world view

Male-dominated cultures throughout the world have negatively interpreted such deep historical, cultural, and physical links between women and nature. Contemporary Western science and philosophy, for example, have a long history of dualism, from Plato through the early church fathers to the late authorities of the nineteenth and twentieth centuries. This intellectual tradition split nature, in which there is no inherent division between material and spiritual, into two nearly exclusive categories: one linking the material with the body, emotions, subjective feelings, private life and natural processes; the other linking the spiritual with the mind, reason, culture, objectivity, public life and economics.

It is commonly 'understood' that women and femininity are linked with the first series of associations, and men and masculinity with the second. These basic human characteristics are divided between the sexes instead of being harmoniously attributed to both sexes. According to this paradigm, the physical is subject to the spiritual (or intellectual); and woman, viewed as part of nature and associated with the physical world, has to submit to the rule of man. A deep dichotomy is thus created between men and women. In this way, the suppression of women and of nature are historically and ideologically linked.

According to a critique of Western dualistic philosophy by feminist theologian, Rosemary Radford Ruether, such dichotomizing has created a strong hierarchical structure which is reflected in the policies and practices of social institutions, including the academy. It has resulted in a relationship where man is the subject, the one who defines, and woman is the object, the one who is defined. As a result, women's own self-definition and perspectives are hardly even heard or incorporated culturally. Women, like all oppressed peoples, live in a culture of silence.[3]

For many of us contemporary women, this principle is still very much alive. Women are confined to silence even in so-called 'progressive countries' like Finland and Sweden. This is evident on the pages of any newspaper where practically only the ruling men are interviewed and referred to, and in the lists of references of any book written by a man.

But the schizophrenic division of basic human characteristics between the sexes resulted in dire consequences for men themselves. Dualist thinking led not only to the interpretation that 'Man' represents mind or intellect, but that he also represents the image of God or soul. Masculinity, defined as the domination of 'inferior' things — the body, nature, women — when exercised to the extreme, develops into a flight *from* body, nature, and women. All that sustains physical life comes to be seen as a realm of death against which a realm of consciousness prevails. For centuries, Western religious consciousness focused its energy on this world-fleeing agenda and developed such adorable heroes as ascetics and hermits who tried to rid themselves of the flesh (the 'feminine' nature), and sever the connections of mind and body, in order to achieve eternal, spiritual life.[4] The belief in technoscientific progress corresponds to the theological body–mind dualism. Both patriarchal religion and industrial society are motivated by the same desire: to deny mortality, and escape the necessity of the coming-to-be-and-passing-away cycle.

The American alternative economist and futurologist, Hazel Henderson, agrees with this analysis. She views industrial 'machismo' — the need to control, dominate, and 'own' not only each other but women, children, animals, plants and all of Mother Nature — as rooted in the fear of death and a sense of alienation from the natural world.

Any separate, egoistic consciousness, to the extent that it feels separated from all life, will fear its individual death as a final extinction, a total loss of meaning that must lead to existential anxiety . . . these same fears of death and loss of meaning led to the neurotic notion of scientific objectivity.[5]

Table 20.1 contrasts the views of men and women as they are suggested by several authors.

The scientific revolution which promised the realization of 'Man's' ancient dream to control nature, and become 'Master' of creation, also combined nature and women. Thus, we have the colourful images used by Francis Bacon and members of the Royal Society of London to describe how by means of new discoveries they would be able to reveal 'the secrets still locked in nature's bosom', enabling them to 'conquer' and subdue her, to shake her to her foundations'.[6] Science and technology, these men believed, would enable them to recover man's 'dominion over creation', which was lost in the Fall due to the temptation of a woman. By 'digging further and further in the mine of natural knowledge the narrow limits of man's dominion over the universe' could be stretched 'to their promised bounds'. They reveal a great deal about the attitudes of the founding fathers of science toward both nature and women. Since the scientific revolution started with these attitudes and aspirations, it is no wonder that it led to our present attitudes regarding women and nature.

Scientific progress implied quite a revolution indeed — politically, culturally, and ethically. For centuries the Church had both spiritual and political power, but with the progress of science it was gradually diminished to the spiritual dominion only. Religion and religious life were privatized, which also meant the beginning of a dual system of morality. Religious virtues were attached to women and family, to be cherished primarily in the homes and churches — by women. Religion was no longer to concern itself with public life, secularized science, expanding industry, trade, or commerce. These were the dominion of men and regarded as the 'real' life of power and importance. Thus, a new dualism was created: on the one hand, feminized religion; on the other, the masculine world of secular power where religious morality had no place.

The life of women was turned upside down in many ways. Motherhood, childcare, and housekeeping became the full-time, life-long task of women, a situation unknown to previous agrarian societies. Marriage became a moral pillar of society, but outside it was the masculine world of egoism, competition, and technical rationality that prevailed.

To the qualitative demands on women, like unselfishness and morality, were added sexual innocence and sexual purity. Sexuality was deemed a male characteristic. The middle-class housewife became an adored but repressed ornament to her home and husband, while working women were exploited both economically and sexually. Women were seen as either too pure and noble or too stupid and trivial to participate in public life. Both views were equally efficient

Table 20.1   Male versus female views

Men	Women
Life	
Life is a problem! Physical life is uncontrollable, threatening. Continuation is uncertain.	Woman's life is part of the eternal cycle of birth, maturation, and death.
Eternal life — true life — transcendental — spiritual — scientific life.	Life is delivered and nurtured by woman and then disappears back into the womb of Mother Earth.
Alienation from the physical.	
Death	
Death is final extinction. Therefore, conquest of death is a superior concern.	Offspring transcend death. Life continues.
The quest for transcendence through spiritual, material, physical, scientific; means 'to have a place in history'.	The protection of life, children, and nature is a way of conquering death.
Deep subconscious fear of death and denial of one's mortality.	
Nature	
Nature is a constant challenge to the desire to control and rule, to be a 'Master'.	Nature is manifestation and sustenance of life.
A constant fight to conquer, exploit, and mould nature.	Mutual nurturance and utilization.
To leave one's mark behind!	Nothing to fear, suppress or fight against.

methods of depriving women of the opportunity to obtain the higher education necessary for democratic participation in society.

Women have paid a high price for their share of today's material improvements and technical advances. The average woman's workload has not in fact decreased. Also, the possibilities of influencing either their own lives or the societies in which they live has declined. Women have been led from one trap to another, from curtailment and persecution under a religious patriarchy to the gilded cages of consumerist societies.

Feminist ecological ethics and male self-criticism

Today dualities manifest themselves in ways which have both ecological and economic implications, and which attempt to confuse women so that they find it difficult to recognize their real challenge. Ruether has predicted that, as the consequences of ecological disregard become apparent, the private sector will be expected to exhibit ecological morality, but public business will continue in its disregard for ecological principles. Token reforms will concentrate on the individual consumer. Women will naturally be pressed into becoming the self-help ecologists engaged in band-aid remedies that only dissipate their energies in trivia but have minimal effects on ecological imbalances. She concludes:

Women must see that there can be no liberation for them and no solution to the ecological crisis within a society whose fundamental model of relationships continues to be one of domination. They must unite the demands of the women's movement with those of the ecological movement to envision a radical reshaping of the basic socioeconomic relations and the underlying values of this society.[7]

To reverse this trend, counter to Western hierarchical thinking, a 'chain of being' which is also a 'chain of command', Ruether introduces a particular interpretation of ecological ethics, which she calls an 'ecological-feminist theology of nature'. It challenges the notions that humans are morally and ontologically superior to other forms of life, or that they are justified in treating non-humans as private property and the material world as something to be exploited. It calls for an unmasking of the structures of social domination, not only male over female but also owner over worker, that mediate this domination. Finally, it calls for a radical rethinking of the model of hierarchy that puts non-material spirit (God) at the top and nonspiritual matter at the bottom, where, because it is the most inferior, it is the most dominated.

From a biological standpoint, as Ruether points out, hierarchy makes no sense, since most complex forms of life are radically dependent on all stages that go before them. Intelligence is not a privilege 'above and against' nature, but a privilege to become the 'caretaker and cultivator of the welfare of the whole ecological community upon which our own existence depends'.[8]

Recently, male-initiated criticism has emerged in the form of 'ecophilosophy'. Ecophilosophy is the study of what has happened to nature and to Western science and thinking as a result of mechanistic empirical cosmology. This philosophy analyses the same processes as does feminism. For instance, the ecophilosopher, Henryk Skolimowski also points to the profound dualism of Western science which divided man himself, separating his knowledge from his being.[9] Skolimowski shows that this process reached its peak in the nineteenth century, when an attempt was made to conceptualize a world and science free of values — free that is, of all but the one value which persevered, that of controlling and ruling everything. Since the scientific and other developments analyzed by ecophilosophers were produced solely by males (women until the twentieth century having had little chance to contribute to the scientific world of the universities at which they were not permitted to study), criticisms of past and present science and its consequences are in fact male self-criticisms.

How much ecophilosophy and feminism have in common is not generally recognized. Both ecophilosophers and feminist thinkers relate the social crisis to the ecological crisis. In their opinion, it is impossible to solve the environmental crisis unless the whole system of social domination is changed. It cannot succeed in conditions where a few top dogs maintain their high profits by passing the costs of environmental damage to the majority of people in the form of low wages, high prices, poor working conditions, and toxic side effects to both human beings and nature. According to Ruether, women, nature, and the liberation of society go hand in hand. The liberation of women will entail the liberation of society and culture from suppressive masculine ethics, resulting in revolutionary changes in both national and international structures. 'Women must be the spokesmen for a new humanity arising out of the reconciliation of spirit and body.'[10]

Both ecophilosophy and feminist thinking, like peace research and development research as recent scientific thinking, deviate from the positivist-empirical trend of past centuries by clearly being value- and goal-orientated. One of the very basic common goals is to eliminate pervasive dualism.

Also typical of these new modes of thought is an interdisciplinary and comprehensive approach. Their aim is to bring about a synthesis after the long tradition of 'pure' analysis and objectivity. Typical of feminist research is a participatory approach, which integrates both the researchers and those researched, and recognizes the subjective experiences of both as part of the acquisition of scientific data.

One can say that feminism and ecophilosophy also belong to the hermeneutic approach to research. They both question the meaning of things and phenomena. Both aspire to explain historical events rather than only describe and register them. They try to penetrate the concepts and expressions of language in a new way and understand the behaviour of individuals and societies more profoundly than these have been understood before.

Feminist researchers speak about the *relationality* of women's existence, ethics, and world view, meaning that a woman's world is based on relationships between people, people and the rest of creation, and nature and divinity. Skolimowski writes about living 'in a multitude of webs'.[11] The Norwegian ecophilosopher, Sigmund Kvaløy, stresses that human life implies existence in constant relationship with other people, animals, and the environment.

Ecophilosophy and feminism also both speak about a recognition of the real necessities of life, though they often use a different vocabulary. Ruether speaks about 'the realm of necessity'; Kvaløy about 'the life necessities society'. Development researchers speak about basic needs; and the women's movement about unpaid labour, caring, and nurturing. These concepts cover the realm of life for which women have always been, and still are, responsible. With regard to survival and quality of life, this realm is irreplaceable. If one does not attend to cleaning and organizing the home, supplying and preparing food, caring for and nurturing both children and adults, existence very quickly becomes unbearable.

These functions are still more or less invisible to economic, scientific, and political theorists. Even if recognized, they are called 'reproduction' or 'informal economics' and considered auxiliary to society's 'productive' activities. In fact, this so-called 'free economy' work conducted outside the monetary economy is a prerequisite for everything else — for the whole national economy and the existence of the society itself.

An emphasis on and awareness of values is also common to ecophilosophy and feminism, although when,ecophilosophers deplore what they call an 'eclipse of values' in modern society, they do not realize that positivist-empirical science was not capable of totally destroying the essential values of human existence; they were preserved in the realm of home and women. In this realm they have been valid all along, and they remain the elements which give meaning and purpose to life. The more alienated and frustrating work done outside the home has become, the more importance and meaning is attached to the private sphere. The family is still the place, perhaps even more than before, where we are somebody, where we are irreplaceable.

Finally, both feminism and ecophilosophy are becoming increasingly orientated towards profound change of the whole society and its culture. Kvaløy defines the concept of ecophilosophy as much more than an academic discipline in the traditional sense — for him, it is a total engagement, and it implies an imperative to act. While feminist understanding, even among women, has been extremely diverse, during this decade it has emerged from traditional, statistical, and technical notions of equality and become a more comprehensive vision of life and society. Feminism is becoming a philosophy of its own with indigenous perspectives on society and politics.

What I experienced at the Third Interdisciplinary Congress on Women in Dublin in the summer of 1987 leads me to believe that feminism is about to shape itself as a philosophy, encompassing three basic elements: equality, ecology, and peace.

Utilizing feminine culture

Hazel Henderson uses the term 'ecofeminism' for the whole process of feminist thinking described in this chapter. This term is a tautology — a matured feminism *is* ecological. It is Henderson's feeling that ecophilosophy and ecofeminism could and should go together like 'warp and weft' to make the fabric of livable, viable life. So far, however, ecophilosophers have paid little attention to feminism and the women's movement. Indeed the two movements have developed almost totally apart from each other, though they document the same insights. Perhaps, as Henderson suggests, this is because they have approached the same phenomena from different directions. Ecofeminists have arrived at their conclusions experientially, from a 'feeling in their bones', while ecophilosophers have searched new insights mainly through theoretical, logical considerations in the traditional male manner. Yet, there are signs that the two separate streams, ecophilosophy and ecofeminism, are now beginning to approach each other, providing a glimmer of hope that they will become parallel streams toward common goals. This is of the utmost necessity. We have to be able to enter into a genuine dialogue on those issues which are of the utmost concern to both sexes; they are issues of life and death to the *whole* of humanity.

Feminism is not, in other words, for women alone. As the first professor of feminist theology in Europe, Catharina Halkes of the Netherlands, explains:

The concept of 'brotherhood' has always been important in the Churches . . . If we now like to speak of 'sisterhood' it is not only as a protest against it, neither is it meant as a polarization and apartheid; but it is a new symbol for those women who are in the process of growing awareness and for all women and men who, wherever and whoever, live in curtailment and non-freedom. Sisterhood . . . opposes the dual morality which condemns women and exonerates men, a superior power which crushes, a technology which dehumanizes and depersonalizes, sexual libertinism which makes woman again an object and sees her only as a body, the exploitation by the supermen and then Capital, of slaves, blacks, the powerless, but also the rape of mother earth, of nature and the whole creation which is becoming unlivable and exhausted.[12]

Skolimowski points out that, though they have the same underlying causes, ecology as a movement has predominantly focused on devastated nature, while humanism has mainly focused on the devastated human being. I wish to point out that women have been and are living in such a relationship with nature and humanity that both of these processes are interwoven in their own life experiences.

I maintain that women are the largest alternative movement in the world, a hidden, subversive, invisible counterculture to the overt masterculture of our time which has brought us to the brink of disaster. Feminine culture could bring an untapped source of traditions, values, skills, and insights to the service of humanity to reconstruct a sustainable way of life and economy for the future.[13]

On the opposite side of the globe, another woman, Ariel Salleh of Australia, has come to the same conclusion:

If women's lived experience were recognized as meaningful and were given legitimation in our culture, it could provide an immediate 'living' social basis for the alternative consciousness . . . The traditional feminine role runs counter to the exploitative technical rationality which is currently the requisite masculine norm. In place of the disdain that the feminine role receives from all quarters, 'the separate reality' of this role could well be taken seriously by ecologists and reexamined as a legitimate source of alternative values.[14]

There are two main obstacles to the utilization of these untapped sources of feminine culture. One is women's unawareness of their own potential, the other is the attitudes of men.

Most women themselves are not yet aware of the value and importance of the culture they represent consciously or unconsciously. Only after they have become aware of their womanhood and of the intrinsic value of being women will they be able to make their indigenous contribution towards a change in politics and culture.

Subjugated men of a patriarchal culture have the attitudes and values of that culture deeply ingrained in their minds. A long process of male liberation is needed before they can rid themselves of their 'masculine mystique' in order to meet feminine culture without prejudices. Ariel Salleh still anticipates a new ally within the personality of men, and it is 'the original androgynous natural unity . . . the feminine aspects of men's own constitution'.

Human beings possess the unique potentiality of developing their humanness, of growing humanly, of realizing their full potential as male and female human beings. That is what is now needed from all of us, men and women. Only then will we be able to take the responsibility which is upon us at this turning point in history.

Notes

1 The World Commission on Environment and Development *Our Common Future*, (Oxford: Oxford University Press, 1987).
2 Lin Pugh and Moniek van der Kroef, 'Before we die' . . .', *ISIS Journal* 15 (1980).
3 Rosemary Ruether, *Liberation Theology* (New York: Paulist Press, 1973). Many thanks to Elina Vuola for allowing me to draw from her MA thesis, 'Uusi nainen — uusi maa' (New Woman — new earth), (Helsinki: Helsinki University, 1985), an analysis and synthesis of the thinking and works of Rosemary Ruether.
4 Rosemary Ruether, *Sexism and God-Talk: Toward Feminist Theology* (Boston: Beacon Press, 1983), 79–80.
5 Hazel Henderson, 'The Warp and the Weft — The Coming Synthesis of Ecophilosophy and Ecofeminism', *Development* 4 (Journal of SID, Rome).
6 Quoted in Carolyn Merchant, *The Death of Nature: Women, Ecology, and the Scientific Revolution* (New York: Harper & Row, 1980).
7 Rosemary Ruether, *New Woman — New Earth* (New York: Dove, 1975), 200–1.
8 Ruether, *Sexism and God-Talk*, 87–8.
9 Henryk Skolimowski, *Ecophilosophy* (London: Marion Boyars, 1981).
10 Ruether, *Liberation Theology*, 124.
11 Skolimowski, *Eco-Philosophy*, 46.
12 Catherina Halkes, 'To a New Image of Man Based on Feminist Theology', paper presented to Groningen International conference, 1977.
13 See Hilkka Pietilä, 'Women as an Alternative Culture Here and Now', *Development* 4 (1984); and Hilkka Pietilä, 'Kinnoperspektiv på nuet och framtiden', in Friberg and Galtung, eds, *Alternativen* (Stockholm: Akademilitteratur, 1986).
14 Ariel Salleh, 'Deeper than Deep Ecology: The Ecofeminist Connection', *Environmental Ethics* 6 (1984): 339–46.

21 Living with nature: Reciprocity or control?

Ariel Salleh

During the 1980s, international agencies have acknowledged the close connection between women and the environment. The International YWCA's Geneva-based Y's EYES campaigns not only for health and human rights, but also on issues of energy use, water supply, and appropriate technology. The Environment Liaison Centre in Nairobi, an independent non-governmental organization (NGO), runs sessions for women on forestry, sustainable farming, and pollution control, and urges political recognition of women's traditional farming expertise. The Rome/Santiago International Information and Communication Services (ISIS) facilitates women's education in similar areas. The International Women's Tribune Center in New York provides leadership skills and resource material on conservation and development to a vast female network. In Santo Domingo, the United Nation's International Research and Training Institute for the Advancement of Women (INSTRAW), works on water management programmes. In Bangalore, an innovative group called Development Alternatives with Women for a New Era (DAWN), is critical of the imported 'growth' ethic and the oppressive gender division this ethic reinforces. World WIDE — Women in Defense of Environment — Washington D.C., is also trying to pre-empt superficial 'development' schemes and 'give voice to the voiceless' in policy.[1]

This recognition of women's involvement in, and concern for, the environment is both essential and rare. For, in the words of Carol Gilligan:

Though we have listened for centuries to the voices of men and the theories of development that their experience informs, we have come more recently to notice not only the silence of women, but the difficulty of hearing what they say when they speak; yet in the different voice of women lies the truth of an ethic of care, the tie between relationship and responsibility, and the origins of aggression in the failure to connect.[2]

Women could contribute to the discussions of environmental sustainability 'the truth of an ethic of care'. Yet, their 'different voice' is seldom heard.

Women as invisible workers

At the celebrated 1985 Nairobi Forum on 'Equality, Development, and Peace', the social and environmental impact of cash-cropping and industrialization were discussed thoroughly, after which the conference resolved to counter harmful development by getting more women into pressure groups, management, and education. The media were asked to promote more constructive images of women, and governments were encouraged to research and modify policies which inhibit women's full participation in community life. These resolutions were adopted by delegates from 157 countries, and later, by the fortieth session of the United Nations General Assembly. The resolutions are to be monitored by the appropriate UN agencies up to the year 2000.[3] Still, the problem remains: just as 'most women's work is invisible, so are our Herculean efforts against [that invisibility], North and South, East and West'.[4]

Some impressive grassrooots projects — the Chipko movement among Indian peasants to preserve forests and limestone deposits from the 'formal' economy; the Greenbelt Movement of Kenya women, led by Wangari Maathai, which won an Alternative Nobel Prize; and model farming by the Ação Femínea Democrática Gaucha in the Amazon — are internationally acclaimed. In official accounts of development, however, women's activities are often passed over. While the UN Economic Commission on Africa found that women and their children produce 70 per cent of the continent's food, are responsible for the transport of that food, and work a 14–16-hour day, the UN Food and Agriculture Organization (FAO) describes only 5 per cent of them as employed. Similarly, national statistics on agricultural production in Peru indicate a female contribution of 2.6 per cent, while local estimates put it at 86 per cent. In Egypt, the same cultural phenomenon occurs: official figures show a 3.6 per cent agricultural contribution by women, whereas local opinion has it at 35–50 per cent. Tourist postcards and agency propaganda shots also tend to portray 'rural workers' as male. Further, while 'women grow half the world's food . . . most agricultural advisors are men — who tend to give advice to men'.[5] And what kind of advice is that? Famine conditions in Ethiopia have resulted from land being taken out of women's hands by those who would render it profitable in terms defined by an abstract and unpredictable global economy.

Sithembiso Nyoni, coordinator of women's rural progress associations in Zimbabwe, believes that consultants and ministers are too concerned about international hobnobbing to remember that 'we are the basis of their power'. Hence, in the South, the debt crisis gets worse as 'aid programmes' open the way for multinational corporations and an increasing concentration of assets among the wealthy. Meanwhile, the female half of the world's population owns less than 1 per cent of world property. Major breadwinners in the Third World, women receive less than 1 per cent of UN aid. Under the present 'relations of production', their access to land is contingent upon marriage, and other forms of credit are invariably blocked by bureaucratic attitudes. A survey of professional staff in environmental agencies and NGOs by Dutch IUCN administrator Irene Dankelman affirms that women are noticeably few at an advisory level.[6] Neither the famous Indian report on the status of women nor India's sixth Five-Year Plan acknowledges problems with water, fuel, and feed. Yet, the daily experience of

The problem of overpopulation is real and needs to be seriously examined. However, given the ethical issues of eugenics/genocide and of a woman's rights over her own body, the targeting of 'population control' has both racist and sexist dimensions. But even as a matter of simple equity, where children provide supplementary farm labour for overworked mothers, it is inappropriate for local men and their international policy advisors to demand population control. Such programmes originated in a post-World War II middle-class urban desire to protect 'the quality of life' — for which read 'levels of consumerism'. Now the argument for population 'control' is formulated more prudently in terms of protecting the Earth's scarce resources. But this injunction as applied to the Third World exclusively is patently hypocritical. Each infant born into the so-called advanced societies will use about fifteen times more global resources during his or her lifetime than a person born in the Third World.[24] Population restraint may well be called for in the West, hopefully complemented by a scaling back of high-technology excess. On the other hand, subsistence dwellers are sometimes producers as much as consumers: as 'prosumers' they are practical examples of human autonomy in a non-exploitative relation to land. To borrow the impoverished language of the dominant materialistic ethos here: in certain circumstances a child born in the Third World could be seen as an 'asset' rather than a 'liability'. What much of the talk about population 'control' may express is a projection and displacement of the guilt experienced by those who continue to live comfortably off the invisible backs of working women in the Third World.

Deeper than this, does the constant focus on population control in development debates even reflect a fear of nature or of female power? Fear of that different voice? If not, then why the obsessive pursuit of status in the economic pecking order and expertise in frankly destructive technologies? Consider this piece from the Kenya *Sunday Nation:*

Only sound social, economic and political policies that favour or promote indigenous scientific and technological potential will help the continent meet its *basic human needs* . . . the minimum target of 1000 scientists and engineers per million inhabitants.[25]

The iniquitous financial transfer from South to North which imported development involves, the predatory consumption of food and energy resources by an industrialized North, lessons from the green revolution — are all glossed over, although they are surely very good arguments for disengagement from the multinational order and for concentrating on the wealth in one's own back yard. What is overlooked again and again is that the self-reliant, life-affirming, bioregional labours of women, 'the informal or free economy, the world of nurturance and close human relations, is the sphere where basic human needs are anchored and where models for humane alternatives can be found'.[26]

As things stand, women, half the world's population, put in 65 per cent of the world's work, and get back only 10 per cent of all income paid.[27] The rationale for this institutionalized theft, and that of the exploitation of nature, has been uncovered by the ecofeminist analysis of patriarchy. But unless the reality of this cultural process is accepted by environmentalists, their handling of the global predicament will fail to make any sense. *Our Common Future*, the 1987 report by the World Commission on Environment and Development, a collection of environmentalists, economists, politicians, scientists, and engineers, is a classic case in point.[28] The wisdom of 'live simply that others may simply live' is lost. Ultimately, its recommendations collapse back into a 'more growth and trickle-down someday' solution to world poverty. Given the metaphysical premises on which economics is currently organized, the costs of the growth will again be levied on women and the environment. Getting more women into advisory positions is only half of the story. The unconscious connection between woman and nature needs to be made conscious, and the hierarchical fallacies of the 'Great Chain of Being' acknowledged, before there can be any real growth towards a sane, humane, ecological future. Once this step is made, the way that women work in reciprocity with nature will become visible as a model to learn from. The result would be a fundamental change in the relations of production, a change summarized by the ecofeminist, Ynestra King, when she says: 'men must stop trying to control nature and join women in identifying with nature'.[29] The personal is indeed political; and struggles for equality and sustainability are interlinked.

Notes

1 *Women and the Environmental Crisis: A Report of Workshop Proceedings at the Nairobi Forum '85: Women in Development* (Philadelphia: New Society Publishers, 1984).

2 Carol Gilligan, *In a Different Voice* (Cambridge, Mass.: Harvard University Press, 1984), 173–74.

3 *Report of the World Conference to Review and Appraise the Achievements of the United Nations Decade for Women — Equality, Development, and Peace, Nairobi, 15–16 July 1985* (New York: United Nations, 1986).

4 Selma James, *The Global Kitchen* (London: Housewives in Dialogue Archive, 1985), 25; Marilyn Waring, *Counting for Nothing* (Sydney: Allen & Unwin, 1989).

5 FAO statistics and quotation from *Women and the Environmental Crisis*, 45.

6 Irene Dankelman and Joan Davidson, eds, *Women and Environment in the Third World* (London: Earthscan, 1988), Ch. 7.

7 Hilkka Pietilä, 'Women as an Alternative Culture Here and Now', *Development* 4 (1984), 60.

8 James, *The Global Kitchen*, 1.

9 *Forward Looking Strategies for the Advancement of Women in Africa Beyond the End of the United Nations Decade for Women*, Expert Group Meeting, Arusha, United Republic of Tanzania, 4–6 October, 1984 (New York: United Nations Economic and Social Council, 1984).

10 Ibid., 10–11.

11 Berit As, 'A Five Dimensional Model for Change', *Women's Studies International Quarterly* 4 (1981): 111.

12 Ruth Schwartz Cowan, *More Work for Mother* (New York: Basic Books, 1983).

13 Lin Nelson, 'Feminists Turn to Workplace, Environmental Health', *Women and Global Corporations* 7, 1 and 2 (1986).

14 Cecelia Kirkman, 'The War at Home', *The Non-Violent Activist* 3 (1986): 7.

15 International Women's Tribune Center Team and Anne Walker, 'Peace Is No Violence Against Women', *The Tribune, A Women and Development Quarterly* (3rd Quarter, 1985): 32.

16 Barbara Ehrenreich, *The Hearts of Men* (New York: Anchor, 1983), 172.

17 Hazel Henderson, 'Indicators of No Real Meaning', in Paul Elkins, ed., *The Living Economy: A New Economics in the Making* (London: Routledge and Kegan Paul, 1986), 33.

18 Rosemary Ruether, *New Woman New Earth* (New York: Dove, 1975); Elizabeth Dodson-Gray, *Green Paradise Lost* (Wellesley, Mass: Roundtable Press, 1979).

19 For a more detailed discussion of this hierarchy, see the essay by Hilkka Pietilä in this volume.

20 Maria Mies, *Patriarchy and Accumulation on a World Scale* (London: Zed Books, 1986).

21 Ibid., 52.

22 'How Food Production is Hit by Population', *The Standard* (2 October 1987): 14.

23 Debbie Taylor, ed., 'Myth Conceptions', *New Internationalist* (October 1987): 8–9.

24 F.E. Trainer, *Abandon Affluence!* (London: Zed Books, 1985), 1.

25 Otula Owuor, 'Sound Science Policies Called For', *Sunday Nation* (4 October, 1987): 17 (emphasis added).

26 Hilka Pietilä, *Tomorrow Begins Today* (ICDA/ISIS Workshop, Nairobi Forum, 1985), 26.

27 United Nations International Labour Organization (ILO).

28 World Commission on Environment and Development, *Our Common Future* (Oxford: Oxford University Press, 1987).

29 Ynestra King, Address to the international conference on 'Eco-feminist Perspectives — Culture, Nature, Theory', at the University of Southern California, Los Angeles, 1987.

Index